S0-AGV-108

THE
ART OF SURVIVAL
IN EAST AFRICA

THE
ART OF SURVIVAL
IN EAST AFRICA

The Kerebe and
Long-Distance Trade,
1800-1895

Gerald W. Hartwig

AFRICANA PUBLISHING COMPANY

NEW YORK   LONDON

A Division of Holmes & Meier Publishers, Inc.

Published in the United States of America 1976 by
Holmes & Meier Publishers, Inc.
101 Fifth Avenue
New York, N.Y. 10003

Great Britain:
Holmes & Meier Publishers, Ltd.
Hillview House
1, Hallswelle Parade, Finchley Road
London NW11

Copyright © Holmes & Meier Publishers, Inc. 1976

ALL RIGHTS RESERVED

LIBRARY OF CONGRESS CATALOGING IN PUBLICATION DATA

Hartwig, Gerald W.
    The art of survival in East Africa.

    Bibliography: p.
    Includes index.
    1. Kerebe (Bantu people). 2. Tanzania—Commerce—History.
I. Title.
DT443.H37   380.1'09678   74-84653
ISBN 0-8419-0182-1

PRINTED IN THE UNITED STATES OF AMERICA

Robert Manning Strozier Library

APR 12 1979

Tallahassee, Florida

Contents

Maps

Preface

To emerge from a tumultuous century changed but still intact as a society, it was necessary to develop the art of survival. What this involved and how it was accomplished for
the Kerebe of Tanzania is the focus of this study. The time
under consideration is the nineteenth century, a century
that has been romanticized to a considerable extent in the
past because this was when East Africa was "opened up." It
was the era in which East Africans of the interior, like the
Kerebe, became active participants in the international
community by exchanging ivory for trade goods produced in
Asia or Europe. As the following pages attempt to convey,
participation in the "opening up" process was by no means
all beneficial. The cost for the Kerebe in lives and values was
significant, yet the cost was less than that paid by some of
their neighbors.

The view of society presented is based upon oral evidence
provided by Kerebe elders, thus an insiders' perspective
from the small former chiefdom of Bukerebe (Ukerewe),
located in the southeastern part of the Victoria Nyanza
(Lake Victoria). The Kerebe were distinctive in their district a century ago: they represented a rather isolated exten-

sion of the awe-inspiring interlacustrine culture zone found
on the other (western) side of the lake and they lived in an
area that received adequate and reliable rainfall. These factors encouraged and enabled the Kerebe to assume a dominant role in their district until the mid-nineteenth century,
after which their dominance was unmistakably eroded.

Long-distance trade was the mechanism by which eastern
Africa was "opened up." Caravans with African porters
carrying burdens of beads, cloth and wire trekked into the
interior in hopes of returning in a year, or maybe two years,
with a bountiful load of ivory—and hence a profit. The
Kerebe received some of these caravans through the century
while supplying their share of ivory to the traders. But this
view of Kerebe involvement in long-distance trade was only
the visible fasade. Behind this exterior a series of other
developments occurred: some men commenced accumulating possessions, proceeds from their trading activities in grain; insecurity increased within the community,
a phenomenon related to the presence of epidemic diseases;
the role of servile persons changed perceptibly; and social
relationships among the Kerebe became strained,
manifested in accusations of sorcery. The Kerebe experienced changes· of this nature and magnitude as the century
progressed. It was the price required for participation in the
international community.

The use of Kerebe terms and names in the text requires
an explanation. A standardized orthography for most
Ekikerebe (the prefix *eki-* is translated as "the language of,"
in this case, the Kerebe) does not exist. Given the in-
terchange of the *r* and *l* sounds in the language and the
possible inclusion of some Jita words that tend to use the *z*
sound in place of the *j* sound of the Kerebe, the spelling is
necessarily arbitrary. The name of the chiefdom and island
is Bukerebe in Ekikerebe and the people refer to themselves
as Abakerebe (singular, Omukerebe). Within the following
pages, the root *kerebe* is used to identify the people as well
as to descibe their possessions, such as a Kerebe canoe. Outside the chiefdom, Ukerewe and Kerewe are used as names

for the chiefdom, island, and people. This usage became common during the nineteenth century when traders from the East African coast replaced the *b* sound of the Kerebe with the *w* sound and then used the Swahili place prefix *U* for the Kerebe *Bu*.

Research in London, Stuttgart, Berlin, Rome, Dar es Salaam and Bukerebe was generously financed by a grant from the Foreign Area Fellowship Program. I am deeply indebted to the Program, who are in no way responsible for the results of my study, for assistance to myself and my family. I would also like to express my appreciation to the Department of History, the University of Dar es Salaam and to the Tanzanian government for their permission to conduct research among the Kerebe and their cooperation during my stay in Tanzania.

Numerous institutions kindly permitted me to use materials for study and assessment. I gratefully acknowledge the use of archival materials in the Tanzanian National Archives, the Mother House of the White Fathers in Rome as well as those sources located at Nyegezi, the Church Missionary Society and the London Society in London; museum collections were also examined at the National Museum of Tanzania, the Museum für Völkerkunde in Berlin, the Linden-Museum in Stuttgart and the British Museum in London.

Because this monograph is predominantly based upon oral sources, the Kerebe who accepted my intrusion with equanimity, hospitality, and valuable information are to be especially thanked. I have endeavored to respect their contributions and sincerely hope I have not abused their trust in me. Interpretations have been freely made from their oral evidence, interpretations that frequently placed events and developments within an East African perspective. Thus the Kerebe data benefited enormously from oral data of other East African societies. My concern is that the Kerebe data has been handled in a manner that will contribute to our better understanding of the East African past.

Numerous individuals have assumed a critical role in bringing this project into being, particularly George E. Brooks and J. Gus Liebenow of Indiana University and Roy C. Bridges of King's College, Aberdeen, Scotland; each has unselfishly contributed time and energy, for which I am sincerely appreciative. I would also like to acknowledge the valuable assistance and encouragement from my colleague John W. Cell of Duke University, from T.O. Ranger of The University of Birmingham and from John A. Rowe of Northwestern University. To Stanlake Samkange and Anza Amen Lema a special tribute is made; they unconsciously—perhaps—made it possible for me to begin the process of understanding and appreciating African culture and values, a process that began in 1961 in Tanzania.

On Ukerewe I benefitted immeasurably from stimulating discussions with Father Henryk Zimoń who was undertaking an ethnographic study of Kerebe rainmakers in addition to a history of the royal Silanga clan. Numerous research assistants aided me during my eight months on the island including Josephat K. Mdono, who introduced me to the island and people of Bukerebe; Edward L. Alphonce, whose patience and ability in transcribing taped interviews has never ceased to amaze me; Joachimus M. Abel, who assisted me ably for five months in acquiring traditions; and Philibert T. Magere, whose interest in Kerebe music and history added significantly to his contribution. Our neighbors, the White Fathers of Murutunguru parish and the personnel of the Tanganyika Cotton Company's ginnery, were most generous of their time and consideration during our stay at Murutunguru. I would also like to note my appreciation for his encouragement of the project to Michael Lukumbuzya, the last Kerebe omukama, who now serves Tanzania in its diplomatic corps.

Throughout the period of research and writing I have been encouraged, queried, assisted and listened to faithfully by my wife, whose presence has made the endeavor feasible, educational and ultimately worthwhile. Her contribution has been immeasurable. I would also like to express my appreciation to Kris, Karl, and Kari for their forbearance and patience while their father trekked about East Africa and Europe; to Kurt I can only express my hope that he too will have the same experiences some day. To my parents for their understanding, encouragement and support, I express my sincere appreciation.

To Shoonie and in memory of
Buyanza

THE
ART OF SURVIVAL
IN EAST AFRICA

Introduction:

The Challenge of Oral History

Namwero said to Myombekere, "My son-in-law, today I have come to take your wife. I shall not leave her here. It has reached us at home that your brothers and sister have been most offensive to your wife here in your house saying 'go away you bitch, go back home at once, what sort of woman are you that has no children? You do not deserve to be married to our brother Myombekere who is in his prime, and we are afraid that you will infect him with your barrenness.' This is the reason why we have come here because to bear children is the gift of God himself. She was most anxious to have a child, but God has not granted her this blessing. She would also like to be like other people in the world. Now, as our child is in danger it is our duty to take her and to care for her at the house of her own parents."

Myombekere's mother-in-law picked up these words saying, "It is true. Is there not a Kerebe saying, a thing that is not valued must go back to its owner, or what is bad to others is beautiful to its mother."

Aniceti Kitereza,[1] an imaginative and articulate Kerebe elder, set forth this interclan dilemma when beginning his lengthy story about a young couple experiencing difficulty in conceiving a child. Throughout his story Kitereza stresses the importance and wisdom of particular Kerebe customs that existed in the mid-nineteenth century, during the reign of *Omukama* Machunda, Kitereza's paternal grandfather. Woven into the story's fabric are proverbs, riddles, stories,[2] and even song texts, all designed to disclose the richness and intrinsic values of Kerebe culture before western culture made its impact. This type of literature helps us understand the complex customs of an alien way of life; yet, it was never intended for us. Kitereza wrote the story specifically for the pupils attending primary school within Bukerebe during the early 1940s.

What could have been an innovative educational experiment stressing cultural values rather than purely factual and, for all practical purposes, barren information of an historical nature, never came to fruition. But not because Kitereza hesitated. He worked for several years on the project, motivated by a desire he articulated in 1970:

> It was my intent to write an account about the habits, customs and practices of our fathers long ago. . . . In the morning, each man went to do the work he felt necessary or to assist a neighbor who needed help. . . . People who shared their work—their hearts were cheerful, without bitterness or strife and their conversation was good.

> It was in my heart to write of these things, of the particular practices and how people worked together to help one another, even those in neighboring villages. Men consulted together and their ways were for the good of all; poor behavior was forbidden and elders were respected.

> For fear that these customs, habits and practices
> of our fathers would die and be forgotten, I began
> to wonder about this and suddenly I realized that
> the traditions of this country would be lost for
> our children and the children yet to be born if
> they were not written down, for how else would
> they be preserved? I was very distressed and I
> sought a way in which to preserve these
> traditions of times past, when people wore goat
> and cow skins and put butter fat on themselves to
> prevent illness. . . Then I selected a method; it
> would be best to put these words in a book. I
> wrote in Kikerebe so that the customs of our
> fathers would be known in this place of
> Bukerebe.

The medium of expression doomed Kitereza's effort to publish his novel. Too few people could read Kikerebe; the potential market simply did not warrant publication.[3] Aniceti Kitereza's dream of combatting an erosion of respect for the past by promoting an understanding of former social values among the educated young of Bukerebe came to naught.

Nonetheless the legacy of Kitereza's accomplishments is incalculable. Because he looked to the "yet to be born" generations and accepted the tenet that "words that are spoken fly with the wind but words that are written live forever," his years of painstaking research and writing can now be appreciated, albeit a full generation after Kitereza sensed the need. Although untrained for ethnographical or historical investigation, he energetically collected cultural and historical oral information from Kerebe elders living during the early 1940s. To seek, find and then share the secrets of life in a bygone era, to discover "those things loved and those things despised" became his goals. Kitereza's burning desire to know what values motivated the everyday activities of his grandfather's generation enables his story to transcend the parochial setting of a small, relatively unimportant chiefdom. It concerns common people, those whose daily unglorified existence and beliefs must be respected because their fundamental concerns are also ours.

It is my desire to transcend the boundaries of a parochial history of the Kerebe in much the same fashion that Kitereza accomplished this feat in his story—by focusing upon similar opportunities and concerns affecting virtually all societies in the western portion of East Africa. Kitereza, for example, uses the theme of barrenness to portray a universal phenomenon. I find this a particularly appropriate theme for the Kerebe of the nineteenth century although I think in terms of depopulation. Kitereza reconstructs an image of a wholesome life during his grandfather's reign, ca. 1835 to ca. 1869. This is also a critical era for me, but I focus on how life was changing because of disruptive new forces.

Relation of Kerebe History

to Existing Studies

This case study basically seeks to answer the following question: What happened to an African community during the nineteenth century as a consequence of its participation in long-distance trade? A description of various trade routes and commodities exchanged is certainly a vital part of this study, but my intention has been to go beyond the descriptive to an understanding of what occurred within Kerebe society, what happened to the values and relationships between people.

As the subject of a case study, the response of the Kerebe to new forces has considerable relevance for our increased understanding of African societies in the century preceding the colonial era. The Kerebe experience contrasted starkly, for example, with that of the Zulu in southeastern Africa. By 1800 the Zulu and their neighbors were blocked in their gradual migratory drift southward. The consequent internal pressures caused by overcrowding gave rise to the leadership of heroic men like Dingiswayo and Shaka who proceeded to reorganize society and to formulate new communal values. This unleashed a military force never before experienced in southern Africa, a force ultimately affecting hundreds of thousands of Africans in the present states of South Africa, Lesotho, Swaziland, Botswana, Rhodesia, Malaẉi, Mozambique, Zambia, and Tanzania.[4] Nor was change within Kerebe society as innovative as that experienced by the Igbo of the Niger delta on the western side of the continent when a new social, political, and economic institution known as the house system appeared.[5]

The numerous variables affecting the Zulu, Igbo, and Kerebe were significantly different in each case. Demographic considerations alone represent two extremes. The Kerebe suffered from depopulation, while the Zulu and Igbo experienced a surplus population. Although portions of the Igbo and Kerebe communities actively participated in trade with international traders, only the Igbo had direct access to them. The Kerebe lived hundreds of miles from the Indian Ocean, a situation limiting their opportunities as well as serving as a buffer from intensive pressures. The Zulu did not turn their backs entirely on trading opportunities, but they did not manifest the same enthusiasm as the Igbo and Kerebe, even though members of the trading community were accessible. In spite of these important variables, all three societies experienced fundamental social changes.

It is precisely because the social and economic history of the Kerebe did not exhibit the drama of the Zulu or the innovation of the Igbo that their case is worthy of examination. Valuable as the knowledge of unusual cases is to our understanding, comprehending the development of the majority of societies is an equally valid goal and perhaps a more important one. While the Kerebe experience was by no means typical even in their region of Africa, the identifiable historical forces confronting them also affected other communities in the continent's eastern interior. These historical forces affecting the entire region must first be identified before human responses can be examined. This monograph was written to facilitate the identification both of impinging forces and of the particularistic responses of one East African society. As should become apparent from the Kerebe experience, there was nothing mundane or pedestrian about their development in the nineteenth century. A great deal was at stake—in fact, their very survival. Aniceti Kitereza's theme of barrenness suggests one ramification

My collection of oral materials on Bukerebe for eight months in 1968-69 benefitted immeasurably from earlier historical studies. Important economic and political issues had been raised in the first volume of the Oxford *History of East Africa,* edited by Roland Oliver and Gervase Mathew. I pursued these particular issues as far as possible. I also learned a great deal from the experiences and results of other historians such as Kathleen Stahl, B.A. Ogot, and Gideon Were.[6] Particularly valuable was the example of each in treating complex lineage traditions. In addition, these studies suggested to me that the very nature of the Kerebe evidence was more suited to shed light upon general questions than upon the reconstruction of Bukerebe's political and economic history. The essays of the contributors to *Tanzania Before 1900,* as well as the valuable remarks contained in editor Andrew Roberts' introductory essay, clearly established a series of historical problems that needed further attention. Together, these scholars provided a methodological and historical base upon which I could build an additional tier. Works such as I.N. Kimambo's *A Political History of the Pare of Tanzania; The History of Tanzania,* edited by I.N. Kimambo and A.J. Temu; and *Pre-Colonial African Trade,* edited by Richard Gray and David Birmingham, appeared after my research on Bukerebe was completed. But they subsequently reinforced my intention to concentrate upon issues relevant to the region as a whole.

Africanist historians have now reached the stage of asking pertinent questions rather than simply recounting past events. Although the published data has thus far been unable to provide the desired answers, it has been instrumental in directing attention to critical problems, a significant contribution in its own right. For example, stimulated by essays on eastern Africa in *Pre-Colonial African Trade* and a Colloquium on Zanzibar and long-distance trade in early 1971 at Boston University, Ralph Austen formulated three basic questions:

1. To what extent were indigenous, as opposed to alien, commercial stimuli responsible for the emergence of market trading in East Africa?

2. What was the relationship between specialized trading and production activities and other roles in East African society, particularly that of the state?

3. Given the stimulus of trade opportunities, what patterns of development followed from them?[7]

More recently there has been a concerted effort on the part of economic historians to avoid a total concentration on long-distance trade. Walter Rodney,[8] Edward Alpers,[9] and A.G. Hopkins[10] are consciously seeking to redirect the emphasis of scholarship away from simple trading activities to those activities associated with the actual production of agricultural and material goods which may or may not be linked to trading. Related to this concern is the use of available resources, such as land, and the use of the labor potential. In a sense these economic historians are requesting that the total economy of a society, a region, or a country be examined, not merely one facet of that economy. Rodney and Alpers explicitly attempt to understand the nature of contemporary African underdevelopment by analyzing the consequences of precolonial trade with non-Africans, a trade in which the African is seen as continually assuming a subordinate economic role. Alpers would like to know why this subordination was such a characteristic feature.[11] The Kerebe evidence provides one set of responses to these questions.

Rationale of Study

The consequences of their participation in long-distance trade affected the Kerebe in an awesome yet insidious fashion. This trade was the major development for them in the nineteenth century. It is theoretically possible to maintain that every feature of Kerebe life, whether related to economic, political, social, or religious matters, was significantly altered by their own or their neighbors' or alien (Arab and Swahili) involvement in long-distance trade.

The purpose of this monograph is twofold: to describe Kerebe participation in trade insofar as this is possible and, simultaneously, to analyze the effects of this participation upon the society. Because trade is the thematic focal point, this may be considered an economic case study of a specific East African society. Yet to declare it as such would be to misrepresent my own intentions. It is definitely broader in scope. I commenced collecting oral data from Kerebe elders in 1968 on economic and political affairs. Kerebe involvement in long-distance trade, in fact, was my initial concern. But an explanatory remark by a respected informant, Buyanza s/o (son of) Nansagate, caused me weeks of puzzlement. The comment flatly asserted that sorcery was a frequent phenomenon after the reign of a particular ruler but not before.

My attempt to understand that chance remark subsequently refocused my investigative purposes. In a very real sense this monograph attempts to explain Buyanza's assertion. Economic factors remained a basic concern, but they became inextricably interwoven with social, religious, and political considerations at one point after another. Hence this analysis necessarily incorporates many noneconomic factors. Without them, the critical economic changes lack a comprehensive rationale. Examining only economic factors to understand a precolonial African society is simply too restrictive, whether it is a question of their increased production of grain or their use of a servile population as a labor force. The societies in question must be initially encountered on their own terms. Once additional case studies are available, each with its own set of specific responses, there will be ample opportunity to generalize and to attain an acceptable basis for reconstructing the social, economic, and ontological developments during the dynamic and disruptive nineteenth century.

At this stage of reconstructing East Africa's social history, it is imperative to identify and analyze the direct and indirect consequences of long-distance trade. Until these forces are discerned, all efforts to assess developments during the nineteenth century will fall short of their mark. Arab, Swahili, and African traders provoked a wide range of complex responses. These very responses comprise the essential Kerebe contribution to our understanding of eastern Africa's history during the 1800s. It is now apparent that the influence of long-distance trade upon societies can be broadly characterized as having provided *opportunities* and/or as having increased *insecurity* within communities, either of which required extensive adaptation from the entire population. Gains were difficult to realize and losses were common. Of necessity, however, communities developed the means to survive or they ceased to exist. The Kerebe survived that tumultuous century, but the community and its values had undergone a metamorphosis as a consequence of long-distance trade. The social cost of participation in trade and of the subsequent acquisition of prestigious commodities was extremely high. An advantage of the experience, if one can call it that, was that to some extent it prepared the Kerebe for further rapid change in the twentieth century. Adjustment to alien and impersonal forces had become a way of life by 1900.

The discussion of Kerebe developments during the nineteenth century basically follows a topical approach, which may well be disconcerting at times. The initial chapter identifies the society and their environment and provides relevant historical background on the Kerebe prior to the nineteenth century. The second chapter traces Kerebe involvement in long-distance trade throughout the century as well as their subsequent relationship to other societies. This chapter concludes with a discussion of the serious impact that the exposure to an apparently new disease environment had upon the Kerebe. Chapter three is devoted to a description of local trade and internal economic changes concluding with an analysis of Kerebe servitude, both as an economic and a social development. Changing political relationships and the altering basis of political authority during the century are examined in the fourth chapter. Chapter five is an analysis of disrupted social relationships as manifested by sorcery, a spiritual as well as a social phenomenon. The final chapter summarizes the Kerebe evidence.

Chapters two through five are devoted to specific topics, and therefore each incorporates evidence from the entire century. Only the chapter describing participation in long-distance trade possesses an easily discernible chronological order. The topics of local trade and servility, political authority and relationships, and sorcery do not lend themselves to such an ordered approach. Fortunately the oral evidence provides some chronology by associating events with a particular *omukama* (chief). By familiarizing oneself with these names and when they ruled, the reader will be able to comprehend the period of time involved. The four key men with their approximate dates in office are:

Mihigo II, ca. 1780 to ca. 1820.

Ibanda, late 1820s to ca. 1835. (By the late 1850s Ibanda was well entrenched in a new, splinter chiefdom that survived until the end of the century.)

Machunda, ca. 1835 to ca. 1869.

Rukonge, ca. 1869 to 1895.

Gaining the most complete understanding of prevailing conditions and of the general processes at work during the nineteenth century is the ultimate goal of all research in East African history, whether a single society or a topical problem involving several societies is studied. The following questions have emanated from the Kerebe oral data and, to a degree, provide a framework for organizing the material:

> What economic changes occurred as a consequence of long-distance trade?
>
> How did participation in trade, regional and long-distance, affect relationships between individuals, between social groups, between neighboring political entities?
>
> How did these presumable altered relationships affect the authority of ascriptive leaders, i.e., those whose role was basically defined by birth? How did these leaders respond? If these leaders were displaced, by whom?
>
> How did commoners respond to the fluctuating economic, social, and political conditions?
>
> Did the role of the servile population alter?
>
> Did increased mortality characterize participation in long-distance trade through disease and/or violence? Was there depopulation? Did new food crops offset depopulation forces?
>
> Did individual and lineage insecurity increase? How was this manifested?
>
> Were religious or ontological beliefs altered or in any way adjusted during this era?

The degree to which these questions can be pursued in other societies is problematical, but, as the Kerebe evidence illustrates, they suggest a potentially rewarding research direction. They recognize the multiple and awesome consequences of long-distance trade. They also alert the inquirer to the disadvantages of focusing too narrowly upon a single aspect of the evidence that can lead to distortion.

If this and the following discussion of Kerebe society tend to emphasize the harsh and opportunistic side of existence, it is because this seems the most valid interpretation of the available evidence. But like Aniceti Kitereza, I feel that something in the Kerebe past needs to be stressed. Kitereza selected communal values and extolled the wisdom of his grandfathers. In contrast, I have sought to reveal, at least partially, the trying conditions under which Kitereza's forefathers lived and why they reacted to these conditions as they did. This approach should, in the end, provide a more complete impression of Kerebe life in an earlier era.

Nature of the Oral Evidence

This monograph presents an interpretation of Kerebe oral data. It must not be construed as a work relying solely upon the literal use of oral evidence. Rather, the evidence has been sifted and analyzed to determine what factors prompted the events mentioned within oral accounts. The present interpretation has developed over a five-year period, during which time the limited archival data from Tanzania and published materials devoted to this region, anthropological as well as historical in nature, have been searched and considered. Consequently, the oral information has been used in conjunction with a wealth of sources devoted to other societies. Unfortunately, as is so often the case in research, only tidbits from a few sources were specifically relevant. All too often the historical studies did not consider developments parallel to those analyzed in the Kerebe experience. Similarly, the anthropological studies possessed little or no historical perspective, describing institutions as they appeared at some time in the twentieth century with no regard for their internal dynamics.[12] Yet I could not have interpreted the oral data without the foundation provided by these earlier studies. That the interpretations presented below require verification and very possibly modification from studies based upon other societies is essential to stress. The Kerebe evidence was frustratingly incomplete but extremely suggestive as well as provocative.

This Bantu-speaking society offered an unusual set of conditions for historical research in the late 1960s. They numbered approximately 70,000 and primarily inhabited a large island in the southeastern confines of the Victoria Nyanza. This restricted geographical area and population enhanced the process of locating persons with knowledge of the past, while simultaneously limiting the potential number of elders possessing historical information. Thus it was not difficult to learn from people which elders in the society possessed historical information. The task of obtaining information, however, was great because no substantial history (nor anthropological study) of the Kerebe existed. To be sure, the archives produced a list of rulers and narrations concerning the ruling clan, collected during the 1920s and 1950s, but the information was sterile when it came to understanding who the Kerebe were and what they had experienced as a society throughout their history. Consequently a great deal of background information had to be acquired simply to understand the nature of the society.

As a result of these conditions, this study is the product of a modified approach to the use of oral data.[13] I assumed during the course of research that a detailed reconstruction of Kerebe political developments would not contribute as much to our knowledge of East African history as would a reconstruction of economic and social developments. This in turn created certain methodological problems. There is, for example, little relevant published information concerning social issues within an historical context. Thus the information on sorcery and its ramifications introduces a topic only recently considered by historians.[14] Likewise,

altering agricultural practices, the assumption of new
political and social roles by nonroyalty and the perplexing
issue of servility within a given community have all been
recently alluded to by Kimambo, Ogot, Roberts, and Were.
But to examine these specific issues had not been the major
concern of these writers. The problem of oral traditions
compounds the difficulty. In his "Introduction" to *Tanzania
Before 1900,* Andrew Roberts discusses what we eu-
phemistically call "oral traditions in eastern Africa." Most
often these traditions are nothing more than responses to
specific questions. They certainly are not elaborate,
memorized texts with historical content. Only one such oral
tradition existed among several Kerebe elders, and that had
to do with the arrival of the royal Silanga clan in Bukerebe in
the seventeenth century.[15]

Consequently, I prefer to refer to Kerebe "oral data" or
"oral information" to avoid misconstruing the existence in
Bukerebe of extensive oral traditions that did exist in some
interlacustrine East African societies and in numerous West
African societies. Given the lack of cohesive oral traditions
among the Kerebe, it was necessary in collecting oral
historical data, which does exist, to determine the nature of
each individual's information and then attempt to extract
this information by asking questions related to his
knowledge. My greatest concern then became what to ask.
And with few published examples of information on social
and economic issues during the nineteenth century available
from other societies, adapting my questions to what
appeared to be a reasonable line of inquiry became the
critical issue.

The frustrations encountered in collecting, validating,
organizing, and then incorporating oral data on non-
political matters into a scholarly account are beyond adequate description for me. A part of this frustration stems
from the very nature of oral data; it does not emerge as pithy
statements of fact that can be easily checked from some
other available source. Each person interviewed must be
subjectively assessed as to extent of historical information;

position within the community; clan membership; what, if anything, that person has to gain or lose by information offered; and the person's basic reliability. Add to this a different ontological and chronological frame of reference for someone like myself and Kerebe elders and you have an extremely complex situation. But perhaps most important to emphasize is that historical information possessed by elders is couched in subjectivity.

The magnitude of my transformation as an historian while with the Kerebe is illustrated by the altered focus of my research activities. My original intention was to focus upon economic developments and intersocietal relations about the lake district. After four months it became apparent that altering social relationships held the greatest potential for investigation. This focus was a realistic response to the actual knowledge possessed by Kerebe elders. Imposing my interest on this historical information (and knowledge) had proven to be an inefficient and frustrating enterprise. I learned, albeit slowly, to use what was available and thereby focused on the strengths of the oral data.

Nonetheless, these strengths, whether a product of oral traditions or oral data, require substantiation from sources outside Bukerebe—which brings us back to the issue of methodology. Historians utilizing extant accounts of travelers and missionaries before 1890 have generally been unsuccessful in finding observations that shed light on the type of questions currently posed by Africanist historians. It now appears that confirmation of the interpretations offered in this monograph will ultimately come from oral sources in other societies in the region, not from archives or published accounts of the nineteenth century. This method will enable historians to verify significant developments— certainly a major concern.

The chronology inherent in Kerebe oral data is the association of particular events with a specific omukama. Because the omukama was the single most important person in the chiefdom, with powers presumed to be far superior to those of others, he was frequently credited with innovations or blamed for misfortunes that occurred during his tenure. Consequently, historical data after the royal Silanga's arrival in the seventeenth century and during the approximately three centuries of Silanga rule contains a degree of chronological order, although comparatively plentiful information is not available for events before the nineteenth century. In contrast, the era before the arrival of the Silanga has very little discernible chronology. The principal remembered events are the movements of small clusters of people from site to site, village to village. This data contains the names of "clans"—a more accurate designation would be "migratory lineage segments"—and occasionally the name of a man, but whether the individuals so remembered were important leaders, clan founders, or prominent hunters is no longer recalled.

Nonetheless, significant information about the way of life in the pre-Silanga era is available, making some reconstruction possible. Kerebe oral data focuses on Bantu speakers who have historically been hunters as well as agriculturalists. The Kerebe have been significantly influenced by pastoralists throughout the centuries and have adopted some of their practices, but the separate identity of the agricultural population remains intact. The Kerebe describe their ancestors as hunters who also practiced agriculture. This distinguishes them from pastoralists such as the Tatog, Hima, and Masai with whom the Kerebe have had contact at various times in the past. Simultaneously their historical data has little to reveal directly about non-Bantu hunters, fishermen or pastoralists who may have been absorbed by the Bantu speakers. The disparate nature of cultural practices followed by Bantu-speaking lineages suggests a movement of small diverse groups of people. While the hunters (identified as ancestors of the Sandawe) and pastoralists (identified as ancestors of the Tatog) preceding the agricultural-hunters in Bukerebe are readily identified in oral accounts, only the later, Bantu population is described in detail.

What oral historical data has been preserved by elders varies from individual to individual. The most detailed traditions usually concern the informant's clan or a particular member of it. If an elder's father or grandfather was involved in some memorable event, it may often be recalled in detail. Few young people growing up at the beginning of this century missed hearing exciting accounts of their forebears which should compose the bulk of Kerebe historical information today. But the effort an elder had to make to retain the affairs of his family was a variable influencing what was remembered. Elder after elder expressed an inability to recall this heritage. Conditions within the chiefdom during the twentieth century fostered this historical amnesia, a situation already noted by Aniceti Kitereza in the early 1940s.

Kerebe history, like history of any centralized political unit, stresses the ruler and his exploits. What the ruler has done at any given time has been accorded signal importance. In contrast to the omukama and the chiefdom, the lineage or clan is a parochial and mundane entity and its importance in "official" histories is measured by its relationship and ability to serve the omukama. Moreover, modern experiences have discouraged the preservation of historical events by introducing new sets of values emphasizing a way of life that has minimal relationship to stories of either the family or the chiefdom. Whether or not they have attended school, young people throughout the present century have seldom been enthusiastic in learning about their past; there has been an aura of irrelevancy about it all. Altered social developments also have hindered the process of transmitting traditions. The time following the evening meal once devoted to informal family education and entertainment has been cut short so that children attending school can obtain sufficient rest. During recent decades, extended family homesteads have been dispersed, with many family units now containing only a small number of individuals. The result is that services of the family specialist in traditions or story-telling are partially lost to the majority of the clan.

The social role of those who remember historical traditions has also significantly influenced the type of traditions passed from one specialist to another. Prior to the present century, an elder held this responsibility within a specific clan. In addition, the omukama required individuals who possessed general information about all clans, attracting to his court those whose knowledge and advice was needed. Some of these men earned the right to be called *enfura* (friends of the omukama); although they held no official position, they were esteemed in society because of their influential relationship with the omukama. One means by which these men could gain recognition was by acquiring an extensive body of historical information that could be used by the omukama to resolve legal cases brought before him. Traditions of this nature were mainly those concerned with clan rights in relation to land: villages where clans had resided, shifts from one village to another within the chiefdom, historical relationships between clans, and different names of the same clan who lived in surrounding districts. The enfura who was an historian was called an *omwanzuzi* (pl. *abawanzuzi*) by the Kerebe; the information itself was *omwanzuro*. Usually no more than four to six men held this enviable position at any particular time. It required an impressive amount of time and effort to become an official (that is, recognized by the omukama) traditional historian. An aspiring historian sought to elicit information from men who were already renowned as historians, which meant in practice that the novice would visit his informants periodically until he had absorbed the desired factual information. Perseverance is a characteristic of an historian, and those in Kerebe society were no exception.

The sole surviving official Kerebe historian in 1969 was Bahitwa s/o Lugambage.[16] The adjective "official" is used in the sense that Bahitwa claimed to be an omwanzuzi and was in turn recognized as such by the community. The Kerebe, in the person of Bahitwa, are thus far the only society studied by historians in Tanzania possessing an institutionalized role for an historian.[17] Bahitwa's knowledge has specific limitations, even though he has attempted to encompass "all" historical information. His most extensive data is on clans, their migratory routes, their important leaders, their villages of settlement and the development of subclans. These accounts are not focused solely on the Kerebe, insofar as most clans have representatives living in many different ethnic communities. Bahitwa has also made himself the repository for events that feature the Silanga, the major royal clan.

Bahitwa's rendition of the royal Silanga history is valuable because he belongs to the Kula, a royal clan that rivaled the Silanga on the peninsula and island from the late seventeenth century until the 1920s, when its ruler was deposed by the joint efforts of the British administration and the Silanga omukama. As a Kerebe historian, Bahitwa has attempted to bridge the difficulties imposed by his descent and his desire to gain recognition as a specialist on all Kerebe history, including those of the Silanga. But his view of royal history is parochial in comparison to his recounting of clan histories. Diplomatic alliances arranged during the nineteenth century by Omukama Machunda, for example, are unknown to him and the relationship between the Kerebe and the Ganda is vague and seemingly unimportant in his recounting of traditions. These shortcomings exist because the knowledge of a Kerebe omwanzuzi was determined by the omukama's need for clan history to resolve cases of litigation. The function of the Kerebe oral history was only partially related to praise of the omukama or the chiefdom; it was also pragmatic in that it assisted the ruler in carrying out his functions.[18]

The system of maintaining oral accounts by means of specialists such as Bahitwa possessed a series of checks to insure accuracy. Bahitwa readily acknowledged that differing versions of men's deeds and their significance existed and maintained that one task of the omwanzuzi was to determine the authentic in conflicting materials. If two versions of an account could not be satisfactorily resolved by intensive questioning of numerous elders, Bahitwa resolved the dilemma by accepting the version held by his most trusted and respected teachers, themselves abawanzuzi. But in giv-

ing information Bahitwa provided only the version he has
accepted as valid, rather than indicating that others held
varying interpretations. Once confronted by a different interpretation, however, he would acknowledge its existence
and, on occasion, could explain the background for the op-
posing views. In the precolonial era, the omukama's method
of checking clan histories was to refer to several abawanzuzi
who would discuss conflicting evidence or confirm the
evidence supplied by litigants in a dispute.

Specific information related to a particular event was
never told the same way by two different informants. But
for a socio-economic history it is still possible to reconstruct
the basic historical framework without the specifics related
to each event, however desirable the specifics may be. Recent historical studies have shown that oral traditions are
reasonably reliable for general information, and Bahitwa's
are no exception. Major discrepancies on basic trends or
developments were infrequently encountered.

The presence of Bahitwa as an individual—he was extremely jealous of his own knowledge and critical of others'
information—and as a representative of a particular
socialized role militated against an avid interest in historical
concerns by other elders, except for their own clan's past. In
these matters, elders would defend their interpretations if
challenged by Bahitwa. It must be emphasized that
historical knowledge itself represents an awesome form of
social power in a community. Every clan has specific
skeletons in its family closet; these things should not be discussed nor even disclosed to others, whether an alien or not.
Hence an historical specialist like Bahitwa is greatly
respected as well as feared. He has made it his business to
know everyone else's past, skeletons and all. Therefore,
many of his clan accounts are adamantly challenged by
others. As for Bahitwa, his inflated conception of his own
role and abilities made it difficult to work with him. To
acknowledge ignorance about something was extremely difficult for him. His standard ruse was to request me to ask
him that question next time; he needed time to think about
it. Frequently he would then try to obtain the information

from other elders so he could have an answer during the next interview.

Bahitwa's advantage vis-à-vis other Kerebe elders is an important consideration. His confidence in his own sources of information—earlier generations of abawanzuzi— enabled him to dispute those with a narrow, clan perspective. Bahitwa's broad perspective thus set him apart and enhanced his value to me. One other Kerebe elder, Buyanza s/o Nansagate, falls into a similar category, that is, a man whose historical horizons extended far beyond the parochial context of clan or chiefdom.

In 1968 Buyanza was estimated to be 86 years of age, about four years Bahitwa's senior.[19] Buyanza was a Silanga, a grandson of the powerful Omukama Machunda. In contrast to Bahitwa, Buyanza was among the first Kerebe to receive formal mission education in the late 1890s, while Bahitwa never received any formal education and is not proficient in Kiswahili. Buyanza acquired literacy by the time he was twenty years old and retained it throughout his life. He had been recruited to serve in the German forces in 1904 and participated in the suppression of the Maji Maji uprising. He remained in the German military forces until 1918, when he was among the force of General Paul von Lettow Vorbeck that finally surrendered in Zambia. His experience outside Bukerebe undoubtedly sharpened his interest and awareness of the distinctive Kerebe past. Upon his return to Bukerebe after the war, Buyanza assiduously sought information from elders concerning the Silanga and the relationship of the Kerebe to neighboring peoples. His historical information is rich in references to the Ganda, Haya, Zinza, Sukuma, Jita (Kwaya), Ruri, and Luo and can be characterized as chiefdom-oriented, in contrast to Bahitwa's information, which is clan-oriented. Although Buyanza cannot be classified as an official historian nor was he regarded as such by the community, he merits the description of an outstanding unofficial historian.

In contrast to Bahitwa, Buyanza represented the other extreme as an informant. He was an extremely confident and successful man. He had lived a full life and was proud of who he was—his Silanga heritage—and what he had accomplished, namely to rear a large family and to educate his sons. His fifteen-year service in the German colonial army, his intimate relationship with the Roman Catholic White Fathers for seventy years, his interest in the Kerebe past and how this related to other East African societies gave him a cosmopolitan perspective which could understand and appreciate my endeavors. It was of no consequence to Buyanza to confess ignorance about something. If there was something sensitive about his clan's past that he did not want to discuss, he would indicate this and let the matter rest at that.

I searched for more informants like Buyanza, but they did not appear. A few elders who may have possessed valuable information refused to be interviewed. A considerable amount of bitterness existed within the community. This emanated from altering social and political conditions of the present era. They represented the displaced Old Guard whose position in society had been severely eroded by educational, political, and economic change. To talk to a stranger about the past was anathema to them. It only emphasized what had happened to them. Buyanza had fortunately never been a part of this former power group. This is no doubt partially explained by his family line. He was a grandson of Machunda, and this line of the Silanga ruling family lost power with Rukonge in 1895. Thereafter the descendants of Ibanda, Machunda's brother, held the position of omukama until the office was abolished in 1963.

Buyanza's knowledge, character, and intelligence qualified him as an ideal informant. His contribution to our knowledge of nineteenth-century history in the lake region is unusually great. The data on which this monograph is based owe much to Buyanza. His storehouse of information contained the kind of data that led me directly into socioeconomic rather than political history.

At the end of my research, once the oral data had been partially organized in my own mind, I presented Buyanza with my interpretation of Kerebe history during the nineteenth century, relating such things as sorcery to disease accompanying long-distance trade. I was curious about his reaction since he had been instrumental in the conception of the interpretation. Frankly, he was nonplussed. Our cultural differences suddenly emerged, something that had not intruded into our relationship earlier. But being the patriarch he was, he could only marvel that someone who had taken so much of his time, information, and food (I gained ten pounds during the last two months of my stay on Bukerebe, primarily because of my frequent visits to Buyanza's home) could emerge with such a strange understanding of what had happened. But in a sense he regarded me as one of his sons, and hence he was pleased that I was so pleased.

Buyanza's perplexed response to my interpretation of the Kerebe past illustrates the problem of interpreting oral data. Particular events from the past have been preserved in the minds of elders for a specific reason. In Bahitwa's case, there was a logic to the collective and remembering process, but to other men it was for some other reason. Buyanza specifically wanted to know about his family's history and the chiefdom's relation to other political units. These elders' remembered events are essentially descriptive. Explanations normally did not accompany the descriptions. Informants therefore had frequently to hypothesize if asked why something happened a particular way.

In determining the increase or decrease of some social development, unusual difficulties arose. Something like the increased production of cash crops during the present century is easy enough because this is within the personal experience of the elders. But was there more grain cultivated in 1875 than in 1825, or was there a larger servile population in 1875 than in 1825? Questions of this nature cannot be answered yes or no. A lengthy discussion was necessary, with question after question posed to determine whether the elder could recall any relevant information about the topic under consideration, then relate it to one omukama as opposed to an earlier one. I vividly recall a two hour interview with Buyanza in which I attempted to determine whether all Kerebe enthusiastically participated in regional trade or merely some of them. After considerable probing on my part and reflection on his part—with hot tea as a lubricant—we arrived at a proportion, approximately one-fourth, that satisfied us both.

Once this type of information was available, it was then necessary to check with other informants to determine if it possessed any validity. This was a tedious but essential process. On major political events verification was a relatively simple although time-consuming matter. But social alterations, such as the development of sorcery or the modified role of the medicine men, were difficult to discern and considerable extrapolation was necessary.

Yet this process alone falls short of an adequate examination. Too much information remains beyond validation: One tentative hypothesis could be cautiously built upon another equally tentative hypothesis. But the value of that type of exercise is limited. Thus the importance of published studies or archival information, particularly from the interlacustrine region, that could reveal similar events or trends. Without them, this analysis could never have been undertaken.

The scholar consults the most reliable and most productive sources in obtaining data. Consequently I interviewed Buyanza and Bahitwa more frequently than other informants.[20] The nature of their data, based upon a broad and essentially cosmopolitan perspective in relation to that of their contemporaries, required this approach. Each man, in his own unique manner, surpassed the norm of a good informant. Bahitwa's social role and Buyanza's personal experiences enabled them to see their community within a larger context and thereby better understand themselves and their society.

Notes

1. Additional information about Kitereza is found in Charlotte M. and Gerald W. Hartwig, "Aniceti Kitereza: A Kerebe Novelist," *Research in African Literatures,* III, 2 (1972), 162-70.

2. Aniceti Kitereza, "How Men and Women Came to Live Together," *Natural History,* ed. Charlotte and Gerald Hartwig, LXXIX, 1 (1970), 9-20. This is a story taken from Kitereza's novel.

3. The manuscript is presently being translated into English for publication.

4. J.D. Omer-Cooper, *The Zulu Aftermath* (London, 1966), 24-48.

5. K.O. Dike, *Trade and Politics in the Niger Delta, 1830-1885* (London, 1956), 28-30.

6. Kathleen M. Stahl, *History of the Chagga People of Kilimanjaro* (London, 1964); B.A. Ogot, *History of the Southern Luo* (Nairobi, 1967); and Gideon S. Were, *A History of the Abaluyia of Western Kenya* (Nairobi, 1967).

7. Ralph A. Austen, "Patterns of Development in Nineteenth-Century East Africa," *African Historical Studies,* IV, 3 (1971), 646. Also see David Cohen, "Agenda for African Economic History," *The Journal of Economic History,* XXXI, 1 (1971), 210, 212, 217.

8. Walter Rodney, *How Europe Underdeveloped Africa* (London, 1972).

9. Edward A. Alpers, "Re-thinking African Economic History: A Contribution to the Discussion of the Roots of Under-Development", *Ufahamu,* 3, 3 (1973), 97-129.

10. A.G. Hopkins, *An Economic History of West Africa* (New York, 1973), 8-77.

11. Alpers, "Re-thinking African Economic History," 116-21.

12. T.O. Ranger has a strong critical statement about the problems of published literature presenting African societies in an historical manner in "Recent Developments in the Study of African Religious and Cultural History and their Relevance for the Historiography of the Diaspora," *Ufahamu,* IV, 2 (1973), 17-34.

13. Information concerning the collection and use of oral data in East Africa can be found in the following: Ogot, *History of the Southern Luo*, 11-20; Were, *A History of the Abaluyia*, 13-27; Andrew Roberts, ed., *Tanzania Before 1900* (Nairobi, 1968), ix-x; Andrew Roberts, *Recording East Africa's Past* (Nairobi, 1968); Isaria N. Kimambo, *A Political History of the Pare of Tanzania, c. 1500-1900* (Nairobi, 1969), ix-xii; Thomas O. Beidelman, "Myth, Legend and Oral History: A Kaguru Traditional Text," *Anthropos*, 65, 1/2 (1970), 74-77; Alison Redmayne, "The War Trumpets and Other Mistakes in the History of the Hehe," *Anthropos*, 65, 1/2 (1970), 98-108; Samwiri R. Karugire, *A History of the Kingdom of Nkore in Western Uganda to 1896* (Oxford, 1971), 6-16; David W. Cohen, *The Historical Tradition of Busoga: Mukama and Kintu* (Oxford, 1972), 28-69; M.S.M. Semakula Kiwanuka, *A History of Buganda: From the Foundation of the Kingdom to 1900* (New York, 1972), 1-6; and Patrick Pender-Cudlip, "Oral Traditions and Anthropological Analysis: Some Contemporary Myths," *Azania*, VII (1972), 3-24; also relevant is Jan Vansina's "Once Upon a Time: Oral Traditions as History in Africa," *Daedalus*, 100, 2 (1971), 442-68.

14. See A.J.H. Latham, "Witchcraft Accusations and Economic Tension in Pre-Colonial Old Calabar," *Journal of African History*, XIII, 2 (1972), 249-60.

15. Bukerebe was a name gradually adopted during the eighteenth century. Earlier, the name of Bukerebe had been associated with the Yango clan when they lived on the west side of the lake; they used the same place name when they settled in the southeastern part of the lake. According to Bahitwa, Bugibwa had been the name of the district before being replaced by Bukerebe. Throughout this study Bukerebe is used to identify the island as well as the chiefdom of the royal Silanga clan.

16. Additional information concerning Bahitwa's training and his historical data is found in Gerald W. Hartwig, "Oral Traditions Concerning the Early Iron Age in Northwestern Tanzania," *African Historical Studies*, IV, 1 (1971), 93-114. The article was subsequently discussed and criticized by Patrick Pender-

Cudlip in "Encyclopedic Informants and Early Interlacustrine History," *The International Journal of African Historical Studies,* VI, 2 (1973), 198-210. My response to Pender-Cudlip's article is entitled "Oral Data and Its Historical Function in East Africa," *The International Journal of African Historical Studies,* VII, 3 (1974).

17. In Uganda, guardians of the royal Ganda tombs possessed historical information about deceased rulers; see Kiwanuka, *A History of Buganda,* 1-4. In Rwanda and Burundi royal traditions were also consciously preserved. Other politically centralized societies in the interlacustrine region no doubt also had specialists devoted to preserving historical information, although representatives may no longer survive.

18. A set memorized tradition was not passed from one omwanzuzi to another as it was by *griots* of West Africa; see Philip D. Curtin, "Field Techniques for Collecting and Processing Oral Data," *Journal of African History,* IX, 3 (1968), 371-76.

19. Buyanza passed away in early February 1974.

20. The oral data of Buyanza and Bahitwa, along with that of other informants, is being prepared for deposit in the University of Dar es Salaam library and the Indiana University Archives of Traditional Music, Center for African Oral Data.

1 The Kerebe and Their Past

The pre-1800 era of the Kerebe past is shrouded with a veil that permits only fragments of information to emerge. Yet it is sufficient to reveal glimpses of who lived in the district and something about how they lived. The image is of a small district blessed with favorable climatic conditions lying adjacent to a region through which many Bantu and Nilotic speaking peoples passed. Few of these migrants stayed long in the adjacent region because it possessed a harsh and exacting environment, one that could not assure reliable moisture. Pastoralists with their livestock found it reasonably attractive, but the island of Bukerebe and the adjoining peninsula was too restrictive. Agriculturalists and fishermen, on the other hand, could make better use of the limited space.

Information about the early occupants lacks a precise chronological framework. We know that hunters initially roamed the district, followed by pastoralists who in turn experienced the gradual infiltration of Bantu hunters who practiced some agriculture. The latter may have started to arrive around 1000 A.D. Then in the seventeenth century a group of refugees from the west side of the lake settled in the district and established a politically centralized system of government. The evolution of this chiefdom introduced a more complex system of government described in Chapter 3. Society also became stratified, based primarily upon cultural differences.

The gradual transformation of relatively independent lineage segments into sedentary agriculturalists with a centralized political system took place over a long period of time, possibly a millennium. The establishment of a royal clan in the 1600s marks the beginning of more rapid change, but it was nothing like the change encountered in the nineteenth and twentieth centuries. A synopsis of the pre-1800 era follows.

Environmental Features

In historical times, it is imprecise to refer to Bukerebe as an island within the Victoria Nyanza (Lake Victoria). In the twentieth century, the German and the British administrations broadened and deepened the narrow, swampy Rugezi canal that separated the island from the mainland to permit the passage of loaded sailing vessels. Previously people had waded across with their livestock, particularly when the water level was low. The explorer H.M. Stanley passed through Rugezi strait in 1875 and penned this description:

> Standing closed to the water at Nifuah we would have imagined that Ukerewe [Bukerebe] was an island separated by a strait about two miles broad, but turning our boat to the north, a couple of hours' rowing brought us so near that we could see that the opposing point of the mainland is joined to the island, or appears to be joined, by a very low bush-covered neck of land a mile in width, which thus separates the waters of Speke Gulf from the great body of Lake Victoria. A still closer examination, however, reveals the fact that this narrow neck is cut by a shallow channel, 6 feet wide and in some places only 3 feet deep ... Hence it will be seen that Captain

> Speke, who called Ukerewe an island, was literal-
> ly correct.[1]

Furthermore, Bahitwa insisted that the peninsula and island formed a single geographical unit prior to the nineteenth century. During the present century the depth of the lake has fluctuated between thirty and forty inches in any given decade.[2] Between 1961 and 1964, with the completion of the Owen Falls Dam at Jinja, Uganda, the lake level rose approximately two and a half meters, and Bukerebe has become an island in every sense of the word. It now takes twenty minutes by ferry to reach the mainland peninsula from the island. Nonetheless, the chiefdom itself was never greatly influenced by whether or not water separated one district from another. Historically, the chiefdom included a major portion of the peninsula in addition to the "island."

The Kerebe are predominantly an agricultural society that has also vigorously pursued hunting, fishing and herding. A fundamental determinant for an agricultural society is the average rainfall and its reliability. Although local variations occur, the entire island receives adequate and reliable rain for the traditional crops of sorghum, eleusine, and legumes. The rains usually begin in late October when the first crops are planted, with the second planting occurring during another wet period from December to February. The heaviest rains fall in April and May; July and August mark the dry season and harvest time. The average rainfall for the island is over fifty inches annually. In contrast, the mainland or peninsula portion of the chiefdom receives only thirty to forty inches.[3] The western portion of the island receives consistently more moisture than the eastern section, the difference being approximately thirty inches; that is, some seventy inches falls on the western end and some forty inches on the eastern end. This has significantly influenced the pattern of settlement.[4] The drier eastern portion of the island provided the most desirable conditions for cattle and the dominant grains:

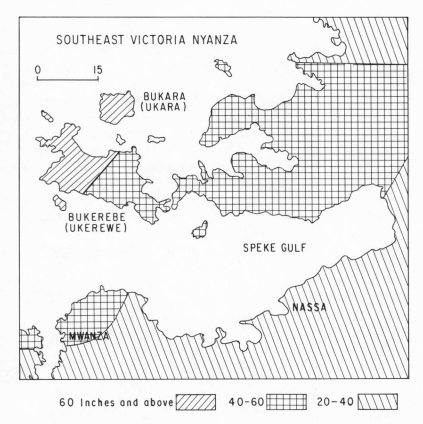

MAP I. RAINFALL DISTRIBUTION IN THE SOUTHEASTERN VICTORIA NYANZA.

sorghum and eleusine. People living on the wetter end of the island depended to a greater extent upon bananas. In the late nineteenth century the population was concentrated on the eastern and northern areas of the island. Elsewhere people tended to dwell along the lake shore leaving a large forested area vacant in the central and western interior. Prior to 1800 people inhabited the central region, but as population declined in the nineteenth century the central region became a preserve for wild animals such as monkeys, wart hogs, buffalo, rhinoceros, leopards, and elephants.

Early Inhabitants

The earliest identifiable inhabitants of Bukerebe were a hunting people referred to as Sandasya (Abasandasya).[5] According to the Kerebe historian Bahitwa, the Sandasya were "tall people"[6] who had previously migrated into the region from the northeast. Apparently they continued their general southward movement when the next group of migrants appeared. The extant descendants of the Sandasya are identified by Bahitwa and other informants[7] as the Sandawe, a Khoisan-speaking people now living some 250 miles SSE of Bukerebe.[8] Recent archaeological excavations of rock shelters by Creighton Gabel on the northeastern shores of the Victoria Nyanza possibly reveal the type of settlement pattern and mode of existence that can be attributed to the Sandasya. The radiocarbon dates for sites excavated by Gabel range from 450 B.C. to 640 A.D.[9] R.C. Soper conducted an archaeological survey to the south of the lake. His findings, of a tentative nature, give additional clues to the life followed by hunters when they occupied the region.[10]

The Kangara (Abakangara), a pastoral people, followed the Sandasya hunters into the region, possibly during the latter centuries of the first millennium A.D.[11] Confusion arises over the present identity of these people. The Kerebe claim that the Kangara called themselves Nyaturu; yet the Nyaturu are a Bantu-speaking, predominantly agricultural society, although they have adopted numerous customs of pastoral people. Traditions collected from Zinza and Sukuma informants also designate early pastoralists in their respective districts as Nyaturu.[12] The German explorer Oscar Baumann who passed through Bukerebe in the 1890s identified the Kangara pastoralists in the vicinity as "Taturu or, as they refer to themselves, Tatoga."[13] Assuming that the Kerebe designation for people they now call Kangara has not been transferred from one pastoral group to another, the original Kangara can be identified as Tatog, a Nilotic-speaking people who are culturally and

linguistically related to the Kalenjin people of western
Kenya such as the Nandi and Kipsigi.

The Tatog (Kangara) brought their cattle and other
livestock with them to their new region of settlement in the
vicinity of the southeastern corner of the lake. Oral sources
claim emphatically that the Tatog did not find any people
practicing agriculture upon their arrival, and although it is
uncertain whether the Tatog found hunters in the district, it
is a distinct possibility. The Tatog remained in the area for
an undefined period of time and, according to Bahitwa,
moved on when their herds became too large. It is apparent,
however, that some of them remained in the general vicinity and exercised a considerable influence over the Bantu
agricultural-hunters who followed in their wake. When the
royal clan arrived in the 1600s, for example, they found Bantu people in the area practicing circumcision, a custom
learned from pastoralists. Since it is reasonably well established that the Masai did not appear in the region until
approximately the eighteenth century,[14] it is necessary to
seek an earlier group, most probably the Tatog.[15]

Either the Sandawe or the Tatog left an isolated example
of "rock art" on Bukerebe. Similar designs and pictorial
representations have been found in numerous East African
localities. Late Stone Age hunters are no doubt responsible
for some, while agriculturalists are definitely associated
with particular representations, such as hoes. Pastoralists
have also been associated with these rock paintings in oral
accounts.[16] Those found on Bukerebe are located on the un-
derside of a rock outcrop some twelve feet above the surface
of the ground near the lake shore on the south central part
of the island. It may originally have been a shelter; the surface of a rock ledge extending directly beneath the design
has been worn smooth, seemingly by human activity. A
series of short vertical red lines, some placed at right angles
to others, reveals no meaningful pattern. There is no oral
information among the Kerebe concerning the lines, a fact
which supports the likelihood that either the early hunters
or the Tatog were responsible for them.

Bantu-Speaking Agricultural-Hunters

The migrants who followed the hunters and pastoralists were Bantu-speaking descendants of peoples who entered eastern Africa in the first half of the first millennium A.D.[17] The Bantu moved from west to east, settling on the western shores of the Victoria Nyanza before some moved to the eastern region of the lake; Kerebe accounts conform to the postulated pattern of migration.[18] Information provided by Bahitwa is sufficiently detailed to reconstruct the migratory movement of numerous clans that have dwelt on Bukerebe at one time or another.[19] His data may also shed some light upon the early Iron Age in the lakes region. Bahitwa insists that there were two major dispersal regions from which people migrated to Bukerebe: Buha and Bunyoro. The majority of clans came originally from Buha, the closer of the two dispersal centers. Bahitwa's concept of the dispersal centers is general rather than specific, and therefore should not be too closely identified with the present locations of the Ha and Nyoro. Unfortunately his information does not include specific details concerning the presumed movement of agricultural-hunters prior to their entrance into Buha and Bunyoro. In fact, he preferred to regard Bunyoro as the area of "creation." He could not provide substantial information about possible migrations before the Bantu entered eastern Africa with the exception of the Gara who definitely entered Bunyoro from the west. Bahitwa's historical orientation for the Bantu is Bunyoro, to the northwest of Bukerebe; there is simply no way to interpret his information to make it conform to the hypothesized migration of the Bantu from the southwest.[20] Rather, it complements the historical reconstruction advanced by Aidan Southall. Southall assumes that a significant portion of the predecessors of the present Bantu population in Uganda gradually moved from western Africa to the east along the northern edge of the equatorial forest zone, thereby reaching the interlacustrine area.[21] From his archaeological work, Robert Soper tentatively supports a similar interpretation.[22]

According to Bahitwa, these Bantu migrants were family units practicing hunting and agriculture. When discussing migrations Bahitwa referred to a specific clan *(oluganda)* not to the Bantu in general. From Bahitwa's usage of "clans" it is impossible to determine if clusters of kinsmen now designated as clans possessed a similar composition in the first millennium A.D. He also fails to distinguish between a clan/lineage and a number of such units which may have formed an ethnic group. Whether the clans/lineages he enumerated and identified as Bantu were so originally creates an additional difficulty in discerning the movement of various people. When asked to name the early groups of people who migrated to Bukerebe, he began with the Sandasya, then proceeded to the Kangara, Gara, Koni, Sohera, Nange, Si, Hira, Twa, etc. He identified the Sandasya as the Sandawe and the Kangara as "Nyaturu" (Tatog), both of whom speak a non-Bantu language. Once groups of agricultural-hunters within the dispersal centers are discussed, Bahitwa ceased to distinguish one cluster or clan from another; they are all indiscriminately included within the basic "clan" list.

The Twa (Abatwa) provide an example of the difficulty in attempting to reconstruct the early era from Bahitwa's information. In Rwanda the Twa compose a pygmoid population that is made up of numerous lineages, whereas in Karagwe there is a Hima (pastoral) clan by the name of Twa. Bahitwa's "Twa" lived on Bukerebe for a time before returning to Rwanda. Although he had no information on the physical characteristics of the Twa to suggest whether they were either short in stature or tall pastoralists, he did know that they were renowned potters, an attribute strongly suggesting that his Twa were related to the Rwandan pygmies, who are skilled potters.[23] The basic problem remains, however; it is impossible to determine whether they were a single clan or composed of a number of family units. A related issue is Bahitwa's identification of pastoral migrants. He identified them as an ethnic group without smaller social units. His four pastoral "brothers" are the Somali, the Kwabi (Masai), the Kangara (Tatog), and the

Huma (Hima, Tusi). He draws a distinction between non-Bantu pastoralists and Bantu, such as the Sukuma, who maintain large herds of cattle. Significantly, he designated the Hima, who now speak a Bantu language, as being different, a circumstance reflecting that their origins differ from other Bantu. The imprecise nature of Bahitwa's data means that it is exceedingly difficult to determine without additional evidence from other oral sources, most of which are as yet uncollected, whether or not some "clans" were originally non-Bantu but then gradually became assimilated by the agricultural-hunters.

Bahitwa attributed a unique migratory route to the Gara, allegedly the earliest Bantu "clan" to appear on Bukerebe. This particular tradition is unique in that it does not begin with Buha or Bunyoro; rather, he claimed that they came from the west, from Gana, in fact "Nkrumah's Ghana." According to Bahitwa, the Gara migrated eastward to Bunyoro where they divided into two major segments. One group continued traveling eastward while tracking a wounded elephant until they reached "Mombasa" (the Indian Ocean). The other segment traveled south from Bunyoro into present-day Buhaya. The hiving-off process of individuals and small clusters from a core group or groups continued and eventually some representatives arrived in Bukerebe; it is from these people that the island of Bukara receives its name according to Bahitwa (at some time the "g" sound being altered to a "k" sound to produce Bukara rather than Bugara). The alleged migration from Gana is staggering in its scope; concomitantly the portion dealing with the movement from somewhere in western Africa to Bunyoro complements existing linguistic evidence.

The Longo (Rongo) are another cluster of people whose designation has caused confusion among historians. They inhabit a portion of Buzinza and have assumed a vital role in the region as smelters of iron ore and as forgers of hoes which became the basic medium of exchange for much of this area in eastern Africa during the nineteenth century. An early twentieth century account of the inhabitants of

Buzinza identified the Longo as a group of clans who were descendants of the original Bantu population.[24] The given identity of the Longo has varied from a distinct ethnic group, on the one hand, to a single clan on the other hand. Bahitwa's data provide significant information because many of the Kerebe clans have ancestors who were Longo prior to their departure from the area. He identified the Longo as a cluster of clans cooperating in iron-ore smelting and hoe production. Nonsmiths, according to Bahitwa, used the name Longo to identify the smiths, deriving the name from the verb *kulongo,* meaning to cooperate in the smelting and smithing process. Bahitwa's own ancestors of the Kula clan at one time worked as smiths in Buzinza and formed a portion of the Longo population.

Bantu Settlement within Bukerebe

In all, Bahitwa enumerated at various times the names of 107 clans and lineages that allegedly settled in the district of Bukerebe at unspecified times; the list provided by him cannot be considered as complete nor beyond correction.[25] Only a minority of these clans still reside in the area while others either migrated to other districts or died out. Bahitwa related the dispersal center from which the ancestors of each clan emigrated—either Buha or Bunyoro—in addition to the general migratory route taken. While some details concerning routes and clan totems, particularly of those who are no longer represented in the chiefdom, may be erroneous, the general pattern of migration that emerges is complex and seemingly reliable.

In all likelihood the clans Bahitwa enumerated were representatives of a general movement of people that entered eastern Africa shortly after the time of Christ. Bahitwa's account suggests that the movement from the dispersal centers was gradual with small groups of migrants moving in virtually all directions with a considerable intermingling of people from Buha and Bunyoro. Bahitwa is relatively specific about the route taken by seventy-eight clans included in Appendix 1. The majority that have resided on Bukerebe trace their origins to Buha, the closer of the two centers. As far as can be determined from Bahitwa's account, only a few representatives of a given clan migrated from the dispersal area at any one time with a nucleus remaining in the center; a few people moved on some distance before settling down again farther east. "Clans" were fragmented during this process and it appears that a new name was frequently given to the "fragment" after its hiving-off, although an identity with the parent group often continued through the centuries. Important variations to the basic eastward migration from Buha occur, particularly for those migrants moving northward who eventually had representatives living on Bukerebe. Some clans moved into the Karagwe area, then representatives backtracked and gradually moved along the southern shores of the lake until reaching the Bukerebe district. Simultaneously other migrants continued their northerly trek into present-day Uganda, then moved east along the northern lake shore, and finally a few moved back south along the eastern lake shore to Bukerebe.

The Bunyoro dispersal center illustrates the same general complex migratory pattern with hundreds of miles traveled, but most likely over hundreds of years. According to Bahitwa, a substantial number of Kerebe clans—twenty-seven—trace their origins to Bunyoro, in comparison to fifty-one from Buha. Three different routes are discernible for those migrants with origins in Bunyoro who eventually arrived in Bukerebe. A general movement to the south from the dispersal center implies that many of the migrants intermingled with people from the Buha center in the Karagwe area. Some of these migrants rounded the lake and joined the movement of clusters from Buha that were moving eastward toward Bukerebe. A group of political refugees representing approximately eight clans came across the lake in the seventeenth century from Ihangiro to Bukerebe; this method of migration was most unusual, and this group is the sole example of immigrants who used water transportation extensively. The third cluster of clans from Bunyoro moved eastward from the center before traveling southward along the eastern lake shore.

One purported impetus for migration was strife between clan members. The consequences of this friction are revealed in the development of subclans of the Silanga and Timba clans which then adopted distinctive names and, in one case, altered the clan totem. The royal Silanga clan traces its origins to the Bunyoro dispersal center from which they traveled eastwards and then south along the east side of the lake. Tradition places them at Isene, a district to the east of Bukerebe, when a quarrel in the clan—called Segena—caused one man to seek his future elsewhere. The individual eventually arrived in Ihangiro chiefdom where he and his family were given the clan name Silanga which was derived from skill in constructing canoes. When his descendants had established their chiefdom in Bukerebe, surviving members of the parent Segena clan from Isene joined them on Bukerebe. Each group retained their separate identity, although both the Segena and the Silanga subclan claimed the same bird and fish totems. Later, two subclans hived off from the Silanga. The Gembe subclan was formed when one "brother" of the chiefdom's founder allegedly selected a hoe when they arrived in Bukerebe, symbolizing his preference for cultivation, while a second "brother" selected a drum, symbolizing his preference for ruling. The Yambi, the second subclan to splinter from the Silanga, came into existence during the reign of the fourth Kerebe omukama when a son of the ruler killed a brother and was ejected from the clan. All subclans that evolved retained the totems of the parent Segena clan from Isene, although a new social unit was created each time another name appeared. The experience of the Timba clan stands in contrast with that of the Silanga. Another clan dispute, possibly in the eighteenth century, caused the ejection of one member who originated the subclan name of Chamba and subsequently acquired two different totems from those of the parent clan.

The bewildering changes in "clan" names and the less frequent adoption of new totems make it difficult, if not impossible, to trace the interrelated clusters of people who share common ancestors merely by names or totems. Bahitwa's clan information, for example, includes as far as he can remember, the clan name of those who dwelt on Bukerebe during at least the past millennium and the name of the parent or subclan that lived in Buzinza, Buha, Bukara, etc., a formidable maze of varying names which reveal the hiving-off process and the tendency to alter the clan name when settling in a new location. Although alterations in clan totems also occurred, an interesting pattern emerges from a survey of those totems provided in Appendix 1. Two basic phenomena appear: the majority of clans that trace their origins to Bunyoro have a wild animal, a bird, or a fish as a totem; in contrast, most clans with origins in Buha have a cattle totem, and in some cases a wild animal is the second totem. It is generally explained by informants that totems originally came into existence either because the particular "thing," whether it be an animal, a bird, a fish, or an object, either had harmed an ancestor and was therefore cursed by him, or had aided an ancestor in some way and was henceforth protected by his descendants.

This available information about clans, totems, and clan origins suggests that the Bantu-speaking clusters at the time of their entry into East Africa possessed totems of which the vast majority were wild animals.[26] Gradually, new totems, reflecting an important event or development for the clan or subclan, were added. Not least of the important events in this area of East Africa was the introduction of cattle, probably during the first millennium A.D., and the clans emanating from Buha were more influenced by pastoralists, as indicated by the cattle totems, than those emanating from Bunyoro and now living in the southern lake region.[27] It appears that either totems of clans in the Buha center were replaced after cattle were introduced or there was a substantial amount of intermarriage between the Bantu population and the Nilotic-speaking possessors of cattle with the result that some pastoralists became sedentary and more dependent upon agricultural produce in addition to acquiring a Bantu language.

The Bantu population of the southeastern lake region was eventually composed of migrants with similar cultural backgrounds from Buha and Bunyoro, although people from the former center had received a more intensive exposure to pastoral values. The language of the Bantu in the interlacustrine area is markedly different from that spoken by the Nyamwezi and Sukuma, which is a related Bantu language. Around the shores of the Victoria Nyanza, the Sukuma and the Nilotic Luo (a completely separate and distinct language family) possess languages that are significantly different from that of others in the vicinity, but the majority speak mutually intelligible languages and these people are the descendants of the early Bantu from Buha and Bunyoro.[28] This population in turn has been influenced by intrusive people speaking other languages, the major event being the appearance of the Hima (Tusi) pastoralists into the interlacustrine region. Although they adopted the language of the agricultural majority, they also altered it significantly. The Kerebe spoke the language of the interlacustrine cultures once the royal clan and its entourage imposed it upon the inhabitants of Bukerebe after they arrived. Their language was probably still intelligible to the earlier occupants whose language is currently spoken by their Kara and Jita descendants.[29]

Hunting, Fishing, and Agricultural Pursuits
of the Agricultural-Hunters

Hunting, both as a food source and for protecting cultivated crops, was important for the early agricultural-hunters in Bukerebe and the neighboring region. The significance of hunting among the ancestral predecessors of most Kerebe clans is provided in the ethnographic notes recorded by A.M.D. Turnbull in the 1920s when he described the ironworking Longo of Buzinza as hunters and recorded nothing about their agricultural interests.[30] As descendants of early agricultural-hunters from the Buha dispersal center, their described preoccupation with hunting reflects a condition that presumably existed centuries ago; Kerebe accounts refer to the importance of hunting, particularly in sparsely populated areas where wild life was abundant and not greatly threatened by man. Oral accounts frequently explain the movement of people by stating that they were hunting an animal that led them to a desirable location and hence they settled in the area.

Hunting is and was a prestigious activity according to elders of today. Men hunted animals for their flesh to supplement the vegetable diet provided by the agricultural activities of the women. Cultivated crops in turn had to be protected from wild animals, and men had the responsibility of preventing burrowing and grazing animals from destroying crops by using trenches and pit traps. As the population increased in agriculturally favorable districts, wild animals were forced to give way to a sedentary population with hunting decreasing in importance for the people who remained in the area. Where various species of antelope existed, hunters used bow and arrow, frequently assisted by their dogs who located, chased, and confused the intended victims.[31] Informants suggest that large animals such as buffalo, elephant, and hippopotamus received very little attention from the early hunters. Not until formal hunting associations were introduced do oral accounts refer specifically to hunting of these larger animals. It is explained that only with an organized group of hunters possessing specific skills in addition to magical knowledge necessary to hunt a particular animal successfully, could the task be undertaken without exposing the participants to unreasonable risks. On Bukerebe men have not always imposed their will on wild animals. Bahitwa maintains that many centuries ago, long before the royal clan arrived in the 1600s, Bukerebe was literally invaded by large numbers of wild life, presumably animals such as buffalo and elephants. The agricultural-hunters of the region were unable to cope with them and were forced to withdraw from the district. Only after the animals had departed could the people once again occupy the area.

In contrast to the early importance assigned by elders to hunting, fishing activities are not accorded much significance, although in recent centuries fishing appears to have increased in importance.[32] Specific methods, implements, and fishing techniques are assigned to particular clans; unfortunately it is impossible to determine the sequence of clan arrivals or even the approximate time of their arrival that a hypothetical reconstruction of early fishing activities necessitates. There is a dearth of published historical evidence from other fishing communities around the lake. Information from fishing populations on the west side of the Victoria Nyanza, for example, would be valuable in understanding their historical role.

Bahitwa's data reveal little about any fishing clans that lived in the southeastern area of the lake before the arrival of the Silanga clan in the seventeenth century. The data, however, indicate that the cultures on the western side of the lake were strikingly different from those on the eastern side, a situation revealed when innovations introduced by the royal clan are enumerated. The royal clan, or someone within their entourage, introduced an unbarbed metal fish hook *(emigonzo)* and a three pronged metal fish spear *(amasaku).*[33] The fact that the Silanga are also credited with introducing the "sewn" canoe enhances Bahitwa's contention that early clans had little to do with fishing.[34] Yet other informants contend that their ancestors preceded the Silanga into the district and had "always" concentrated on fishing.[35] These clans utilized basket traps *(emigono)* and possibly fence traps *(emibigo)* and consequently did not depend upon canoes for fishing since both devices are used along the lake shore. Kerebe accounts thus reveal some complexities that will be involved in eventually reconstructing the history of fishing populations.[36]

While Kerebe data suggest that hunting clans originally had a separate identity from fishing clans, they associate agricultural innovations with the hunters, but early fishermen may have practiced agriculture as well. Bahitwa confidently contends that the agricultural-hunters who were in the Buha and Bunyoro dispersal centers cultivated a number of food crops but the extent to which hunting and gathering supplemented other food acquiring activities remains unclear although soil and climatic conditions would limit the role of cultivation. All informants agree that the earliest types of cultivated grain were sorghum *(omugusa)* and eleusine *(endwero)*. Bahitwa also stated that the earliest clans cultivated two species of legumes *(enkole* and *enzutwa)* in addition to two species of ground nuts *(empande* and *enkuku)*.[37] The Kerebe acquired at least one type of banana in the 1600s; later, about 1800, they experienced a veritable revolution in agriculture that accompanied the era of long-distance trade and travel which is discussed in Chapter 3.

Especially noteworthy is the fact that the banana (or plantain) was not known to the early clans in Buha and Bunyoro and was not introduced to the southeastern area of the lake until the royal clan brought suckers of the plant with them from Ihangiro on the western lake shore.[38] Bahitwa's understanding of the dispersal of bananas within the interlacustrine zone indicates that the early migrants did not yet have them when the pastoral Tatog passed through the country west of the lake. Bahitwa assumes that this plant was brought into the lake region from the north, although this is inconsistent with a recent historical hypothesis that it was introduced into the interlacustrine area from the Zambezi basin far to the south.[39]

The Introduction of Iron Technology

Bahitwa's traditions indicate that the early agricultural-hunters in Buha and Bunyoro possessed the knowledge of iron working, both smelting and forging. He stated in addition that "all" early clans had smiths *(abahesi)* within their midst; his traditions, however, did not differentiate between smelters of iron ore, practitioners of a highly specialized skill requiring sophisticated technical knowledge, and forgers, who only reworked iron.

Smithing has not been a prestigious occupation among the Kerebe for a number of centuries, an attitude possibly acquired from the Tatog pastoralists. Members of Kerebe smithing clans have been restricted in their marriage arrangements to the extent that they could marry only into other smithing clans or with the royal Silanga clan. Silanga women, unlike others, had no fear of marriage with smiths because they possessed "medicine" sufficiently powerful to protect themselves from a skin disease associated with people who worked with iron. Bahitwa and other informants did not satisfactorily explain the origin of social restraints imposed upon smiths, a development dating at least from the 1600s, but informants agree that a significant proportion of the early clans had smiths (forgers) within their midst.[40] But by the nineteenth century only one Sese clan, the Bago, continued to forge iron while a second clan, the Gabo, provided a few iron ritual objects for the abakama. Otherwise all smiths were immigrants of either Jita or Zinza extraction, and in the present century only the descendants of Jita migrants have remained active in this work. The trend has consistently been for smiths to abandon this occupation because of the social impositions.

The Victoria Nyanza region is reasonably well endowed with iron ore deposits. In the southern lake district the richest deposits were located in Buzinza while minor deposits were found to the east and south of Bukerebe Island. It is apparent that ore from Kulwirwi, a highland massif on the peninsula just to the east of the island, was smelted by Kerebe smiths before 1700.[41] The smelters belonged to the Gabe clan who resided on Kulwirwi until the 1700s when they were driven from it by the Silanga.

With the Gabe smelting iron ore on Kulwirwi, the mountain served as the center for hoes which were also made by the smelters and then bartered for livestock or grain. When hoes had been worn down by use (the attrition rate of the untempered metal used in hoes was relatively high), the remaining blade and tang—the portion inserted into the handle—was reheated and reworked by local smiths (forgers) to make such objects as arrowheads, spears, and knives. In the 1600s, according to the elder Buyanza, the hoe made by the Gabe smiths was called *ebyebwe* and was smaller in size than the Zinza type later used. Some form of the word *gembe* was also used at approximately the same time in relation to the hoe since the Gembe, the subclan of the Silanga mentioned above, acquired their name from their choice of a hoe in preference to a drum. The word *gembe* shares a common root, *-embe,* with the Kiswahili word for hoe, *jembe.* The hoe used by the Kerebe since the eighteenth century is called *enfuka* and was acquired from the Longo in Buzinza.

Centuries ago, according to Bahitwa, local forgers were numerous and common, particularly in clans settled in sparsely populated districts. Given higher concentrations of population, specialization apparently emerged within specific clans, a development primarily dependent upon the extent of political and religious authority with which each clan was imbued, the greater the authority the more likely that a clan's members ceased smithing. Specialization in iron working by particular clans commenced before 1600 among the Kerebe, a fact which implies significant interdependence among clans in the area. Consequently the Gabe clan, who controlled the iron ore sources on Kulwirwi, assume an important role in Kerebe traditions at the time the Silanga arrived; they were in a position to command respect and cooperation although they were confined territorially to Kulwirwi. This arrangement was dramatically altered in the eighteenth century when a military encounter between the Gabe and Silanga dispersed the former, who subsequently occupied a subordinate ritual role in relation to the Silanga. The Kerebe were left without a local source for hoes, making it necessary to acquire them by barter in Buzinza.

Cattle and the Agricultural-Hunters

Bahitwa relates that the migrants who emigrated from Buha and Bunyoro had sheep, goats, dogs, and chickens, but not cattle. He emphatically asserts that the Tatog, speakers of a highland Nilotic language,[42] introduced cattle to the Bantu, presumably the short-horned type. The Tatog, according to Bahitwa's information, moved westward with their cattle through present-day Uganda from Mount Elgon and then moved southward through the interlacustrine region into central Tanzania.[43] During this migratory period, the pastoralists encountered the Bantu, who acquired cattle when the pastoralists exchanged them for grain during times of food shortages. From Karagwe, a kingdom west of the lake, there are oral accounts claiming that the agricultural population there possessed short-horned cattle before the Hima pastoralists arrived with the long-horned breed by the fourteenth century, thus supporting Bahitwa's contention that the Hima-Tusi did not introduce the short-horned cattle into the interlacustrine zone.[44]

Kerebe accounts unfortunately provide few insights into the probable integration process that occurred between the agricultural-hunters and the pastoralists. It is likely that this took place to a greater degree with the first wave of pastoralists, particularly in and around the Buha dispersal center, since the later Hima wave has retained its identity in the interlacustrine zone over at least a five-hundred-year period. No clan that settled in Bukerebe has a pastoral identity or background recalled in traditions, although in the mid-1800s an omukama had some twelve Tatog (Kangara) wives. Yet the elders recognize any contributions from the pastoral Tatog. The care and treatment of cattle, for example, is accepted as particularly significant. Within the spiritual realm, Rugaba was respected by the Kerebe as the protecting guardian spirit for cattle. This same spirit assumed an important role in the spiritual realm of the various states west of the lake where the spirit was generally, though not always, associated with cattle.[45] Bahitwa also made the revealing comment that the Tatog taught the Kerebe to work and socialize together, reinforcing the impression that agricultural-hunting clans were virtually self-sufficient, autonomous units that reluctantly merged with their neighbors into larger corporate entities.

The Establishment of a Chiefdom

Kerebe society appears to have been relatively homogenous before the arrival of the royal Silanga clan. Diversity no doubt existed, particularly in terms of hunting and fishing activities as well as in possession of livestock. But with the exception of smiths and potters, rigid social and economic levels appear to be absent. Politically, the era before the mid-1600s had evolved a system of government focusing upon several dominant clans (for example the Hira, Gabe, Kula, and Zigu). Each of these clans provided a semblance of leadership to other clans residing in the same vicinity. The politically subordinate clans had representation in a body of elders, a form of advisory council. Therefore all clans normally had an opportunity to assist in decision making, particularly in cases of litigation between clans. When clans fell outside the effective control of a dominant clan, it is very likely that an elder within the social unit provided effective leadership.

Existing social, political, and even economic patterns received an abrupt shock during the mid-seventeenth century. The Silanga contingent, along with a sizable group of followers—large enough to have an impact militarily—arrived and proceeded to subdue piecemeal the existing dominant clans. Henceforth the Kerebe form an integral part of the interlacustrine culture zone, both linguistically and ethnographically.[46] Their political system is discussed below in Chapter 4.

The royal Silanga clan itself possesses an interesting and complex past.[47] Oral accounts trace the origin of the clan to the Bunyoro dispersal center from which they had migrated as hunters to the east, eventually turning south and approaching the southeastern corner of the Victoria Nyanza along the eastern shore line. At Isene, a community directly east of Bukerebe on the plains, the clan was splintered by a family quarrel. The incident encouraged a young man and his friend to seek their future elsewhere. The two companions walked from Isene in a general westward direction and eventually found themselves in Ihangiro, a kingdom already under the authority of Ruhinda the Great or his immediate descendants.[48] While the two men stayed in Ihangiro they improved their status, rising from a position of servitude to one of confidence. The duration of their sojourn there may very well have exceeded one generation. The migrant from the east, or his descendant, eventually aroused the animosity of important men who counseled the ruler. Intrigues occurred which in turn stimulated Katobaha, the probable leader of the Silanga clan at this time, to develop plans for escaping from Ihangiro with his followers. Indeed, a small band soon surreptitiously departed from Ihangiro by canoe and moved directly eastward across the open waters of the Nyanza.

There are rich oral accounts concerning the trek from Isene, the stay in Ihangiro, the journey to the east, and the encounter with the inhabitants of Bukerebe, called Bugibwa at the time. Significant issues that emerge are centered around the establishment of a royal dynasty. The founder of the royal clan for example, is assumed to be the son of Ruhinda by the royal clan, yet other renditions effectively contradict this contention. The need to identify with Ruhinda the Great is obviously important, and it is certainly not incorrect to recognize that Ruhinda the Great was in every sense the spiritual father of the royal clan. The totems of the royal Silanga clan (*enfunzi,* a small bird, and *omusilionjio,* a type of fish) together with their close identification with fishing and hippo hunting, however, reveal a background that is associated with agricultural-hunters, not pastoral rulers.[49] The humble background of the migrants from

Ihangiro may partially explain the outbreak of fighting when Katobaha attempted to impose his authority on the existing population of Bukerebe.

The immigrants introduced a series of innovations, in addition to the political changes, that initiated significant modifications in everyday life. Agriculturally, the banana was brought by the newcomers from the western shore of the lake to the southeastern region, and initially this impressed the inhabitants of the region more than any other factor about the immigrants. A second innovation was a new style of fishing, using an unbarbed metal hook, that enabled the fishermen to catch fish in deep water, thus concentrating on heretofore uncommon species of fish. Associated with fishing were the sewn plank canoes; however, it is impossible to determine whether these canoes were absent before 1650, though it is definite that the migrants possessed them. In hunting, the royal clan while in the west lake district had acquired the knowledge required to hunt the hippopotamus on an organized basis using a metal harpoon. Whether an earlier system of killing the animal existed and was merely supplanted or whether the animal was generally unmolested earlier is unknown. Social changes occurred as well; for example, the concept of domestic servitude appeared. The language and customs of the interlacustrine community became the accepted norms and the inhabitants apparently adapted themselves to the imposed standards. A seven-stringed trough zither made its appearance at this time also; it represents the first stringed musical instrument for the Kerebe.[50] On the other hand, circumcision, an earlier custom adopted by agricultural-hunters from the Tatog but anathema to the migrants, was discouraged in the Silanga controlled area.

Impact of the New Order

The royal Silanga clan arrived in the southeastern lake region during the seventeenth century, along with representatives from seven other clans. This nucleus of eight clans successfully imposed their language and customs on the inhabitants of what became Bukerebe. This politically and culturally dominant group called themselves Sese and set themselves apart by means of language and custom. Before the arrival of this contingent from the west lake district, the language spoken was presumably one closely related to that now spoken by the inhabitants of the island of Bukara and by the Jita (Kwaya) on the southeastern shore of the lake. All of the languages around the lake are mutually intelligible, with the major exception of the Nilotic Luo of Kenya on the northeastern corner of the lake. The language of the Bantu Sukuma is also difficult to understand within the lake complex. As in any society, the language or dialect spoken by inhabitants was partially determined by the social stratum in which they found themselves. Those persons appearing frequently at the royal court found it necessary to adopt its usages; a court language developed that was based on proverbs, nuances and indirect speech; only frequent attendance at court could keep a man abreast of current idiomatic expressions. Since vast powers were presumably centered within the person of the omukama, the various clan representatives aspiring to become a part of the Sese community and share their prestige adopted the language of the influential minority. In the present century the Sese language has become virtually obsolete because of a steady influx of immigrants (Jita, Kara, and Sukuma), a tendency to use Kijita in dance associations, and the impact of Swahili, which is taught in the primary schools.[51]

The people currently refer to themselves as Kerebe, but this is a recent development based on the island's name. The proud Sese reluctantly adopted the more imprecise name. Among the Sukuma living across Speke Gulf the word =*sese* meant slave; Omukama Gabriel Ruhumbika (1907-1938), sensitive about his people's image, advised the Sese to use the name "Kerebe," which had the added attribute of including all inhabitants of the chiefdom. Earlier, "Sese" had designated only a minority of the population, albeit the "important people" descended from clans claiming relatively recent ties to lacustrine societies to the west.[52] The royal

Silanga clan was naturally the leading representative of the
Sese. We may conclude that Sese clans permitted others to
join their ranks, because in 1968 informants gave a broad
definition of the term Sese. Furthermore, distinctions could
not be readily made on a clan basis; representatives of a clan
living on Bukerebe may have been Sese, while members of
the same clan living on the eastern mainland were not
regarded as Sese.

By 1900 three ethnic terms were used to differentiate
non-Sese portions of the population, who together composed the majority of the people. The largest group was and
remains the Jita (Kwaya), who began their sporadic emigration in small groups from the east coast of the lake by at

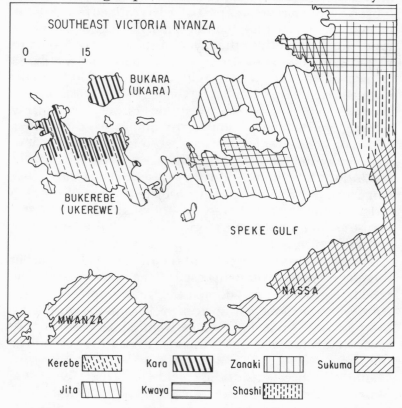

MAP II. ETHNIC DISTRIBUTION IN THE SOUTHEASTERN VICTORIA
NYANZA.

least 1800. Another important group had come during the nineteenth century from the island of Bukara and was referred to simply as Kara. The third group was the Ruri, who composed the vast majority of the servile population. They originated from the region north of the Jita and came from a number of different ethnic stocks such as the Suba, Luo, Kuria, and Kwaya. In the 1800s both the Kara and Ruri occupied low social positions, although the former group can best be described as agricultural laborers. The Jita and Kara migrated into the chiefdom when conditions in their own country forced them to seek a more favorable place in which to live. The Jita experienced periodic famine due to drought and to attacks from pastoralists in the nineteenth century. The attackers are invariably designated as Masai, but additional candidates for the role are the Kuria and the Tatog (Taturu). The Kara, on the other hand, experienced a shortage of food caused by a high population density, so their problem existed on a recurrent and virtually annual basis. The servile Ruri were usually children brought to Bukerebe and sold by men needing food during times of famine. In the present century Sukuma and others also began to migrate into Bukerebe in significant numbers.

When migrants entered Bukerebe, they generally did not stress their ethnic and language differences; rather, they emphasized their clan affiliation. With approximately seventy-five different clans and subclans found in this region of the lake, any one clan may have had representatives living among half a dozen different ethnic groups. Although the different ethnic representatives of a clan may identify themselves with a distinctive name, they nonetheless are well aware of what their relatives call themselves in other districts. Thus when the Sukuma immigrated into Bukerebe in this century, they reduced Kerebe suspicion of themselves as outsiders by announcing their clan ties and identifying their brothers (cousins) and fathers (uncles) within the chiefdom. All immigrants could claim their own land within the chiefdom, providing they went through the proper administrative channels. Uncultivated land was available to them and although an exception to this policy occurred in the post-World-War-II period, this barrier was soon removed. Today the Sese, Jita, Kara, Ruri, and Sukuma make up the Kerebe, that is, the inhabitants of Bukerebe. Throughout this century there has been a growing tendency for differences separating the ethnic groups to decrease in importance. Intermarriage is becoming more frequent, although total integration remains to be achieved.

The earliest population estimate (in 1907) was based on a hut count for tax purposes. The population was then given as 30,000 for the island, some 13,000 for the peninsula, and 2,000 for the numerous small islands that are included within the chiefdom. The large island of Bukara (Ukara) to the north of Bukerebe has never been a part of the chiefdom. In 1932 the population of Bukerebe was reckoned to be 65,000 with 47,000 living on the island, giving a population density of 218 per square mile, in contrast to the drier peninsula with a population density of about 48 per square mile.[53] In recent years the island's population has been estimated to be 70,000.

Notes

1. Henry M. Stanley, *Through the Dark Continent,* I (London, 1878), 160.

2. Heinz Dieter Ludwig, *Ukara—Ein Sonderfall tropischer Bodennutzung im Raum des Victoria-Sees* (Ifo-Institute für Wirtschaftsforschung München: Afrika-Studienstelle, Nr. 22, München, 1967), 57. Ludwig has assembled an extremely valuable set of geographical statistics for the southeastern lake region that includes population data on an ethnic basis, soil and vegetation information, and rainfall data. He has compiled all available statistics for the twentieth century. Therefore any variations that may have occurred in the lake level from decade to decade are taken into consideration.

3. E.C. Baker, "Report on Administrative and Social Conditions in the Ukerewe Chiefdom," Cory Papers No. 9, University of Dar es Salaam Library.

4. Ludwig, *Ukara,* 39.

5. The majority of information on the pre-Silanga period is the contribution of Bahitwa s/o Lugambage. Beginning in August 1968, Bahitwa was interviewed occasionally until January and February 1969, when he was interviewed weekly. Makene s/o Ikongolero contributed important supplementary information that clarified and modified Bahitwa's information for the pre-Silanga era. Makene's clan, the Hira, was important in the region before the arrival of the Silanga. Although certainly not as knowledgeable as Bahitwa, he was extremely helpful in independently validating some of the latter's assertions. Makene was initially visited in August 1968 and then again on several occasions in February 1969. Hans Cory, a sociologist under the British colonial government, collected historical information about the Kerebe during the 1950s. His notes substantiate the information collected although it is possible that the same informant, Bahitwa, was also used extensively by Cory. The latter's material was collected in the presence of *Omukama* Michael Lukumbuzya; presumably other informants were also present: see "Ukerewe Local Government and Land Tenure," Cory Papers No. 420, University of Dar es Salaam.

6. Bahitwa was insistent that the Sandasya hunters were tall in stature even though hunters are commonly described as short. For the sake of perspective, it is necessary to realize that Bahitwa's height is approximately 5'4".

7. When "Kerebe" or "informants" is used in the text to identify the source of information, it means that the information was given by numerous persons, regardless of clan affiliation.

8. J.E.G. Sutton, "The Settlement of East Africa," *Zamani; A Survey of East African History,* eds., B.A. Ogot and J.A. Kieran (Nairobi, 1968), 85-86. An excellent discussion of precolonial Sandawe history is provided by Eric ten Raa in "Sandawe Prehistory and the Vernacular Tradition," *Azania,* IV (1969), 91-104.

9. Creighton Gabel, "Six Rock Shelters on the Northern Kavirondo Shore of Lake Victoria," *African Historical Studies,* II, 2 (1969), 219.

10. R.C. Soper and B. Golden, "An Archaeological Survey of Mwanza Region, Tanzania," *Azania,* IV (1969), 15-80.

11. See Christopher Ehret, "Cushites and the Highland and Plains Nilotes," *Zamani,* 166-68; Soper and Golden, "An Archaeological Survey of Mwanza Region," 59; also note the term Kangara in Zinza oral accounts.

12. A.M.D. Turnbull, "Notes on the History of Uzinza, Its Rulers and People," and O. Guise Williams, "Tribal History and Legends-Sukuma," Mwanza Province Book, National Archives of Tanzania; Soper and Golden, "An Archaeological Survey," 17.

13. Oscar Baumann, *Durch Massailand zur Nilquelle* (Berlin, 1894), 168.

14. Sutton, "The Settlement of East Africa," 94.

15. Ehret, "Cushites and Nilotes," 163-68.

16. Soper and Golden, "An Archaeological Survey," 48-53; Merrick Posnansky, "The Prehistory of East Africa," *Zamani,* 65-68; R.E.S. Tanner, "A Series of Rock Paintings Near Mwanza," *Tanganyika Notes and Records,* 34 (1953), 62-67; R.E.S. Tanner, "A Prehistoric Culture in Mwanza District, Tanganyika," *Tanganyika Notes and Records,* 47 (1957), 175-86.

17. Archaeologists associate dimple-based and channeled pots with the spread of iron working; simultaneously the Bantu are assumed to have produced the aforementioned pots hence they are credited with the spread of iron working. It is a tentative hypothesis.

18. The most recent archaeological information relating to the Bantu migration is found in R.C. Soper, "A General Review of the Early Iron Age of the Southern Half of Africa," *Azania,* VI (1971), 5-38; Bahitwa's migration pattern conforms to the existence of known Urewe pottery, attributed to the Early Iron Age Bantu—see Soper's map on page 9. Another valuable discussion is by J.E.G. Sutton, "The Interior of East Africa," *The Iron Age in Africa,* ed. P.L. Shinnie (Oxford, 1971), 142-82.

19. See Appendix 1.

20. Roland Oliver, "The Problem of the Bantu Expansion," *Journal of African History,* VII, 3 (1966), 375. In the case of a significant portion of the Nyamwezi-Sukuma population, a migration from the southern Zaire dispersal center appears sound. This issue is discussed at greater length in Hartwig, "Oral Traditions Concerning the Early Iron Age," 99-107.

21. Aidan Southall, "The Peopling of Africa—The Linguistic and Sociological Evidence," *Prelude to East African History,* ed. Merrick Posnansky (London, 1966), 74; also relevant are G.W.B. Huntingford, "The Peopling of the Interior of East Africa by Its Modern Inhabitants," *History of East Africa,* I, eds., Roland Oliver and Gervase Mathew (London, 1963), 80-81, 85; A.M.D. Turnbull, "Wahima," Cory Papers No. 231; University of Dar es Salaam; Hans Cory "(Banyamwezi) The Country and Its Inhabitants," Cory Papers No. 43, University of Dar es Salaam.

22. R.C. Soper, "Iron Age Archaeological Sites in the Chobi Sector of Murchison Falls National Park, Uganda," *Azania,* VI (1971), 84-87.

23. See Soper and Golden, "An Archaeological Survey," 57-58.

24. Turnbull, "Notes on the History of Uzinza." Bernard Golden discusses the Longo at some length in Soper and Golden, "An Archaeological Survey," 55-76. A description of Longo smelting methods is found in C.C. De Rosemond, "Iron Smelting in the Kahama District," *Tanganyika Notes and Records,* 16 (1943), 79-84.

25. In Appendix 1, 109 groups are listed, but two of them, the Sandasya and the Kangara, are non-Bantu and are not included within the discussion of agricultural-hunter migrations.

26. I wish to acknowledge the many profitable discussions on the problems of clans and their totems that I have had with Carole A. Buchanan, who conducted historical research in Bunyoro.

27. Hans Cory and M.M. Hartnoll provide information on Haya clans and their totems. Generally their data provide a mixed picture and do little to clarify the Kerebe data. It is significant to note, however, that the majority of Hima clans have one type of

cow or another as a totem. Unfortunately, data are incomplete on
the Hima but a sizable minority did not possess cattle totems. An
impressive number of non-Hima clans also had cattle totems:
Customary Law of the Haya Tribe (London, 1945), Tables 1-45,
287-89. Valuable information concerning clans in Bunyoro is also
available, see Carole A. Buchanan, "The Kitara Complex: The
Historical Tradition of Western Uganda to the 16th Century"
(unpublished Ph.D. dissertation, Indiana University, 1973).

28. Malcolm Guthrie, *Classification of the Bantu Languages*
(London, 1948), 42-43.

29. An excellent map illustrating the location of people speaking
various languages in East Africa and also distinguishing between
those people around the Victoria Nyanza influenced by the Hima
and those who missed their influence can be found in the supplement provided by Franz Stuhlmann, "Ethnographische Über-
sicht der Völker des äquatorialen Ost-Afrika," *Mit Emin Pascha
ins Herz von Afrika* (Berlin, 1894).

30. Turnbull, "Notes on the History of Uzinza," also see Soper
and Golden, "An Archaeological Survey," 55-76.

31. See Aniceti Ketereza, "How Men and Women Came to Live
Together," 9-19.

32. Comparative information on Kerebe and Haya fishing prac-
tices in the present century is described by H.A. Fosbrooke,
"Some Aspects of the Kimwani Fishing Culture," *Journal of the
Royal Anthropological Institute,* LXIV (1934), 1-22.

33. Fishing implements and techniques are discussed and illustrated by S. and E.B. Worthington, *Inland Waters of Africa*
(London, 1933), 142-51.

34. J. Hornell, "Indonesian Influence on East African Culture,"
Journal of the Royal Anthropological Institute, LXIV (1934),
324-25. Illustrations of canoe types found around the Victoria
Nyanza are in Worthington, *Inland Waters of Africa,* 157-62.

35. Neki Kageri, Makene s/o Ikongolero, and Mpehi stated that
fishing clans preceded the Silanga, in contrast to Bahitwa who

claimed that the fishing clans arrived with or later than the Silanga.

36. Information on early fishermen near Lake Tanganyika is found in Andrew Roberts, "The Nyamwezi," *Tanzania Before 1900,* ed., A. Roberts (Nairobi, 1968), 118; P.H. Gulliver, "A Tribal Map of Tanganyika," *Tanganyika Notes and Records,* 52 (1959), 74; and J.E.G. Sutton and A.D. Roberts, "Uvinza and Its Salt Industry," *Azania,* III (1968), 45-86.

37. Refer to David N. McMaster, *A Subsistence Crop Geography of Uganda* (Bude, England, 1962), 48-59, 72-87; also P.J. Greenway, "Origins of Some East African Food Plants," *East African Agricultural Journal,* vol. 10 (1944), 34-39, 115-19, 177-80, 251-56, and vol. 11 (1945), 56-63; and Hartwig, "Oral Traditions Concerning the Early Iron Age," 101, 108.

38. G.W. Hatchell, "The History of the Ruling Family of Ukerewe," *Tanganyika Notes and Records,* 47/48 (1957), 198; "History of Ukerewe Chiefdom," Cory Papers No. 290, University of Dar es Salaam.

39. Sutton, "Settlement of East Africa," 92; see also D.N. McMaster, "Speculation on the Coming of the Banana to Uganda," *Uganda Journal,* XVI (1952), 145-47; and Cohen, *The Historical Tradition of Busoga,* 55-56, 75.

40. Although this is Bahitwa's contention, Makene s/o Ikongolero of the Hira clan, a clan that lived in the region for an extended period before the Silanga arrived, confirmed that at one time his ancestors had smithed. The Hira eventually dominated other clans around them and became dependent upon the subordinate population for smithing services. As evidence that another particular early clan had smithed, Bahitwa claimed that he had found waste materials associated with smithing while cultivating a garden in a village formerly occupied by the clan (Gara) who left the island years ago.

41. Magoma s/o Kitina, in addition to Bahitwa, maintained this point of view. Unfortunately members of the Gabe clan refused to discuss their role in smelting and smithing, a product of the stigma attached to the occupation.

42. Ehret, "Cushites and Nilotes," 163-67.

43. The evidence to support this migratory route is limited but complementary; see Hartwig, "Oral Traditions Concerning the Early Iron Age," 111-13; G.M. Wilson, "The Tatoga of Tanganyika," *Tanganykia Notes and Records,* 33 (1952), 35, 40-41, 43, 45; Turnbull, "Notes on the History of Uzinza," Mwanza District Book; C. McMahon, "Ethnological and Anthropological Notes: Notes on the Wasukuma Inhabiting Shinyanga District," Mwanza District Book, National Archives of Tanzania, Dar es Salaam; and Christopher Ehret, "Cattle-Keeping and Milking in Eastern and Southern African History: The Linguistic Evidence," *Journal of African History,* VIII, 1 (1967), 3, 6, 13.

44. J. Ford and R. de Z. Hall, "The History of the Karagwe (Bukoba District)," *Tanganyika Notes and Records,* 24 (1947), 4. Also see Gideon S. Were, "The Western Bantu Peoples from A.D. 1300 to 1800," *Zamani,* 179.

45. Hans Cory, "The Earliest History of Bukoba," Cory Papers No. 79; Cory, "Bantu Religion of Tanganyika," Cory Papers No. 41; Cory, "The Bahinda in Bumbwiga (a Bukoba Chiefdom)," Cory Papers No. 40, University of Dar es Salaam.

46. Malcolm Guthrie, *Comparative Bantu* (Farnborough, England, 1970), III, 13. A chart illustrating the linguistic classification of all East African languages together with suggested terminology is found in Sutton, "The Settlement of East Africa," 80-81. For ethnographical information see Brian K. Taylor, "The Western Lacustrine Bantu," Ethnographic Survey of Africa, Part XIII (London, 1962). Although this survey does not specifically include the Kerebe, it describes the type of society with which the Kerebe cultural heritage is inextricably linked. The most comprehensive ethnographic survey of the Kerebe in print is Father Eugene Hurel's "Religion et vie domestique des Bakerewe," *Anthropos,* VI (1911), 62-94, 276-301. An historical reconstruction of the royal Silanga clan has been published by Henryk Zimon, which is to be followed by a detailed anthropological analysis of Kerebe rainmakers; "Geschichte des Herrscher-Klans Abasiranga auf der Insel Bukerebe (Tanzania)

bis 1895," *Anthropos,* 66, 3/4 (1971), 321-72 and 66, 5/6 (1971), 719-52.

47. Oral information on this topic was provided by Alipyo Mnyaga, Buyanza s/o Nansagate, Magoma s/o Kitina, Aniceti Kitereza, Palapala s/o Kazwegulu, Kaliga s/o Lwambali, Simeo Rubuzi and Bahitwa. Archival sources include A.M.D. Turnbull, "Tribal History and Legends on Ukerewe Chiefdom," Mwanza District Book, Tanzania National Archives; "History of Ukerewe Chiefdom," Cory Papers No. 290 and Hans Cory, "The Coming of the Wasilanga Chiefs," Cory Papers No. 30, University of Dar es Salaam. Published versions can be found in G.W. Hatchell, "History of the Ruling Family of Ukerewe," 198-200; Eugene Hurel, "Religion et vie domestique des Bakerewe," 65-68; Henryk Zimoń, "Geschichte des Herrscher-Klans Abasiranga auf der Insel Bukerebe." A list of the Kerebe abakama and their approximate time in office is provided in Appendix 2.

48. Ruhinda the Great is used to distinguish the various rulers with the name Ruhinda from the founder of the Hinda dynasty in the west lake district. The descriptive word "Great" has been suggested by Israel K. Katoke in "A History of Karagwe: Northwestern Tanzania, *ca.* 1400-1915" (unpublished Ph.D. dissertation, Boston University, 1969), 35. Katoke estimates that Ruhinda the Great lived between 1450 and 1520.

49. See I.K. Katoke, "The Kingdom of Ihangiro," *Journal of World History,* XIII, 4 (1971), 700-14.

50. Gerald W. Hartwig, "The Historical and Social Role of Kerebe Music," *Tanzania Notes and Records,* 70 (1969), 46-47.

51. The impact of singing and dancing associations upon Kerebe society is discussed in more detail in Hartwig, "The Historical and Social Role of Kerebe Music," 41-56.

52. Kerebe elders did not establish a link with inhabitants of the Sese Islands in the northwestern part of the lake, regardless of the common name.

53. Baker, "Report on Administrative and Social Conditions in the Ukerewe Chiefdom."

2 The Kerebe and Long-Distance Trade

Kerebe involvement in long-distance trade is outlined in this chapter and set within the context of regional trading patterns throughout the nineteenth century. Two perplexing issues are discussed within the framework of the Kerebe oral data: when and how the interior trading network was meshed with that of the Indian Ocean coast, and when and by whom the traffic in ivory on the Victoria Nyanza was begun. Buganda's hegemony over communities in the southern lake region is an equally important issue. Yet trading in ivory, and even slaves, and the subsequent political relationships between societies like the Ganda and Kerebe represent a relatively sterile concern if the consequences of these actions upon the people themselves are omitted. To grasp the awesome nature of the "opening-up" process we must take into consideration one of the most disruptive and damaging forces of the century: alien diseases that accompanied long-distance trade. Only when the dramatically increased death rate experienced by the Kerebe in the first decades of the nineteenth century is considered do their subsequent economic and social developments, examined in subsequent chapters, assume a comprehensible pattern.

Economic Change and Trade

Throughout the 1960s, historians interested in trade during the nineteenth century concentrated upon Arab and Swahili initiative and involvement.[1] This process was facilitated and no doubt prompted by the very nature of the available archival and travel literature. But since the publication of *Pre-Colonial African Trade,* edited by Richard Gray and David Birmingham, attention has been drawn to the meager state of our knowledge about African economic activities in eastern Africa before the colonial period. To their credit, Gray and Birmingham attempt to identify the many economic factors associated with long-distance trade operating in eastern and central Africa during the nineteenth century. The presence of traders from the Swahili coast; markets in the interior in which traders exchanged their beads, cloth, and wire for ivory and slaves; the increased importance of various specialists from within the communities of the interior—including the learning of new economic roles; and the use of currency to facilitate trade—all receive attention.

Two diametrically opposed economic systems—a subsistence-oriented economy and a market-oriented economy—are presented by the editors as the two ends of a continuum. In the former type of economy, existing trade is "closely associated with subsistence agricultural production, and is subservient to the local kinship system."[2] Those goods that do exchange hands in this system make little or no impact on the subsistence economy. New or expanded economic activities remain absent. If luxury goods appear, they are assigned a conventional social value, a development that precludes a universal monetary value being given to the object. In contrast, market-oriented trade is economically innovative and dependent on commercial rather than social realities. Diverse items, such as ivory, slaves, or cattle, acquire a new economic value. Markets usually develop and an indigenous or imported currency appears. "New means of capital accumulation [are] formed, a new field of consumer demand for imports [is] created, and, above all, new forms of economic specialization [are] stimulated."[3] Export goods are sought or produced, and professional merchants arise from within the community.

Gray and Birmingham readily acknowledge that conditions in the nineteenth century had not promoted societies that matched their model of a market-oriented community. Variations within eastern and central Africa were the general rule, with some societies such as the Nyamwezi, Kamba, and Yao approximating the market-oriented economy much more closely than most others, which remained less involved in market activities.

Ralph Austen has critically characterized the above model as one of "proto-modernization," since it "emphasized rational maximization [in western eyes] of economic opportunities within the relevant specialized African sectors."[4] Austen argues that this model necessarily becomes irrelevant for African societies by 1900, since they could not compete with the technologically and commercially more developed societies which displaced the indigenous entrepreneurs in the colonial period. He claims that a more viable model is that of the "predatory" society which used the direct or indirect application of violence to achieve what is misleadingly referred to as "economic growth," since the growth was almost invariably illusory. Leaders such as Mirambo (Nyamwezi), Nyungu-ya-Mawe (Kimbu), and Mutesa (Buganda) can be placed in this category. But Austen would prefer to regard the economic developments experienced by most African societies during the nineteenth century as "instituted adaptation." According to this categorization, "economic growth is contained (but not necessarily prevented) by structures and values serving the function of maintaining legitimate order."[5] From this perspective the technological advantages of colonial and postcolonial regimes represent an expansion of the development scale, but not necessarily a qualitative breakthrough to full modernization.

Currently available studies of the nineteenth century generally lack specific information about the production of goods by Africans. Rather, they emphasize the trading of commodities, an approach fostered by the very nature of the written sources used by investigators. Thus a preferred model cannot be selected without substantially more relevant information. And while the Kerebe experience can unhesitantly be placed within Austen's "instituted adaptation" model, it is apparent that the Kerebe are no more typical than any other society one cares to analyze. Their experience does provide a useful case study to illustrate the numerous external and internal forces at work.

To concentrate upon the economic consequences of long-distance trading, however, is to impose restrictive limits on the analytical process. On this issue I must take a stand that differs from those advocating a disciplinary approach. I contend that long-distance trade cannot and should not be understood solely as an economic phenomenon. Even using the word "economic" implies erroneous conditions. The Kerebe still retained a basically subsistence-oriented economy by the 1890s although one certainly modified from that existing a century earlier. In contrast, social relationships and values reveal significantly greater divergence when those of 1890 are compared to those of 1790. These social changes are inextricably bound to the long-distance trading activities of the 1800s and must be recognized before "economic" developments can be placed in their proper perspective.

Origins of Long-Distance Trade

When did long-distance trade in the interior begin? How did it commence? Who provided the stimulus that integrated the interior trading networks with those of the coast? Questions of this nature have seriously concerned historians of eastern Africa since the publication of Oxford University Press' *History of East Africa*. In his essay, Roland Oliver cautiously accepted Ganda tradition that imported goods, specifically plates, cups, saucers, and glassware, arrived in Buganda during the last quarter of the eighteenth century.[6]

Yet working with Nyamwezi oral data, as well as archival and published sources, Andrew Roberts could not find evidence to shed any additional light on when the enterprising Nyamwezi began participating in long-distance trade. Consequently, he left the question open and simply suggested that the "development took place around 1800."[7] The disparate time indicated by the Ganda oral evidence on the one hand and the Nyamwezi on the other becomes crucial, since the imported objects in Buganda most likely passed through Nyamwezi hands. Therefore the Nyamwezi should have been active in long-distance trade anywhere from twenty to forty years before 1800. Edward Alpers, working from a coastal perspective, assigns renewed Omani (Arabs from the Sultanate of Oman) economic interest in East Africa to the "middle of the eighteenth century."[8] Archaeological evidence also suggests a date in the late 1700s for the presence of trade items presumably originating from traders residing along the East African coast.[9] While the available evidence can certainly be interpreted as indicating that the eastern African interior was opened up to long-distance trade in the late eighteenth century, this represents only one facet—and by no means the most significant one—to the questions posed above.

How long-distance trade began is a more perplexing matter. On this issue there is virtually no agreement. A linkage of interior trading patterns to long-distance trade is assumed with some confidence, but how this was achieved remains unclear.[10] In this instance, Kerebe oral evidence suggests one example of trade integration.[11]

Bukerebe began participation in long-distance trade during the reign of Mihigo II. Mihigo's tenure bridges a transitional period in Kerebe history, one that the oral data treat in a fascinating manner. Prior to the involvement of the Kerebe in long-distance trade, Bukerebe and its environs had been insulated from direct and continuous influence emanating from the Indian Ocean coast. Earlier history was characterized by parochial developments. There had been

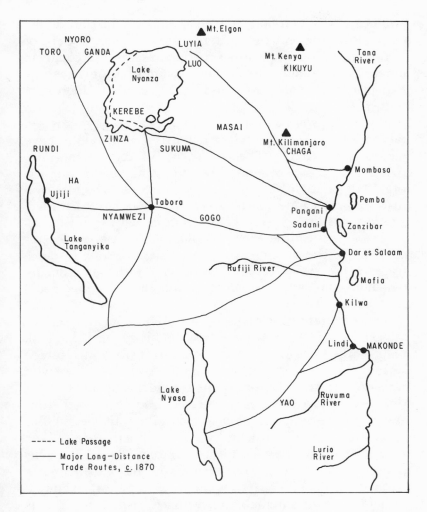

MAP III. MAJOR LONG DISTANCE TRADE ROUTES, ca. 1870

no major discernible regional developments since the arrival of the pastoral Tatog and Hima (Huma) and the royal clan.

Unfortunately for chronological purposes, the time of Mihigo's reign is uncertain and the ascribed dates of 1780 to 1820 are simply an approximation. Kerebe informants usually estimate the length of an omukama's reign by the number of children born to his wives. Bahitwa, the Kerebe traditional historian, figured it this way: "Toward the end of Mihigo's life he had had so many sons that he could no longer remember all of their names." Consequently, Bahitwa attributed to Mihigo II a very long life and reign, longer than any of his successors. Based upon information from written sources, the calculation of average reigns and the length of a ruling generation, Mihigo appears to have died around 1820.[12] The length of his reign is another matter. In this case oral date indicating that Mihigo II ruled longer than his grandson Rukonge, ca. 1869-95, and his son Machunda, ca. 1835-ca. 1869 are accepted. Therefore, a forty-year reign is hypothesized, placing his installation some time around 1780. These estimated dates conform to the probable commencement of long-distance trade in the region, as well as providing the time during which all the historical events attributed to his reign could have occurred.

Two meaningful symbols—a spear and a "man/beast"—may be used to represent the momentous changes that took place while Mihigo II was omukama transforming Kerebe society. The man/beast was Butamile, a "creature" who terrorized the Kerebe for a number of years during Mihigo's time and who persists as a personalized beast in the imagination of young Kerebe even today. Butamile personifies the increased insecurity and irrational death that stalked Bukerebe in an inexplicable manner in the 1800s. This phenomenon is analyzed in Chapter 5. The *endirima* was a spear introduced to kill the formidable elephant, an animal previously not hunted on an organized basis. It represents the search for ivory and the implied presence of different ideas and technology emanating from the East African coast, whether introduced by Africans of the interior, Arabs, Swahilis, or Europeans.

The endirima spear was the instrument—the technology—that enabled the Kerebe to acquire ivory destined for international markets. It was approximately four feet in length and, being heavily weighted, could penetrate the hide of the largest creature. This weapon and the necessary procedures for using it were introduced to the Kerebe by hunters who entered the chiefdom while tracking a wounded elephant. They comprised the advance wave of men whose goal was to extract wealth that could be exchanged for trade goods from the East African coast.

The Kerebe considered specific weapons, hunting techniques, and accompanying rituals necessary to hunt certain large animals. Although organized groups of hunters previously existed to hunt the hippopotamus and buffalo, organized elephant hunters were not present until Mihigo's reign. No doubt a similar situation existed in other societies in the interior of East Africa. Tracing the growth of formal elephant-hunting associations may cast considerable light upon how the local and the long-distance trading networks became integrated.[13] The Nyamwezi interest in trade and ivory, for example, may have been related to the westward movement of people (hunters?) into Unyamwezi from the major dispersal area of Usagara, a process that predated 1800 by decades.[14]

The ancestors of the Hesere clan were responsible for introducing the techniques for killing elephants into Bukerebe. The origin of the hunters was Kanadi, a large, sparsely populated eastern Sukuma district, located approximately 135 miles southeast of Bukerebe. According to informants, the hunters inadvertently found themselves within Mihigo's chiefdom while on a hunting expedition.[15] They presumably explained to Mihigo the existence of men to the east who desired ivory and who exchanged commodities such as beads for elephant tusks. Mihigo was sufficiently impressed with the possibilities of exchanging ivory for trade goods to ask the hunters to remain in Bukerebe to form the nucleus of a hunting organization that his men could join. The hunters agreed to stay, although they asked permission to return to their home in Kanadi before settling in Bukerebe, allegedly to bring their families. Mihigo granted them permission, and eventually the founder of the Hesere clan in Bukerebe returned to Mihigo and thereupon established residence in the chiefdom.

The identity of the Hesere clan is not difficult to trace when using Bahitwa's data. While designated as Sukuma, the district of Kanadi is situated far enough to the east to raise questions about whether the Hesere actually may not have been representatives of a coastal hunting expedition. Yet there is no oral evidence to support this possibility; according to Bahitwa, whose specialty is clan histories, the Hesere had migrated from the Buha dispersal center to the west centuries ago. When and where the hunting society of which they were members had come into being remains a fundamental problem. It was definitely a Sukuma hunting association by the time it reached the Kerebe, and even on Bukerebe it remained essentially a Sukuma organization until its demise late in the 1800s. This is most vividly revealed by the song texts which were sung in Kisukuma after a successful hunt and are still extant among descendants of the Hesere clan.

The men on Bukerebe who joined the elephant-hunting group were called Abagunda. Giving a name to the adherents of a social organization was the standard procedure for any group of men who joined together for a common purpose. Membership was open to any man who was interested in hunting elephants; many of the men from all clans, including the royal Silanga clan, participated in the organization. Leadership of the Abagunda was retained by members of the Hesere clan because they apparently kept sole possession of the magical knowledge believed essential in successfully killing an elephant. According to informants, most elephant hunting was done within the chiefdom on the western portion of the island where the topography, vegetation, and sparse population provided an ideal home for elephants. Various caves in the region are still remembered as camping sites for the hunters.

The Kerebe procedure for killing elephants remained the same throughout the nineteenth century. Once a potential victim was chosen, the hunter with his spear ascended a tree under which the elephant was likely to pass. Other hunters then moved into position and attempted to move the elephant or elephants under the tree in which the hunter was poised to thrust his heavy endirima down into the shoulders of the animal. Even after wounding an animal the hunt was usually far from over. Next came the tracking, stalking and, hopefully, the eventual killing of the animal.

The prize of the hunt—the ivory tusks—was presented to the omukama, a policy instituted by Mihigo II. In some districts of East Africa the chief claimed only a single tusk from a kill, particularly from roving bands composed of nonsubjects, but the Kerebe omukama received both. The successful hunter was well-rewarded for his prowess, usually receiving two head of cattle. Following the presentation of tusks to the omukama, an extended period of feasting ensued, courtesy of the ruler. The district in which the Kerebe hunters searched for their game was restricted, and the number of kills in any given year was certainly limited. A more productive group of hunters would have had to travel at least fifty miles to the east before approaching satisfactory hunting ground on the mainland, and the Kerebe simply did not undertake such ambitious hunting expeditions.

Early Ivory Trading and Its Benefits

How was trade organized in this period? In the early 1800s caravans of Swahili and Arab traders from the coast did not travel from one district to the next in search of ivory, nor did the traders have their agents posted at strategic locations to collect ivory from hunters and chiefs as they did later in the century. Mihigo found it necessary at the outset to organize his own caravans of Kerebe porters to take his ivory to "Takama," where it was exchanged primarily for beads. "Takama," unfortunately, is not a place name but rather a Kisukuma word meaning "south." The destination of the ivory seems to have been somewhere south of Mwanza Gulf, where the ivory may have been exchanged with either Sukuma or Nyamwezi middlemen.

The movement of ivory from Bukerebe to Takama was by water and by land. Kerebe canoes took ivory to Sukuma chiefdoms, where the Kerebe porters disembarked and proceeded to Takama. Mihigo's marriage alliances with two Sukuma chiefdoms, Busukuma on the shore of Speke Gulf and Burima on the eastern side of Mwanza Gulf, indicated two probable routes.[16] As far as can be determined, Mihigo

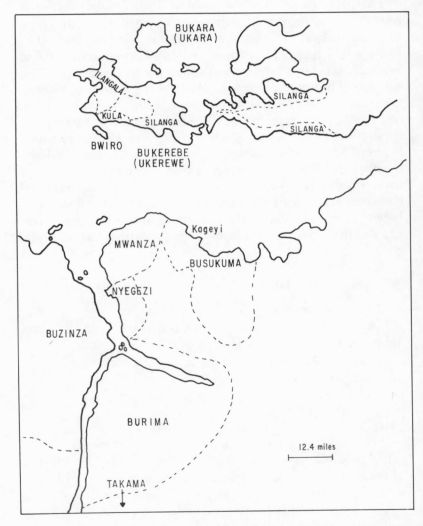

MAP IV. KEREBE CHIEFDOMS AND THEIR SUKUMA ALLIES

was the first Kerebe omukama to establish marriage alliances with any Sukuma chiefdom, and it is assumed that this was done to expedite his interests in moving ivory southward.[17] The Sukuma chiefdoms in question were in an area familiar to the Kerebe, since annual journeys were made to Buzinza for hoes and hoe handles. Buzinza was located on the western side of Mwanza Gulf opposite numerous Sukuma chiefdoms on the eastern side. Had Mihigo moved his ivory in any other direction, he probably would have needed political alliances with the people to the east and southeast. None are remembered. The Kerebe normally traveled during the dry season, June through August, and this was also the time when ivory caravans made trips to Takama.

What were the consequences of this trade for the Kerebe? One basic long-term advantage that evolved from trade was the acquisition of new food crops, a result of the extended travel involved in porterage of ivory.[18] This illustrates Kerebe initiative when meaningful opportunities appeared; their response was undoubtedly characteristic within the region.

It was under Mihigo II's direction that cassava,[19] maize (corn), and new varieties of sorghum and millet were first planted in Bukerebe. None of these food plants was brought by Arab or Swahili traders. In each instance Kerebe porters who had taken ivory to Takama returned with samples of different food crops to the omukama. He then had each new sample, whether seed or shoot, planted near his residence to determine for himself its potential use and value when later harvested. Whether Mihigo instructed his men to seek unfamiliar food crops (or new ideas in general) or whether the porters were merely intrigued with these new foods and returned with samples in hopes of pleasing Mihigo is a moot point. The significant fact is that the Kerebe exhibited a receptiveness to unfamiliar food crops and demonstrated considerable initiative in acquiring them.

Whether a particular plant was eventually accepted and incorporated into the agricultural cycle depended upon other factors, not least of which was the response of the omukama to the novelty. Though neither cassava nor maize replaced the earlier varieties of sorghum and eluesine as the basic food, they did provide feasible dietary options. Conversely, some of the new varieties of millet and sorghum were welcomed to such a degree that the standard species of grain used in 1750 were virtually replaced with new and preferred varieties of sorghum and millet by 1875.[20]

Mihigo's caravans most frequently obtained luxury items in exchange for their ivory. Dark blue beads were the most prized item. These beads, with cloth and the copper used in bracelets obtained later in the century, were greatly desired by the omukama, who redistributed them. Superficially, the primary function of the trade goods appears no more important than as a source of prestige items for the upper strata of society. The advantage of participating in the long-distance trading network seems meager within this context. But an intangible value placed upon prestige goods is doubtlessly the primary issue, and it had wide-ranging consequences, which are discussed in Chapters 4 and 5.

While the political consequences of seemingly trivial luxury goods upon the loyalties of the omukama's clansmen may have been of the utmost importance during the 1800s, in immediate economic terms participation in the ivory trade had few positive results. Diplomatically, however, the Kerebe now had added incentive for fostering formal relations with Sukuma chiefdoms to the south, with whom the Kerebe in all likelihood had bartered agricultural goods on a limited scale prior to Mihigo II's time. Mihigo's response to the opportunities of participating in the ivory trade certainly indicates an enterprising leader.

The Cost of Participation in Trade: Disease

There are indications of other significant changes beyond the political and economic spheres. Butamile, the man/beast, represents negative aspects of Mihigo's reign. The unrest and evil that Butamile connotes in Kerebe lore have become firmly entrenched in society, and "he" appears as a mythical symbol of death. While children on Bukerebe today may never have heard of the endirima, the spear for killing elephants, they are virtually certain to have a vague conception of Butamile.

Butamile is usually described as a lion with human characteristics that stalked the chiefdom, terrorizing people by pouncing on the top of their huts and either forcing his way into the structures to attack the occupants or springing upon them as they fled from their homes. He roamed about for years, maiming and killing, before he himself was eventually killed. The central portion of the island was inhabited at the beginning of Mihigo's reign, but by the end of his reign the region was uninhabited and had reverted to bush. Reoccupation did not begin until after 1920, during which time evidence of the earlier occupation was found in the grinding stones that had been used by women in the preparation of millet. Informants such as Bahitwa and Buyanza attributed the exodus from the central portion of the chiefdom to the harassing tactics of Butamile. They claim that some of the people moved to the lake shore while others left the chiefdom completely.

According to Buyanza, the Kerebe most knowledgeable about nineteenth-century history, Butamile was the creation of Mihigo himself. Butamile was, in fact, a member of the Silanga clan who had been cursed by Mihigo and had "become" a lion—"become" in that he was obligated to live an isolated life in the bush like an animal. In addition, he draped a lion skin over his shoulders and attached lion's claws to his hands. As the man/beast, Butamile was instructed by Mihigo to strike families or individuals alleged to be troublesome within the chiefdom. Once Butamile had successfully cleansed the chiefdom, Mihigo had him hunted down and killed.

Who or what Butamile actually was cannot be determined. He is a mythical creature today. Mihigo's involvement is also problematical. According to the oral data, nothing could occur in Bukerebe during Mihigo's reign that did not have the ultimate sanction of the omukama; whether rain or drought, life or death, it was always the affair of the omukama. Mihigo emerges as a "larger than life" leader, an omukama to whom important developments and awesome powers are attributed. Consequently, Mihigo's alleged responsibility for creating Butamile in the first instance must be treated cautiously. To question the existence of Butamile is an entirely different matter; however, his existence was real enough. Whether he was a demented individual assuming a lion's character to kill on his own accord, whether he was acting at the behest of Mihigo, or whether he was in fact a man-eating lion, we can never know.

Butamile's continued existence in Kerebe traditions indicates the impact of an era of intense insecurity. The violence represented by Butamile's actions is undoubtedly only a single facet of an exceedingly complex situation. Alien diseases appeared at this time and they too took a heavy toll in human life. The unseen killers, cholera and smallpox among them, were also the responsibility of Mihigo according to oral sources. The explanation given is the same as for Butamile. The omukama sought to destroy his enemies within the chiefdom. He therefore appealed to the pastoral Tatog for the necessary "medicine" to carry out his wish. This request was supposedly granted by the Tatog and in this manner new diseases were introduced into Bukerebe.[21]

The devastation caused by new diseases could have been staggering for Bukerebe and the entire region. It is assumed that an isolated human community has a specialized and distinctive disease environment.[22] This condition in turn leaves the population extremely susceptible when alien diseases appear for which the existing disease environment has provided no source of immunity; high death rates are the natural consequences. Since the societies in the interior of East Africa were relatively self-contained before trading in ivory began, the threat of imported diseases was extremely serious. Even later in the 1800s, peoples of the East African interior suffered enormously from the ravages of cholera periodically introduced by trading caravans from the coast.[23] Although disease as an historical factor in eastern Africa has not yet received more than passing attention by historians, primarily because evidence is difficult to obtain, it is reasonable to assume that the interior population was severely affected by new diseases as a result of long-distance trade.

When exposed to a new disease, the Kerebe undoubtedly experienced a high mortality rate, given the density of population in Bukerebe's favorable agricultural areas. The emigration of people from Bukerebe under Mihigo may have been more closely related to diseases than to the creature known as Butamile. It is probable that the Kerebe experienced considerable depopulation at this time as a consequence of the "opening-up" of the interior, although Butamile is assigned this responsibility in traditions. There is little oral evidence that deaths from diseases placed an unbearable stress upon the Kerebe; rather, these diseases are incorporated unobtrusively into the lore accompanying the name of Mihigo II. Since he had allegedly introduced diseases for reasons best known to himself, the matter was questioned no further. Disease was generally regarded as a form of magical knowledge or medicine that could be manipulated by powerful individuals.[24] Just as a ruler might seek power to destroy life by introducing disease, he might also expend considerably more energy in seeking power to control harmful conditions, since he was ultimately responsible for his community's welfare. Traditons abundantly accord Mihigo with both powers. In a sense he was the last traditional omukama. No successor is ever credited with the same profound authority and power. This conception of Mihigo identifies his reign as the transitional period between the old and the new, thus further emphasizing the significance of long-distance trade.

The appearance of new diseases into Bukerebe introduces a complicating factor. Mihigo sent his porters and ivory by canoe to Busukuma and Burima, and the ivory was transported southward from there. On the other hand, Mihigo reportedly "acquired" cholera from the Tatog who lived to the east. It would be logical to assume that diseases would be associated in oral accounts with the ivory trade to

Takama, since Kerebe porters very likely returned with infectious diseases on occasion. Yet the eastern direction from
which the diseases were "acquired" by Mihigo indicates that
carriers of new diseases from the Indian Ocean coast may
have approached the Victoria Nyanza from the east.
Historians have assumed that the Arabs and Swahili arrived
in the Unyanyembe (Tabora) region in Unyamwezi to the
south before they arrived at the lake. Yet the association of
diseases with the east rather than the south suggests that
traders first approached the lake by crossing the Masai-
steppe. Oral information itself does not mention traders
coming from the east, yet there is abundant evidence to indicate that this was the case by mid-century.[25] Indeed,
Kerebe oral data are generally distorted to the extent that
non-Kerebe receive little attention and are consequently
soon deleted from historical accounts. Therefore the oral information cannot be relied upon to provide evidence about
traders approaching from the east. The disease factor may
be the more reliable indicator that there was trading activity
in the vicinity of Bukerebe around 1800.

Altered Conditions

Mihigo II's reign effectively bridged the gap between the
seemingly stable era of the eighteenth century and the uncertain era of the nineteenth century. Mihigo was the most
powerful and therefore the most successful Kerebe
omukama since the founder of the royal clan in the
seventeenth century. The position of omukama never again
achieved the same exalted level. In the eyes of their subjects
Mihigo's successors lost a portion of their "control" over
events. As a "traditional" ruler, Mihigo II ranks supreme in
the eyes of the Kerebe. It was he who "created" and
manipulated Butamile against troublesome people; it was
he who "brought" in diseases to perform a similar function;
it was he who initiated the ivory trade and "introduced" new
food crops for his people; and it was he who sired many
sons, thereby earning the deepest respect from his family
and subjects.

The Kerebe entered the nineteenth century under the pervasive authority of Mihigo, struggling to comprehend the indiscriminate terror that was unleashed in their midst by the arrival of diseases alien to them. Attributing the deaths to Butamile and Mihigo at least made them more comprehensible. As long as a strong omukama held office, the old order and rationale associated with it remained intact. But this facade crumbled with Mihigo's death ca. 1820.

Not until the mid-1830s did a leader with similar stature emerge. During the interlude, political affairs were in a constant state of flux. With Bukerebe alternately battered by too much rain and parched by drought, the rulers seemingly lost control over their environment. Death struck two incumbents, Katobaha and Golita, shortly after their installation, while Ruhinda and Ibanda could not control environmental conditions and were deposed. Mihigo's successors and their relationship to him is illustrated in the genealogy. With the reign of Machunda, one of the youngest of Mihigo's sons, the omukama once again established an effective control over Kerebe affairs, although the basis of his authority was altered. Equally important, the Kerebe role in trade changed.

At midcentury, long-distance trade for the Kerebe still centered around ivory. Trade necessitated diplomatic

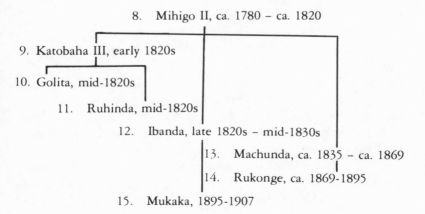

8. Mihigo II, ca. 1780 – ca. 1820

9. Katobaha III, early 1820s

10. Golita, mid-1820s

11. Ruhinda, mid-1820s

12. Ibanda, late 1820s – mid-1830s

13. Machunda, ca. 1835 – ca. 1869

14. Rukonge, ca. 1869-1895

15. Mukaka, 1895-1907

arrangements between cooperating leaders. The Kerebe abakama since Mihigo II had marriage alliances with at least two Sukuma chiefdoms (Busukuma and Burima) and with important elders from the district north of Bukerebe along the eastern lake shore, in addition to a kinship tie with the ruling clan in Nassa, another Sukuma chiefdom. Machunda retained these alliances and made additional arrangements with a Ziba chief from the northwestern side of the lake and with an unidentified Haya ruler on the lake's west coast. In contrast, the Kula chiefdom, a small community dwelling on Bukerebe's southwestern corner and periodically harassed by Machunda's chiefdom, had a marriage alliance with Mwanza, a Sukuma chiefdom at odds with Busukuma. As expected, the rival chiefdoms of Bukerebe did not maintain relations with the same authorities in other chiefdoms. Machunda also maintained diplomatic relations with the leaders of Buganda and Buzinza. A basic reason for cordial relations with Buzinza, besides a close cultural link, was the established trade in hoes, since Buzinza neither supplied the Kerebe with ivory nor provided a route by which ivory could be transported southward. Thus a formal diplomatic arrangement was not essential between the Kerebe and Zinza. The Kabaka of Buganda needed Kerebe assistance to transport ivory; hence the initiative for establishing a diplomatic tie rested with him and the exchange of gifts apparently served this purpose.

The sequence of some major developments affecting participation in the ivory trade by the Kerebe and their neighbors is difficult to discern. Oral information about the elephant hunting society, Mihigo II's participation in the ivory trade, and his marriage alliance is explicit; the sequence of events seems clear up to this point. But subsequent developments are not discernible. Specific information pertaining to the arrival of Arab and Swahili traders in the chiefdom or to the commencement of Ganda canoe journeys to the island of Bukerebe is lacking. European sources reveal only that coastal traders had reached the lake and begun trading with the Kerebe by the 1850s,[26] and that the Ganda had established cordial relations with the Kerebe by 1862.[27] The Kerebe elder Buyanza suggested that the Arabs or Swahili may have initially visited Bukerebe sometime during Ibanda's reign, presumably in the early 1830s. His evidence for this assertion is that one of Ibanda's sons was named Mzungu. He was most likely named for an Arab, although *mzungu* is a generic Swahili term now used to designate Europeans because of their light skin color. This is only suggestive, but it becomes more probable when coupled with the information that smallpox and cholera arrived from the east before 1820. Therefore the route from Tanga and Pangani via Kilimanjaro to the lake region could have been used by traders to penetrate westward earlier and farther than merchants using the Unyamwezi route.[28]

Trade at Midcentury

By 1858 Machunda's pattern of trade was no longer characterized by the need to seek a market for ivory as Mihigo's had been. Coastal traders now sought out Machunda's ivory. Richard Burton described it in this way:

> In Ukerewe, which is exceedingly populous, are two brother sultans: the chief is "Machunda;" the second, "Ibanda," rules at Wiru, the headland on the western limit. The people [Kerebe] collect ivory from the races on the eastern mainland and store it, awaiting an Arab caravan. Beads are in most request. . . . The Arabs who traffic in these regions generally establish themselves with Sultan Machunda, and send their slaves in canoes around the southeast angle of the lake to trade with the coast people. . . . The savagery of the races adjacent to the Nyanza has caused accidents among traveling traders.[29]

Although Burton's comments on the Kerebe were based upon information given to him by Arab traders at Unyanyembe, the trading arrangements he described are no doubt reasonably accurate. Information on internal political affairs is also basically correct. Only the place where one of the "two brother sultans" ruled is inaccurate (Ibanda ruled at Ilangala, while the Kula chief was in "Wiru" or Bwiro). Burton's account makes it clear that the Kerebe omukama was far more cooperative with traders than any of his eastern neighbors. Machunda was actually acquiring ivory from people along the eastern lake shore and stockpiling it for the anticipated arrival of Arab caravans. What is not clear from Burton's information is whether the traders posted agents with Machunda who were then responsible for the acquisition of ivory for particular traders. Oral data are simply not detailed enough to clarify such issues.

Machunda's willingness to cooperate with traders in this way illustrates a particular type of response from an interior African leader. He assumed the role of the facilitator, one who served alien trading groups. Before him, Mihigo had been a trading ruler, one who sought ivory and then sent it to a market center in Takama. The presence of ivory in the southeastern lake district eventually attracted Nyamwezi-Sukuma, Arab, and Swahili traders, who were persistently drawn to regions with abundant "cheap" ivory. Machunda did not pursue an independent trading course. Competition did not appeal to him as it did to other African leaders.[30] The explanation lies partially in the limited size of his chiefdom, but, more importantly, in the nonmartial nature of the Kerebe. Yet although the Kerebe abakama lacked an awesome military force, they still held a trump over their immediate eastern neighbors. This was their uncontested supernatural power as rain-makers, an authority that could provide as well as withhold rain. The reliability and amount of rainfall in this vicinity clearly favors the island of Bukerebe.[31] In the eyes of his less fortunate eastern neighbors, the Kerebe ruler was an authority to be respected and served. From this position, Machunda could seek cooperation, cemented with marriage alliances, and obtain ivory in exchange for trade goods.

Machunda's position vis-a-vis the traders was still precarious. He could insure the acquisition of imported goods only as long as the elephant population in the region satisfied the rapacious hunters' quest for ivory. It was a short-term business. When ivory was no longer readily available, traders drifted to regions further west. Machunda's relations with numerous alien traders, as described by Burton, could endure for only a few seasons. This was apparently the peak. Thereafter, Machunda welcomed fewer caravans; due to its scarcity, ivory decreased in relative importance, although it remained a highly desirable commodity.

Early Ganda Trade Relations

Mention has been made of Kerebe trade relations with the Nyamwezi-Sukuma and Ganda. Information on this is sparse because European sources dwell on Arab-Swahili trade, not on African trade, even though the same commodities were involved. Kerebe oral information is almost as barren. But a piece of sculpture which I had seen on display in the British Museum in London stimulated me to question Buyanza on this point and he responded with enough information to reveal the existence of Ganda-Kerebe relations sometime around midcentury.

Buyanza's information goes some distance in answering two perplexing questions. When did the lake assume a transportation role linking the northern kingdom of Buganda to the southern Sukuma chiefdoms? At whose instigation was the route opened—Arab, European, or African?

The latter question has been variously answered many times by European travelers of the nineteenth century. Their answers also invariably imply a time when the lake route was opened. In his book *Through the Dark Continent,* Henry Morton Stanley proudly claimed to have initiated a lake route from Buganda to Kageyi in Busukuma in 1875 by pointing out the advantages of the water route over a land

route to Kabaka Mutesa. The Kabaka was reportedly impressed by Stanley's wisdom and proceeded to implement
his advice.[32] Stanley contradicted himself on this point,
however; earlier in the same volume he provided conflicting evidence indicating the earlier existence of the very
trading pattern he claimed to have suggested.[33] Comment-
ing on the use of Ganda canoes in transporting goods from
one end of the lake to the other, a White Father missionary
noted that before Mutesa (1856-84) "canoes did not come to
the southern end of the lake, though for the past several
years the Ganda have transported the Arabs and their ivory
to Kageyi."[34] Robert Felkin, of the Church Missionary
Society, was not explicit on when and by whom the traffic
was initiated but he contended that the Arab and Swahili
trade with Buganda had "increased immensely in the last 10
years," that is, during the 1870s. It was standard policy in
Buganda, he noted, to provide traders "with canoes to
transport ivory and slaves they have obtained from Nteb-
bi . . . to Kagei,"[35] Franz Stuhlmann made an
"authoritative" statement on the same subject. He noted
that "the Ganda were induced by the Arabs and Europeans
to send their canoes to the south end of the lake to trade
tusks, but it was inadequate; hence the Arabs built several
large sailing vessels."[36]

These sources fortunately dispel the misconception that
canoes could not be used to transport ivory.[37] On the other
hand, they suggest that it was either Arab or European
initiative that brought about the lake transportation system.
James Grant reaffirmed this view when he stated that in
1871 Kabaka Mutesa had requested the Sultan of Zanzibar
to send craftsmen to Buganda to construct sailing vessels. In
Grant's opinion, Ganda canoes were "quite unfit for
anything beyond coasting or ferrying; no native of the interior would ever risk his life or property in crossing the
lake; they would never move out of sight of land."[38] That
canoes never crossed the lake is a sound generalization
because traffic closely hugged the western coastline. Ven-
turing any distance from the shore was an invitation to disaster, given the occurrence of sudden storms on the lake. But

the coasting mentioned by Grant was the means of moving trade goods between Buganda and Usukuma.

But what of the piece of sculpture? It is a unique object. About a meter in height, it represents a young girl, with realistically proportioned head, torso, and limbs. The Reverend John Roscoe acquired the figure in Buganda and subsequently deposited it in the British Museum in 1909. According to Roscoe's information the statue belonged to Kabaka Suna, who died in 1856. No other information was provided by Roscoe and no similar objects have been collected or noted in Buganda. The origin of the figure was Bukerebe.

Buyanza had heard the story about this figure on numerous occasions because it was related in Kerebe lore to a similar male figure that was taken from Bukerebe in the late 1890s by German authorities and subsequently deposited in the Museum für Völkerkunde, Berlin.[39] Both figures had been made for Machunda by craftsmen accompanying Nyamwezi-led caravans to Bukerebe. According to Buyanza, Machunda later sent the figure of the young girl to Buganda as a gift. He also was aware that even though the object had been damaged while in Kerebe possession, the Kabaka still welcomed the gift. The statue does have a very noticeable flaw: The left arm is broken off at the shoulder.

These statues relate to three significant issues: the nature of indigenous African trade, the specific relationship between Machunda of Bukerebe and Suna of Buganda and the approximate time of both. In the first place, the production of these figures by Nyamwezi craftsmen occurred while caravans visited Bukerebe. (The very different styles of the two pieces suggests two different sculptors.) They were meant to please the omukama, who used them as he saw fit. This fact gives the impression that this was a period when diplomatic niceties were expected and practiced. The violence accompanying trading activities later in the century seems inconsistent with these gifts. That traders other than Swahili and Arabs ventured forth for ivory is just as significant at this stage. Secondly, the Ganda presence does not appear to have been a dominating one while Suna was kabaka and there was no marriage alliance, merely an exchange of gifts. And thirdly, the cordial relationship between the Kerebe and Ganda was established before Suna's death in 1856. Contrary to the sources cited above, Mutesa did not initiate interest in the southern lake region; he was following his father's example.

Additional oral information confirms that Machunda assisted the Ganda in moving ivory southward.[40] Unfortunately, the time of this cooperative endeavor is unknown. Whether it occurred while Suna or Mutesa was kabaka remains unclear. On at least two occasions a flotilla of Ganda canoes arrived at Bukerebe, and the Ganda spokesman asked Machunda for porters to take his ivory to Takama. The omukama consented and directed a Sukuma refugee living in the chiefdom to lead the Kerebe caravan. The use of a speaker of Kisukuma to lead the caravan is an interesting bit of information, but two other details are possibly contradictory. Kerebe sources identify the Ganda spokesman as an "Arab." The presence of an Arab suggests a date during the 1860s when Songoro, a Swahili trader, worked under Mutesa's direction. If Songoro is the man in question, we know that he was in Buganda by 1862.[41] He continued to work under the aegis of Mutesa until he was killed in Bukerebe in 1877.[42] Songoro had also developed a trading establishment on the island while Machunda still reigned, hence it is possible that the two expeditions took place in the 1860's. On the other hand, the Kerebe no longer regularly dispatched caravans to Takama in the 1860s. This whole story bears the mark of an earlier era; but unless the reigning kabaka is identified, the issue must remain in limbo.

Ganda Hegemony over Lake Traffic

The lake trading system apparently existed by midcentury, prior to Mutesa's reign in Buganda. All European sources to the contrary cited above must therefore be discounted, although no direct evidence in support of this contention is available. One major set of contenders should be considered, however—the Arab and Swahili traders themselves. They do not appear to have been innovators in seeking or acquiring either ivory or slaves. The reverse appears to be true, that is, that the traders cautiously entered a region in which ivory was already a viable commodity, as exemplified by the Kerebe experience. They then surveyed the existing trading network and gradually worked themselves into it, often in competition with indigenous traders. Some chiefs resented and resisted the traders' intrusion; others, like the Kerebe abakama, attempted to accommodate them and gain thereby.[43] But striking off into unknown areas to establish trading bases where routes were nonexistent simply does not appear to be characteristic of the Arab and Swahili traders.

Since evidence proving that coastal traders initiated lake traffic is lacking, it is reasonable to hypothesize that traders found Ganda or other canoes operating in the southern part of the lake. Although the precise basis for Machunda's relationship with Suna is unknown, the initiative for the cooperation undoubtedly came from the Ganda, who would profit most from it. The Ganda may actually have been one of the suppliers of ivory to Bukerebe at midcentury. Neither John Speke nor Burton make reference to this possibility, yet Speke, as well as Kerebe sources, refers to Kabaka Suna's interest along the eastern coast of the lake.[44] Some ivory may have been acquired in this region and then moved southward to Bukerebe, where traders could easily have attached themselves to the Kabaka's court and served as valuable agents for the Ganda as men understanding the mechanisms of the ivory trade from the merchants' as well as from the ruler's vantage point. Even more conclusive evidence that traders did not initiate long-distance trade on the lake is that they abandoned the southeastern lake region around 1860, but did not abandon their interest in Buganda. They merely used the overland route, via Karagwe, to reach their destination. If they had developed or encouraged lake traffic in any way, they certainly would have welcomed the opportunity to reduce their arduous overland trek to Buganda.

While the initiators of the lake trade remain problematical, two factors favor the interpretation that the Ganda began trafficking on the lake by midcentury under Kabaka Suna: the tendency of merchants to follow existing trading patterns and the absence of traders operating independently of the kabaka on the lake before 1875. Traders, except for those Swahili or African individuals who willingly served the Ganda kabaka in a trading capacity,[45] felt no compulsion whatsoever to depend upon Ganda canoes for transportation—until circumstances forced them to do so in the late 1870s. Another alternative open to traders was to construct sailing vessels (dhows) for their own use on the Victoria Nyanza, as they had before 1858 on Lake Tanganyika.[46] While a number of factors undoubtedly contributed to their reluctance to build dhows, certainly a primary consideration was that traders could not be assured of a measure of freedom on the lake of the Ganda.

For all practical purposes, the Victoria Nyanza came under the influence of Buganda once the ivory trade commenced across its surface. The Kerebe under Machunda were gradually drawn into Buganda's ever-expanding sphere of domination, although initially their relationship was cooperative. Diminished supplies of ivory served to undermine Machunda's trading opportunities as well. Before his death, ca. 1869, Machunda had only Songoro's establishment in his chiefdom to remind him of more active trading days. Yet Songoro was seldom there. He possessed a second base at Kageyi in Busukuma where he spent most of his time. Bukerebe had fallen into a backwater in the ivory trade. Even the Ganda had little need to visit Bukerebe. They went directly to Kageyi with their ivory.

Diminishing Ivory Trade

Machunda was no longer a supplier of substantial quantities of ivory, certainly an unstable economic base for a community not devoted to dominating its neighbors by military means. A reduction in the amount of imported goods was an obvious consequence of this change. Even more significantly for Machunda, his relations with other rulers—relations dependent upon cooperation for trading purposes—atrophied. Gray and Birmingham correctly emphasize "what is probably the most important single consequence of trade—the creation, maintenance, and expansion of lines of communication. . . ."[47] Ivory had been the commodity of greatest initial concern to all parties participating in long-distance trade. With its importance reduced, either substitute commodities had to appear or the trading network would wither like leaves on an uprooted plant.

Substitutes did appear to supplement the diminished ivory export. Relations continued with other rulers; gifts continued to be exchanged. These gifts included people whom I prefer to regard as serviles rather than as slaves, since they possessed a social, not an economic value. The "commodity" most widely sought by rulers of the interior in the latter half of the nineteenth century was knowledge, that is, useful information to combat conditions threatening the welfare of communities. Much of this knowledge can be classified as *dawa* (medicine) and was supernatural in character. But by no means all knowledge could be placed in this nebulous category. Just as neighboring communities requested the Kerebe abakama for rain-making medicine, now Machunda and his successor, Rukonge, avidly sought medicine from other renowned ritual authorities to overcome problems confronting them. For example, around 1890 Rukonge sent a small group of emissaries to an unidentified site in eastern Zaire, beyond Burundi, to exchange ivory for medicine. The desire to control forces looms large; survival was not taken for granted. Although purely economic motives expanded interior lines of communication, noneconomic factors required the continued maintenance of communications. The extent of the omukama's day-to-day role of course became greater during this century. Monopolizing all aspects of long-distance trade was a new set of functions, but even as trade decreased the abakama's noneconomic responsibilities required buttressing. For this assistance Machunda and Rukonge looked beyond their own community, something Mihigo II did not do.

During the 1870s, Bukerebe's role in the lake trading network altered perceptibly. Songoro's establishment of a trading base on Bukerebe in the 1860s commenced the process. Machunda was obviously willing to have Songoro in his chiefdom. Machunda gave one of his daughters in marriage to Songoro, creating a bond between himself and the trader. The latter's ties with Mutesa of Buganda meant that the Kerebe were indirectly linked to the Ganda. Songoro's desire to locate on Bukerebe was related to the chiefdom's former role in the ivory trading network, particularly its relationships with people along the eastern lake shore. But more importantly, Bukerebe became a resource base for the trader. And it was as a resource center that Bukerebe became important in the last quarter of the century.

Entanglement with the Ganda and Europeans

A new form of water transportation appeared on the Victoria Nyanza in 1877, a sailing vessel modeled on the Indian Ocean dhows. Craftsmen constructed four dhows between 1874 and 1888 for use on the lake. One vessel was constructed outside Bukerebe while three dhows were constructed within Bukerebe during Rukonge's reign, ca. 1869-95. The dhows were related to the increased use of the lake route under Buganda's control and to the arrival of European missionaries. Rukonge essentially ruled as master of his own house from his accession to power ca. 1869 to 1877, during which time one dhow was constructed. Between 1878 and 1889 two other vessels were completed. During this period the Ganda dominated the external affairs of Rukonge. The presence of Europeans inadvertently set the stage and triggered the events which were to rapidly diminish Rukonge's sovereignty.

The explorer H. M. Stanley visited Rukonge in 1875 and subsequently provided the international community with an initial positive description of the Kerebe and their omukama.[48] As a consequence of Stanley's appeal for Christian missionaries to bring the gospel to central Africa, the first respondents to his call appeared before Rukonge less than two years later on their way to Buganda. The relationship of the Kerebe to the Anglican Church Missionary Society (CMS) representatives began amicably in early 1877; but by the end of the year Rukonge's subjects had killed two of these missionaries, and his chiefdom's very existence was in grave danger.

Acting upon the recommendations of the explorers Grant and Stanley, the CMS had planned to establish mission centers in Buganda and Karagwe. They intended to follow the major caravan route west from Bagamoyo to Unyanyembe and then north to Kageyi on the lake. Here boats were to be launched and used for transportation, emulating Stanley's efforts. Because timber was required for construction purposes and it was unavailable in the vicinity of Kageyi, the missionaries determined to go to Bukerebe, where timber was abundant. Once the missionaries completed their own boats they planned to depart from Bukerebe for Buganda.

In this endeavor they followed in the footsteps of Songoro, who in 1874 began constructing his dhow on Bukerebe. By 1877 Songoro's settlement there numbered around eighty persons, both freemen and slaves, who were responsible for a sizable herd of cattle plus stores of trading goods. In the summer of 1877 the missionaries purchased Songoro's unfinished dhow.

Even though the missionaries assumed the responsibility for completing the vessel in mid-June, Rukonge did not understand the transfer of ownership. Not until November when the missionaries attempted to launch the completed vessel did they learn that Rukonge would not permit them to leave. An involved controversy ensued over the next few weeks. Eventually a fight broke out in which two missionaries, Songoro, and some fifty others lost their lives.[49]

Rukonge's action set in motion a complex series of diplomatic exchanges between such diverse individuals as Kabaka Mutesa of Buganda, the Nyamwezi leader Mirambo, Sultan Barghash of Zanzibar, and John Kirk, the British Consul of Zanzibar. Each party had specific interests at stake. Songoro's mercantile associates in Unyanyembe, for example, demanded that the merchandise on Bukerebe be restored to them. Sultan Barghash of Zanzibar was concerned about maintaining secure trade routes in the interior to facilitate trade by his subjects. Also concerned was the British Consul on Zanzibar, who wished to encourage cooperation along the caravan routes and to secure the physical safety of his countrymen who had begun penetrating the interior in significant numbers after 1876. While the incident on Bukerebe was not the first of its kind in the interior, it did serve to remind Sultan Barghash and the trading community that their commerce rested on the goodwill of Africans in the interior. Any action that the Sultan or the British Consul may have decided upon in response to Rukonge's deed could be implemented only by moral suasion or by a strong leader such as Mirambo to act on their behalf. The latter alternative became feasible when Sultan Barghash used the Kerebe incident to temporarily heal a breach between himself, as the representative of the Arab trading community, and Mirambo, the Nyamwezi leader who had been harassing the Arabs since at least the early 1870s.[50]

Mirambo also welcomed the diplomatic opening to offer his services to the Sultan. Mirambo was pleased when subsequently he received encouragement from Sultan Barghash to secure a more stable and peaceful route, because it gave him approval (and gunpowder) from Zanzibar to increase his influence in the region. This rapprochement was a brief respite in his normally tense relations with the trading community. Mirambo made a military foray in the direction of Bukerebe in 1878. No serious threat ever developed, although the action revealed the extent of Mirambo's desire for empire as well as the limits of his power. Rukonge's island was too distant and therefore a refuge from Mirambo, who was more interested in diplomatic recognition from Zanzibar than he was in Rukonge's future.

Ganda Domination

Talk of revenging the deaths on Bukerebe could be heard even in London where the Church Missionary Society attempted to dissuade Kabaka Mutesa of Buganda from attacking Rukonge, stressing that the "revenge we want is the privilege of preaching the gospel there."[51] The mission society had no more realistic means of dealing with the Kerebe omukama than did the British Consul, the Sultan of Zanzibar, the merchants at Unyanyembe, or the powerful Nyamwezi. The sole individual with this power was Kabaka Mutesa, who eventually sent a flotilla of canoes filled with warriors to Bukerebe. Mutesa's motives for the expedition appear more related to a desire for obtaining plunder than for revenging deaths, but this appearance is misleading. Kabaka Mutesa had a vested interest in the people killed by Rukonge, since Songoro had been assisting Mutesa by moving Ganda ivory from Kageyi to Unyanyembe and the two missionaries had been bound for Buganda where Mutesa awaited their arrival. Mutesa regarded the missionaries, no less than the trader, as representatives of an alien group whose presence in the region could be justified only as long as it served the Kabaka's interests. Rukonge's deed had therefore deprived him of additional clients.

The Ganda military flotilla arrived in late 1878 and the expected encounter occurred, but not with the expected outcome. Rukonge successfully diverted the revenge of the Ganda to his enemies on the western end of the island, making Ilangala the center of military action. The cost of Ganda military aid was not inconsiderable. By using Ganda military assistance in this fashion, Rukonge implicitly acknowledged Buganda's suzerainty. He who possessed power controlled. The omukama's request for Ganda aid was in fact an acknowledgment of the Kerebe's dependent relationship to the Ganda. It affirmed Rukonge's subordination to Mutesa and implied his willingness to respond to Ganda demands, making provisions for Ganda canoemen, for example. The immediate cost to Rukonge, according to Buyanza, was canoe-loads of "gifts"—foodstuffs, slaves and ivory—for Mutesa. Only when the canoes were filled to capacity did they embark on their two-hundred-mile voyage to report Ganda success to Mutesa.[52] Still, the omukama's chiefdom now included the entire island; his rivals on the western shores of the island no longer existed as viable entities.

The deaths on Bukerebe in 1877 and the death, seven months later, of Rumanyika, omukama of Karagwe, were fundamental causes for the traders' general abandonment of the overland route from Unyanyembe to Karagwe. The Ganda moved into Karagwe after Rumanyika's death, principally to control the traffic flowing northward from Karagwe into Bunyoro. They did not wish their enemies to acquire trade goods, particularly guns and gunpower, from the Zanzibar traders.[53] By redirecting the Arab and Swahili traders over the Unyanyembe-Kageyi-Buganda route the Ganda maintained control over their trade goods, since the traders normally were obliged to rely upon Ganda canoes for their transportation. The Kabaka's policy was partially subverted by the continued presence of Nyamwezi and Ziba traders along the Karagwe route.

By 1879 the village of Kageyi had become an important caravan terminus, a position it maintained until the mid-1880s when the *hongo* (tax) rate rose to such heights that the Arabs moved their route and their camp eastward. The Catholic and Protestant missionaries used similar routes to the lake and consequently also constructed quarters near Kageyi, on Mwanza Gulf. The Roman Catholic White Fathers appeared on the lakeshore in 1879 and assumed an important role in the development of Bukerebe after 1893. The CMS representatives shifted their supply depots to avoid harassment on three separate occasions in the 1880s, which illustrates the turmoil of that decade. The routes and settlements themselves were vulnerable to ever-increasing demands from innumerable Sukuma chiefs and headmen. The settlements on the lake, essential supply depots for the mission and mercantile representatives in Buganda, were also vulnerable to Ganda political machinations and rumor constantly encouraged fear of imminent attack. In 1884 a White Father recorded a sentiment that must have been shared by Africans, traders and Protestant missionaries alike—"My God, these Ganda cause us uneasiness."[54]

The Ganda periodically appeared in the southern end of the lake from 1879 until 1890, primarily to ferry goods from one end of the lake to the other. Kabaka Mutesa and Kabaka Mwanga after him controlled the movement of aliens about the lake until the end of the decade. The CMS, for example, decided to relocate a supply depot from Kageyi to Bukerebe in 1883 because Rukonge had remained on good terms with the CMS and continually expressed a desire to have his people taught by Europeans. Final arrangements for the shift had been made when Mutesa suddenly learned of the proposal. He warned the missionaries that anyone locating with Rukonge would be killed. Not wishing to harm their already precarious position in Buganda, the CMS immediately gave up its intended move. The men sent by Omukama Rukonge to transport the missionaries were simply informed that "Mutesa wanted us in his own country and did not want us to go to Ukerewe. These words were enough. They were content."[55] Rukonge would no doubt understand.

Bukerebe's subordinate or tributary relationship to Buganda was based on the recognition that the Ganda had greater access to power in the sacred, as well as in the secular realms. The military power of Buganda was merely a manifestation of its spiritual power. Therefore it was a matter of expediency for Rukonge to cooperate with the Ganda, since the association could benefit the Kerebe—a case of the weak attaching itself to the strong for sustenance. Kerebe informants acknowledge Rukonge's "friendship" with the Ganda, particularly with Kabaka Mutesa (1856-1884). The "friendship" in practice meant that Ganda canoemen would be welcomed in Bukerebe (fortunately for the Kerebe, the chiefdom was not immediately adjacent to the major water route), that the two rulers would occasionally exchange gifts and that the Kerebe did not compete with the Ganda in affairs of the latter's own choosing. This relegated the Kerebe to involvement only in the domestic trade.

Bukerebe became the home of a considerable number of Ganda during Rukonge's reign, although their precise status is difficult to determine. Some were slaves given to Rukonge by Mutesa; an earless craftsman is particularly well remembered for his drum-making abilities. Some Ganda came with their wives to settle in the chiefdom, while others came singly and married Kerebe women. Whatever their social status, oral information describes them as agents of Rukonge. A few Ganda were actually accorded the position of *omuzuma* (messenger), but their real asset for the omukama was their allegiance to him, rather than to the Kerebe at large. Rukonge used them to solidify his position in office.

A New Role for the Kerebe

Bukerebe's economic role altered as trading networks fluctuated and political conditions became more oppressive. The water route and Buganda's control over it enveloped the Kerebe. Traders as well as missionaries looked to Rukonge for timber to construct vessels, for which the omukama received compensation. These same groups, in addition to the Ganda in the southern lake region, obtained food supplies from the Kerebe. Excellent climatic conditions and a cooperative ruler meant that as a center for timber and food resources Bukerebe remained involved in trading activities, although in a very different fashion from earlier in the century.

In the five years prior to Rukonge's deposition by German authorities in 1895, the new economic role of the late 1800s was starkly emphasized and carried a step further. The German Anti-Slavery Society focused its attention on the Victoria Nyanza. Since they too needed lumber, Bukerebe became their base of operations. Now Rukonge's subjects had to perform the unskilled labor necessary for numerous projects, including the cutting and transporting of timber for the construction of three vessels and the building of a mud-brick station. Rukonge, of course, had no choice in whether to provide laborers or not; maintaining his position was dependent upon his cooperation. The colonial era was beginning.

In political terms the Kerebe under Mihigo had been independent, a condition gradually lost when the Ganda established hegemony over the chiefdom. But this generally affected only external affairs. The German presence brought internal control as well. Economically, long-distance trade involved exchanging ivory for imported luxury items. But as the supply of ivory decreased, the Kerebe turned to supplying resources from their island to enable others, including traders, missionaries, and the Ganda, to carry out their activities. With the presence of representatives of the German Anti-Slavery Society, the Kerebe became a subject people, supplying foodstuffs, timber and their own labor at the request of their overlord.

This outline of economic and political activities during the nineteenth century is important in its own right. But what happened to the values and relationships within the Kerebe community as a result of such forces is undoubtedly more significant.

Notes

1. See Norman R. Bennett, "The Arab Impact," *Zamani; A Survey of East African History,* eds. B. A. Ogot and J. A. Kieran (Nairobi, 1968), 216-37; and within the same volume Edward A. Alpers, "The Nineteenth Century: Prelude to Colonialism," 238-64.

2. Richard Gray and David Birmingham, "Some Economic and Political Consequences of Trade in Central and Eastern Africa in

the Pre-Colonial Period," *Pre-Colonial African Trade; Essays on Trade in Central and Eastern Africa before 1900,* eds. R. Gray and D. Birmingham (London, 1970), 3.

3. *Ibid.,*4.

4. Austen, "Patterns of Development in Nineteenth-Century East Africa," 646.

5. *Ibid.* Alpers is as critical of Austen's analysis as he is of that presented by Gray and Birmingham; see "Re-Thinking African Economic History," 98.

6. Roland Oliver, "Discernible Developments in the Interior, c. 1500-1840," *History of East Africa,* eds. Roland Oliver and Gervase Mathew (London, 1963), I, 190.

7. Andrew Roberts, "Nyamwezi Trade," *Pre-Colonial African Trade,* eds. R. Gray and D. Birmingham (London, 1970), 49.

8. Edward A. Alpers, "The Coast and the Development of the Caravan Trade," *A History of Tanzania,* eds. I. N. Kimambo and A. J. Temu (Nairobi, 1969), 45.

9. Merrick Posnansky, "The Excavation of an Ankole Capital Site at Bweyorere," *Uganda Journal,* XXXII, 2 (1968), 171-72, 174; Charles M. Good, *Rural Markets and Trade in East Africa,* The University of Chicago, Department of Geography, Research Paper No. 128 (Chicago, 1970), 164; I. K. Katoke, "Karagwe: A Pre-Colonial State," *Journal of World History,* XIII, 3(1971), 533.

10. Alpers, "The Coast and the Development of Caravan Trade," 48-51; Roberts, "Nyamwezi Trade," 48-49.

11. Principle informants for events associated with Mihigo II's reign include Buyanza s/o Nansagate, Bahitwa s/o Lugambage, and Magoma s/o Kitina.

12. See D. H. Jones, "Problems of African Chronology," *Journal of African History,* XI, 2 (1970), 163-72; D. W. Cohen, "A Survey of Interlacustrine Chronology," *Journal of African History,* XI, 2 (1970), 177-202; Karugire, *A History of the Kingdom of Nkore,* 16-32; Zimoń, "Geschichte des Herrscher-Klans Abasiranga,"

366-72; David P. Henige, "Reflections on Early Interlacustrine Chronology: An Essay in Source Criticism," *Journal of African History*, XV, 1 (1974), 27-46.

13. See Aylward Shorter, "The Kimbu," *Tanzania Before 1900*, ed., A. Roberts (Nairobi, 1968), 106-07; Andrew Roberts, "The Nyamwezi," *Tanzania Before 1900*, ed., A. Roberts (Nairobi, 1968), 125-26; and Terence O. Ranger, "The Movement of Ideas, 1850-1939," *A History of Tanzania*, eds., I. N. Kimambo and A. J. Temu (Nairobi, 1969), 167-68.

14. Shorter, "The Kimbu," 100; Aylward Shorter, *Chiefship in Western Tanzania; A Political History of the Kimbu* (Oxford, 1972), 180-226; Roberts, "Introduction," *Tanzania Before 1900*, xi-xii.

15. Makeremu s/o Manyanga, Alipyo Mnyaga, Buyanza, and Bahitwa.

16. Busukuma is the important trading chiefdom in which the village of Kageyi was located. "Usukuma" is used to designate the country in which all the Sukuma chiefdoms are located.

17. Buyanza is the principle source of information on political alliances.

18. See Andrew Roberts, "The Nineteenth Century in Zambia," *Aspects of Central African History*, ed., T. O. Ranger (London, 1968), 83.

19. See William O. Jones, *Manioc in Africa* (Stanford, 1959), 232.

20. Buyanza and Bahitwa.

21. Informants such as Buyanza, Bahitwa, Magoma s/o Katina, Alipyo Mnyaga, and Kaliga s/o Lwambali were not as consistent about when diseases were introduced as they were about the introduction of food crops. This can be partially explained by the lack of importance attached to diseases as killers. An alien disease like cholera did not simply appear one day. It was present because an agent like Mihigo II introduced it. The actual threat to life was the agent who introduced it, not the disease itself.

22. Philip D. Curtin, "Epidemiology and the Slave Trade,"

Political Science Quarterly, LXXXIII, 2 (1968), 195

23. See James Christie, *Cholera Epidemics in East Africa* (London, 1876); also the comments by Robert W. Felkin, "Notes on the Waganda Tribe of Central Africa," *Proceedings of the Royal Society of Edinburgh,* 13 (1886), 704.

24. The Kerebe explicitly associate only one infectious disease to non-Africans: Syphilis is attributed to Arabs, although the Ganda are recognized as the direct agents of introduction.

25. Christie, *Cholera Epidemics;* see the accompanying map; J. A. Grant, "Summary of Observations on the Geography . . . ," *Journal of the Royal Geographical Society,* XLII (1872), 257-58; Gerald W. Hartwig, "Bukerebe, the Church Missionary Society, and East African Politics, 1877-1878," *African Historical Studies,* I, 2 (1968), 212-13; Eunice A. Chacker, "Early Arab and European Contacts with Ukerewe," *Tanzania Notes and Records,* 68 (1968), 75-77.

26. "Excerpt from Proceedings of the Royal Geographical Society concerning Erhardt's Map," *Church Missionary Intelligencer,* VII (1856), 190, 192; Grant, "Summary of Observations," 257-68.

27. John H. Speke, *What Led to the Discovery of the Source of the Nile* (Edinburgh, 1864), 318.

28. Stahl, *History of the Chagga People,* 49; Richard F. Burton, "The Lake Regions of Central Equatorial Africa," *Journal of the Royal Geographical Society,* XXIX (1859), 262.

29. Richard F. Burton, *The Lake Regions of Central Africa* (New York, 1860), 415-16.

30. John Speke particularly refers to a ruler who complained of Arab and Swahili competition in *Journal of the Discovery of the Source of the Nile* (Edinburgh, 1863), 131.

31. See Map I, p. 31.

32. H. M. Stanley, *Through the Dark Continent* (London, 1878), I, 329-30.

33. *Ibid.,* 220.

34. *Près des Grand Lacs par les missionnaires de S. Em. le Cardinal Lavigerie* (Paris, 1885), 35.

35. Robert W. Felkin, "Uganda," *The Scottish Geographical Magazine,* II (1886), 217.

36. Franz Stuhlmann, *Mit Emin Pascha ins Herz von Afrika* (Berlin, 1894), 733.

37. See Gerald W. Hartwig, "The Victoria Nyanza as a Trade Route in the Nineteenth Century," *Journal of African History,* XI, 4 (1970), 536.

38. Grant, "Summary of Observations," 279, 281-82.

39. Both figures are illustrated in Gerald W. Hartwig, "A Historical Perspective of Kerebe Sculpturing—Tanzania," *Tribus,* 18 (1969), 87, 88.

40. This quite detailed information was provided by Chavery Wanzura s/o Magoyelo, whose father participated as a porter in the two caravan journeys mentioned.

41. Journal of Lt. Shergold Smith, 19 November 1877, C. A6/0 22, Church Missionary Society Archives, London. Also J. M. Gray, "Arabs on Lake Victoria. Some Revisions," *Uganda Journal,* 22 (1958), 76.

42. Further information on this incident is in Hartwig, "Bukerebe and the Church Missionary Society."

43. Speke, *Journal of the Discovery of the Source of the Nile,* 131; Oscar Baumann to the Executive Committee of the Deutsch Anti-Sklaverei Lotterie, Coblenz, November 2, 1892, Korrespondenz mit der Anti-Sklaverei-Lotterie, G 1/30, National Archives of Tanzania; R. C. Bridges, "Introduction to the Second Edition," *Travels, Researches, and Missionary Labours,* J. Lewis Krapf (London, 1968), 23.

44. *Journal of the Discovery,* 401.

45. John A. Rowe, "Revolution in Buganda, 1856-1900, Part One: The Reign of Kabaka Mukabya Mutesa, 1856-1884" (unpublished Ph. D. dissertation, University of Wisconsin, 1966), 73-74.

46. Burton, "The Lake Regions of Central Equatorial Africa," 238.

47. Gray and Birmingham, *Pre-Colonial African Trade,* 11.

48. *Through the Dark Continent,* I, 12, 16, 121-28, 175-77, 187, 194-201, 207, 329; Wilson to Wright, 2 March 1877, C. A6/0 25, Church Missionary Society Archives; Hartwig, "Bukerebe and the Church Missionary Society," 213-14.

49. Detailed information on the conflict and its repercussions is found in "Bukerebe and the Church Missionary Society," 211-32.

50. Background material is found in Norman R. Bennett, *Mirambo of Tanzania, ca. 1840-1884* (New York, 1971), 46-68.

51. CMS to King Mutesa, 8 May 1878, C. A6/L 1, Church Missionary Society Archives.

52. Mackay to Wright, 17 November, 5 December, 26 December, 1879, C. A6/0 16, Church Missionary Society Archives. Background information on Buganda during this period is found in M. S. M. Semakula Kiwanuka, *A History of Buganda* (London, 1971), 136-72.

53. See R. W. Beachey, "The Arms Trade in East Africa in the Late Nineteenth Century," *Journal of African History,* III, 3 (1962), 451-67.

54. Bukumbi Diary, 8 March 1884, White Fathers, Regional House, Nyegezi, Tanzania.

55. Gordon to Lang, 5 November 1883; also Ashe to Lang 13 March 1883, and O'Flaherty to Wigram, 19 June and 1 July 1883, G3. A6/0 1, Church Missionary Society Archives.

3 Regional Trade and Internal Developments

The momentous effect of long-distance trade upon the Kerebe is partially evident from the preceding chapter. But how were the lives of the vast majority of people in Bukerebe affected by the new hunting organization, the presence of smallpox and cholera, imported luxury goods, and involved diplomatic and trade ties with neighboring peoples? This chapter will focus upon local economic production and trading (as distinguished from long-distance trading) as well as the function of servility in Kerebe society.

Questions have been raised and assertions made by Gray and Birmingham in *Pre-Colonial African Trade* and by Claude Meillassoux in his introduction to *The Development of Indigenous Trade and Markets in West Africa* to which the Kerebe data should also be applied. For example, did a royal monopoly over the major exported (ivory) and imported (beads and cloth) commodities inhibit the development of a market-oriented commerce among the Kerebe?[1] Did the demand for imported goods grow? Did acquisition of wealth become more important? If so, how was it acquired? And if acquired, how was it used? Was it consumed, stored, or channeled into pre-exisiting social categories such as bridewealth (thereby withdrawing it from an economic category)?[2] Did agricultural production increase? If so, did this affect social relationships? What was the role of servility? Did changes in production affect it? Were servile people only a means of social reproduction or were they actual producers?[3]

Meillassoux also states that personal or lineage wealth acquired through commerce or from labor by persons or groups not of the privileged ranks was a threat to the foundation of the subsistence-oriented society because it favored individuals outside the authority hierarchy. The persons in authority, he contends, formed the conservative element and restricted potential economic and social changes.[4] Meillassoux's hypothesis can be better examined in eastern Africa by analyzing the Kamba, Yao, Bisa, Nyamwezi, or Ziba, in which commercial entrepreneurs emerged on a significant scale. The Kerebe did not produce such individuals. The omukama steadfastly controlled participation in long-distance trading activities, thereby leaving the traditional power structure intact from that potential source of disruption. Imported goods did remain within the pre-existing redistributive social network. But the fact that there was something new to redistribute was important.

Nonetheless the disruption to the earlier system was substantial, but as is discussed in the succeeding chapters, more in social, psychological and political, than in economic, terms. Even without the presence of local trading entrepreneurs, basic changes beyond the control of the existing political authority occurred in the economic sphere. The agricultural producer is the key to understanding Kerebe economic developments; Meillassoux's hypothesis will be examined in light of developments by agricultural innovators.

Local Production and Trade

The definition of wealth among the Kerebe in 1800 should be established before alterations in this concept during the nineteenth century are discussed. Using the reign of

Mihigo II as a baseline, ca. 1780 to ca. 1820, the Kerebe economy can be described as virtually self-sufficient and self-sustaining. Except for the dependence upon Buzinza for metal hoes and hoe handles, the Kerebe extracted what was essential for sustenance and comfort from their immediate environment. According to Meillassoux, goods within this kind of community circulated "through a network of kinship, affinity, and clientage, through presentation, redistribution, or gift exchange. Wealth, as an instrument of social control, was a privilege of rank or birth."[5] This description requires qualification for the Kerebe. The elders of commoner clans held their respective family's wealth, particularly livestock, in a state of trust and used it to enhance the clan's well-being. Wealth as "a privilege of rank or birth" within a commoner clan must be seen within the context of group enhancement, not simply of social control for the sake of aggrandizing the elders' personal positions. The royal clan's position, however, more closely adheres to the situation described by Meillassoux. It used wealth to augment its political and social dominance.

Before the nineteenth century, the Kerebe role in local trade consisted of occasionally bartering locally produced or locally acquired items for nonessential but desirable goods such as quality salt and cattle. Only hoes and hoe handles represented essential items not available locally. The basic measurement of wealth at this time—and for many persons until the present century—was in terms of cattle and family: a wealthy individual in Bukerebe was a man with a sizable herd of cattle and a large family. Bartering seems to have depended on need. When hoes were required, they were sought. When neighbors needed foodstuffs, they would approach the Kerebe.

During the early nineteenth century, conditions and socio-economic values changed dramatically. Although the elders Bahitwa and Buyanza disagreed on the specifics, they both stated that a fundamental measurement of value increased in the 1800s, that is, bridewealth. Bahitwa contended that the number of items necessary for bridewealth increased to twelve, while Buyanza insisted that the number remained constant but that the value of the items increased.[6] In either case, the result was an emphasis on greater material wealth, revealing both the availability and the desire for such items as hoes and livestock. It is also apparent that the Kerebe increased their participation in interregional trade.

During the 1800s the major Kerebe export became grain. Those Kerebe wanting to acquire goods found it necessary to produce a grain surplus. The amount of land cultivated by those Kerebe aspiring to accumulate more wealth increased markedly by Machunda's reign. Yet by no means all Kerebe demonstrated the same aspirations. Buyanza estimated that only a fourth to a fifth of the family heads were actively seeking to increase their wealth and, significantly, some recent immigrants were among this group. The previous system of subsistence agriculture had encouraged cultivators—the women—to sow only the approximate amount of grain necessary to feed those for whom they were responsible.[7] When the Kerebe adopted grain as their major export, cultivators had to take into account the desirability of producing a surplus for trading. An increasing desire for wealth in the form of hoes and livestock meant that an increasing amount of land had to be cultivated to produce the surplus grain.

The practice of bartering goods certainly became more prevalent during this era. The best illustration of this development is the acquiring of hoes in Buzinza. The Kerebe had two options. Either expeditions of twenty to thirty men could travel together, taking with them goods such as dried fish, grain, or goats to be exchanged for hoes, or they could go to Buzinza as individuals or in small groups to work two or three months collecting iron ore for the smelters, in exchange for a portion of the hoes made from the ore. Buyanza's information, in addition to that of other elders, implicitly suggests that the exchange of labor for hoes was common earlier but decreased in the late nineteenth century. The decrease in the practice of labor for hoes occurred simultaneously with increased hoe productivity in Buzinza when labor would have been most appreciated. But the threat of violence, as much as the wish to avoid labor service and thereby expedite the exchange transaction, encouraged the Kerebe to travel in sizable groups with goods for barter.[8] Although a party laden with foodstuffs invited attacks by nonsmithing Zinza, it afforded greater protection to the individual. These parties consequently approached Buzinza well-armed and constantly prepared for a hasty withdrawal when necessary. Foodstuffs no doubt facilitated the procedure for obtaining hoes and bartering became the preferred method for acquiring hoes by the mid-1800s.[9]

Bukerebe acquired a reputation as the granary of the southeastern lake region because of the chiefdom's reliable and abundant rainfall. Drought was not unknown but it was not a frequent problem, particularly when compared to the neighboring districts. Once the Kerebe began consciously exploiting the agricultural potential of their island for purposes other than their own sustenance, they were in a position to benefit from any disadvantages experienced by their neighbors. Hence essential needs continued to determine local trading. Just as the Kerebe depended upon favorable climatic conditions for their surplus in grain, so they also depended upon unfavorable climatic conditions in other regions to gain desired items. Famine in Bururi meant that it was an auspicious time to acquire slaves. Bukara and many of the Sukuma chiefdoms possessed cattle; during drought these were most actively sought by the Kerebe. Oral evidence from a Kwimba chiefdom in Usukuma recounts a serious famine between 1860 and 1870 that is referred to as "the famine of the profiteers, in which residents of Ukerewe came to sell food supplies at an exorbitant price."[10] Hoes from Buzinza of course remained a constant Kerebe need, but even these valued items could be acquired on better terms when adverse conditions existed in Buzinza.

Kerebe exports during the nineteenth century included dried fish, canoes, oars, sheep, goats, grain, and worn-out hoes.[11] A hoe with the blade entirely worn away by use (hoe blades wore out fairly rapidly since the metal was not tempered) retained great value because the tang or shaft which was wedged into the handle was composed of considerable iron. The shafts represented the raw material from which any necessary tool was made. Kerebe smiths themselves had no other access to iron and therefore depended upon them and other discarded implements. They would reheat and rework the iron shafts into implements such as knives, arrowheads, spears, and adzes. Iron, in the form of these shafts, could be readily exchanged with most people along the eastern lake shore for small items. Luo canoemen, for example, came to Bukerebe with salt and eagerly exchanged a packet of salt for a hoe shaft.[12] When the importation of Zinza hoes is viewed from this perspective, their essential nature can be better appreciated.

The Kerebe were also noted as fishermen. They made lengthy journeys to the Buzinza and Bururi coasts during the months of June through August for the purpose of catching fish which were dried and then exchanged for goods the fishermen needed.[13] This particular form of trade may have decreased in the latter half of the 1800s, given the increased political unrest in Buzinza and the presence of the aggressive Ganda. On the other hand, the hunters of the hippopotamus (abanyaga) apparently did not curtail their expeditions to Buzinza and Bururi, journeys that provided the Kerebe with yet another commodity for trading purposes—hippopotamus meat.

The Kerebe generally regarded the inhabitants of Bururi as the most proficient hippo hunters in the region and would join forces with them. This cooperation permitted the Kerebe hunters to range beyond the territorial limits of the chiefdom in company with another community, the only example of a "formal" Kerebe hunting association that cooperated with non-Kerebe. The hunters traveled along the southern and eastern coasts in search of their prey. When a supply of meat was available it was then exchanged for other goods.[14] A favorite region for the hunters was the Luo coast, south of Kavirondo Gulf, where the flesh could be exchanged for the excellent salt found in the area, a commodity that also attracted the Ganda to the same source.[15] This salt trade may have had its origins before the nineteenth century, enabling the Kerebe to supplement their low-quality local vegetable sources.

Hoes, slaves, cattle, and salt formed the bulk of Kerebe imports by 1850. Hides imported from Usukuma and Bukara were made into articles of clothing and represented an additional minor item of exchange that continued from earlier times into the 1800s. By the latter half of the nineteenth century both Ruri and Sukuma tradesmen provided tobacco for the Kerebe; prior to this time local varieties of "tobacco" had been used for both smoking and chewing.[16] The Sukuma also supplemented the Kerebe salt supply from Kenya (Bugaya) by offering another variety obtained from Lake Eyasi.[17]

The desire by the Kerebe for nonessential local commodities and forms of wealth increased during the era of long-distance trade. According to oral evidence their interest in livestock, salt, tobacco, and servile persons was greater in 1875 than in 1800.[18] Their socio-economic values perceptively altered, although their less fortunate neighbors do not appear to have demonstrated the same tendency. These neighbors had no use for Kerebe grain unless climatic or other conditions forced them to find an outside supply. Superficially, the subsistence economy of the region remained intact. Yet the Kerebe proclivity for exploiting their neighbors' suffering, particularly in their acquisition of highly valued cattle and people—neither essential to the immediate survival of the Kerebe—reveals a modified set of values.

Regional trade of this sort was by no means an unregulated activity. A tax was assessed on all major imports by headmen on the omukama's behalf. Whether hoes or salt, a percentage of the commodity was designated as the omukama's share. The details of the system are not altogether clear, but as an illustration, Buyanza reported that after a war in which captives were taken, the omukama

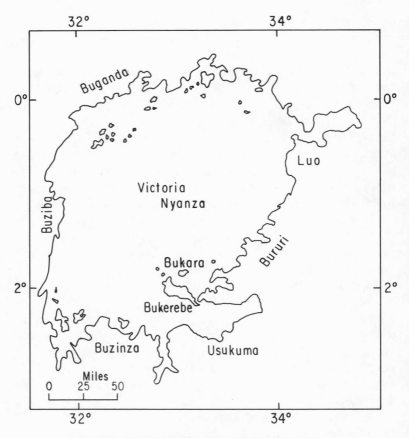

MAP V. REGIONAL TRADE: KEREBE IMPORTS

People	Commodities
Ganda	Bark Cloth
Ziba	Coffee Beans, Bark Cloth
Zinza	Hoes
Sukuma	Salt, Cattle, Hides
Kara	Cattle, Hides
Ruri	Servile People, Tobacco
Luo	Servile People, Salt

received the first prisoner from his subjects and fifty percent of those remaining. This policy was seemingly flexible; the ruler could return a single captive to the captor, but the gesture of recognizing the omukama's right to the first captive was important. As with all goods received through taxation, the omukama used his discretion in redistributing them. Members of the royal clan received the largest single portion, while others who were socially near the seat of authority could expect consideration. Nonetheless, it was also a matter of policy to retain a reserve supply of nonperishable goods to meet unexpected emergencies.

Two other imports, coffee beans and bark cloth, also appeared within the chiefdom during Machunda's reign. These products were in a transitional category between interregional and long-distance trade. They were produced and traded by Africans, but they formed a part of the omukama's trade that bore all the characteristics of a royal monopoly similar to the ivory trade. The Ziba, who live north of Bukoba on the west side of the lake, were primarily responsible for dispersing coffee beans grown in their vicinity throughout the lake region.[19] Although their major interest was ivory, the Ziba were always welcomed when they visited Bukerebe because they brought coffee beans which the elders enjoyed chewing. The Kerebe omukama exchanged ivory for coffee beans in addition to other commodities, then freely dispensed the beans to advisers and *enfura* (friends of the omukama) who appeared at his court. Bark cloth obtained occasionally from the Ziba and Ganda represented another highly prized luxury commodity; it too was a by-product of the ivory trade, hence a monopoly of the omukama.

Social Factors

Those who most enthusiastically participated in local trade manifested not only a change in socio-economic values but also an effort to enhance their social position. The Kerebe were a highly stratified community in the nineteenth century, with social status in most cases firmly based on ethnicity. The royal Silanga clan formed the privileged first rank of the community, with the omukama as its head. The Sese clans formed the second major social stratum. They were primarily the descendants of people coming from Buzinza and Ihangiro whose language and customs were similar to that of the royal clan. The Jita (Kwaya) and the Kara, representing the third and fourth social strata, respectively, were distinct ethnic groups living within the chiefdom by the 1800s. There was no inter-marriage between these social and ethnic divisions, with the exception of the royal clan, whose role permitted and necessitated intermarriage with all ranks.

Conversely, allegiance to the omukama bound the diverse population into a single political entity. The extent of the omukama's authority should be borne in mind before analyzing servitude, the lowest of social ranks. Aniceti Kitereza described the theoretical powers of the omukama's office in the following manner:

> The *omukama* was greatly respected by his peo-
> ple as manifested in greetings and ordinary
> speech. . . . This respect was especially paid to
> him and no one else in the chiefdom. He was
> above all and most people feared him. He had
> power over all things possessed by his subjects,
> livestock and crops for example. He could order
> any death, or the plundering and destruction of
> any homes he wished. He was expected to be the
> elder of everyone in the chiefdom and nobody
> else held these same powers. He was the light,
> elder, sun, lion, creator, etc. [titles of praise].
> When officially greeting him people took gifts
> such as goats or cattle or millet or hoes or beer.
> He received presents [tribute] once a year from
> each home in the villages. Headmen and nobles
> [usually members of the royal clan] did not con-
> tribute to this.[20]

This passage does not indicate that his subjects, particularly the advisers from nonroyal Sese clans, had the right to depose an omukama if he did not serve the community satisfactorily. Nonetheless, the enormous powers of the omukama imply that obedience to him was normally in the subjects' best interest. Within this context, the omukama's power over both life and property was significant. This is the aspect of the omukama's authority, referred to by Meillassoux, which prevented subjects from upsetting prevailing relationships by accumulating too much wealth. At the ruler-subject level it was a form of patron-client relationship with reciprocal rights recognized by both parties. Kerebe traditions definitely extol the generous abakama and denounce those who abused their prerogatives by plundering subjects. The annual tribute (taxes) to the omukama was regarded as normal, but he was expected to assist subjects in time of need. This held true for all subjects, regardless of their social strata.

Three forms of work activity also either determined or influenced one's position in Kerebe society. As mentioned here previously, smiths (males) and potters (females) belonged to a unique low stratum of society. Endogamous marriages were the rule for these clans, that is, marriage could only be arranged between other smithing or potting clans. Again, the royal clan was an exception; its members could marry across this barrier. Since all Kerebe are agricultural Bantu-speaking people, regardless of social strata, this presents an interesting situation. In fact, most Sese clans are alleged to have practiced smithing at one time in the distant past. But even before the 1800s there was a definite trend to foresake this activity, since a social stigma evolving from the not too distant past accompanied the work. Machunda encouraged a number of Jita and Zinza smiths to immigrate to his chiefdom to ensure the presence of these vital specialists.[21] Agricultural work also influenced one's social position.

Routine agricultural work normally was performed by women, with men assisting during the beginning of the agricultural cycle. But as ambitious heads of nuclear and extended families began to cultivate a surplus grain crop there was a simultaneous development to find a labor source to assist the women—no doubt an emulation of the omukama's family, as his wives were freed from agricultural labor. Women of high status were distinguished by their personal ornamentation. They wore heavy metal bracelets of copper or iron that effectively prevented the wearer from using a hoe without considerable discomfort. The bracelets marked the wearer as a woman above menial work, thus reflecting well on her husband's ability to relieve her of agricultural drudgery.[22]

Servility before 1800

What effect did this desire for wealth and high status have upon the role of a servile population? An adequate answer to this question can only be given by determining what servility had been before agricultural production assumed an important function within the trading system.

Defining servitude is basic to this analysis. One recent definition of African slavery calls it "the legal institutionalization of persons as property."[23] Yet this definition does not reflect the type of social relationship that *aberu* (males) and *abazana* (females) are said to have had in Kerebe society. Property connotes a market-oriented economy of which aberu and abanza simply were not a part. For the Kerebe an *omwiru* (one male) or an *omuzana* (one female) can be defined as a dependent individual outside the pale of his/her clan who subsequently acquired a socially servile position inheritable by his/her descendants within a different clan.[24]

A basic assumption within the Kerebe community was that each individual's identity was determined by his membership within a particular clan. For all practical purposes each clan was a self-sufficient economic, social, and political unit. The spiritual concerns of the clan, as well as judicial and economic functions, remained under the control of the clan elders if only members of that family were concerned. Clan elders could petition the omukama for assistance if they felt their powers were inadequate for a given situation. If a clan was not self-sufficient in specific spheres, such as smelting iron ore, its material needs had to be met through a barter or exchange system. While individual property rights scarcely existed within a clan, clan property rights did. Interclan relations also were characterized by a high degree of recognized property rights or rights over the services of individual members.

Outside the clan structure an individual possessed neither an identity nor a claim to the normal rights and security afforded by the family unit.[25] To accommodate dependent individuals, that is, persons who for a number of reasons no longer possessed membership in a clan, the Kerebe followed a practice that incorporated these dependent persons into a new clan, although in a servile status that was inherited by the next generation. This social arrangement is variously referred to as "benign" or "domestic" slavery. The words *aberu* and *abazana* were taken from the vocabulary of the interlacustrine peoples who also used it to designate persons of low status. The existence of the words in Kikerebe is specifically linked with the arrival of the royal clan. The antiquity of servitude dates to at least the time when the chiefdom was formed in the 1600s.

Just as the omukama's generous giving represented the most praiseworthy attribute of a great man, so the inability to provide for one's own sustenance represented one of the most despised attributes of a poor man. He was dependent upon others and had to place himself in their charge to maintain his existence. Whether a victim of famine or a war captive, the lone individual was regarded as incapable of sustaining life outside his clan and therefore totally dependent. The Kerebe treated all such individuals identically, regardless of their reason for being in a state of servility. They were given sustenance, and thus life, in exchange for rights over their services. In common with other African societies, the Kerebe regarded people as their most precious possession; in economic terms they were the "real key to production and prosperity."[26]

In Bukerebe, as in most societies, hospitality was accorded to one's social equals and superiors; that is, it was practiced between equally independent persons with distinct clan identities. Charity also flourished, but within the clan. Non-members were expected to repay what was borrowed and to reciprocate hospitality. Dependent persons—those without a clan identity—were in no position to do either. The most charitable thing an elder could do was to permit the dependent person to become his omwiru or omuzana. Some persons opted for social servitude because of circumstances which forced them from their formerly secure niche into a situation in which they were no longer able to claim such membership. They had to become dependent upon some other group for sustenance.[27] In exchange for food and shelter they readily gave up their position of clanless limbo. Men who voluntarily sought this form of welfare from either the omukama or other wealthy Kerebe were called aberu w'enzara; women, abazana w'enzara. Persons who came specifically because of hunger were called either aberu w'engoyelo or abanza w'engoyelo. It is important to note that only wealthy Kerebe took aberu and abazana, that is, wealthy insofar as they had sufficient food reserves to feed more people.

Since the Kerebe occupy a district with relatively high, reliable rainfall, in contrast to their neighbors along the eastern lake shore who suffer periodic drought, Bukerebe has periodically served as a refuge for those seeking either more favorable agricultural conditions or emergency food supplies. Approximately one third of the Kerebe population in 1900 was composed of Jita immigrants. These people had entered the chiefdom not as servile individuals, but as independent nuclear family units or individuals who had requested and received permission to settle and cultivate. Because they were able to care for their own personal needs, they did not enter the servile status. Therefore strangers entering the district were not automatically placed in a servile role, although in the case of the Jita their cultural distinctiveness formed the basis for a social stratum.[28]

Servitude was the Kerebe equivalent of a welfare system; it was also the Kerebe equivalent of a penal system. While some aberu and abazana acquired their status through need, others acquired their status of servitude through the operation of the omukama's justice. For example if a member of one clan seriously harmed or killed a member of another clan, compensation was made most frequently by the transference of a person, usually a young girl, from the attacker's clan to the clan of the victim. According to the elder Makene whose clan held a leadership capacity prior to the establishment of the chiefdom, the power of the omukama to arbitrate cases of this nature, and thereby curtail the necessity of blood revenge, was one of the most beneficial attributes of chiefdomship. In other legal situations fines could be imposed upon individuals for serious infractions; if livestock was unavailable to pay the fine an individual could be transferred to satisfy the court's punishment.

A third means of acquiring aberu/abazana prior to 1800 was by obtaining captives during skirmishes with neighbors. While Kerebe traditions make little mention of serious military encounters until the latter half of the nineteenth century, it is apparent that endemic hostility existed between the royal Silanga clan and their immediate neighbors and rivals, the Kula. The Kula controlled the southern, the Silanga the northern, portion of the peninsula in the 1600s. By intermittent forays the stronger Silanga gradually forced the Kula from the peninsula onto the island, until by 1850 the Kula could claim only the southwestern corner of the island. Whatever ignited specific quarrels, the usual consequence of an encounter left the Silanga with the upper hand.[29]

In the 1800s, control of strategic land was a factor in the disputes, but before that time the Silanga desire to plunder cattle from the Kula and their subjects seems to have been the main irritant. Occasionally mere cattle raids occurred, while at other times battles ensued, the aim of which was to acquire as many captives as possible to hold for ransom in livestock. In one encounter the Kula ruler was captured, which was a boon for the Silanga. His ransom price was significantly higher than that of an ordinary subject.

The captives taken during these encounters, called *aberu* or *abazana w'ichumu* ("servants or slaves of the spear"), were primarily a means of acquiring coveted livestock. The Kerebe practice was very unlike reports emanating from Buganda during the late 1800s, for instance, when only women and children were taken captive as a means of rewarding warriors and increasing the servile population.[30] By indicating that male captives were as welcome as female, the Kerebe evidence implies that the aberu/abazana w'ichumu were essentially hostages to be exchanged for the wealth actually sought—cattle. Those warriors who took captives were obliged to give approximately half of them to the omukama. But if a successful ransom was arranged by the omukama, all captives were returned to their homes with the warriors receiving their share of cattle. Apparently the division of spoils among the Kerebe was essentially the same as that of Mirambo in Unyamwezi.[31]

Nature of the Servile Relationship

The procedures by which aberu and abazana could be redeemed shed some light upon the shadowy role of servitude in eastern Africa that has caused such consternation for European observers. It is not uncommon to find an explorer such as James A. Grant remarking within the same paragraph that "slavery is the curse of the country and the African races will continue this practice of buying, plundering, and selling slaves to traders as long as the Zanzibar Government . . . supports it," and that slaves are generally "treated with kindness," conditions being "bad" only in the hands of a dealer.[32] Robert W. Felkin, a doctor sent to Buganda by the Church Missionary Society, recorded similar impressions: "Slavery has existed in Uganda from time immemorial . . . the number of slaves held varies necessarily with the position and wealth of the owner. They are well treated."[33] Toward the end of the nineteenth century another observer frankly confessed that slavery in eastern Africa was "a complicated system," hence it could be described as either "beneficial—or abhorrent," depending on whether the slave trade with "all its deadly characteristics" or the domestic slavery which "is only a kind of feudal system," was being described.[34] What these commentators were describing was an aberration of the earlier system of servitude, which had been modified and distorted by fundamental changes accompanying long-distance trading opportunities, including slave trading.

Servitude was not necessarily a permanent condition for the aberu and abazana. Regardless of why a person became an omwiru or an omuzana, he or she could be redeemed and thereby removed from the servile state. Two options are frequently mentioned in oral sources. Individuals from Kerebe clans who became aberu/abazana because of famine or wrongdoing could be redeemed by their kin once compensation was arranged. The rate of exchange for redemption was based upon cattle. An omuzana could be freed with one cow. If this was impossible, then twelve goats or twelve hoes or twelve large containers of millet, or any combination of the last three which totaled twelve items would free her. For an omwiru, a bull or steer or six goats, hoes, or containers of millet were sufficient. The redemption compensation apparently remained the same regardless of the age of the individual or the duration of servile status. A further ritual was required for the redemption of aberu/abazana from Sese clans. In addition to the normal compensation, a hoe or goat was sent to the omukama and the person being released from servility was taken to a crossroad where his or her head was shaven to symbolize the loss of servility.

The other possibility for regaining an independent status was apparently chosen most frequently by those who had migrated into the chiefdom because of famine, those who had no relatives able or willing to provide the redemption fee. If these persons were men (aberu) and if they had a good relationship with their master, they could acquire the use of land to cultivate their own millet. By steadfastly working toward their goal of producing a surplus millet crop, these individuals could redeem themselves over a period of years. This could be accomplished within three to five years. A young marriageable omuzana could also be redeemed if her master took her as a concubine and a child was subsequently born. She then could become his wife and her children possessed full legal rights.[35]

Even with these opportunities for redemption some aberu/abazana remained in a state of servitude which was then inherited by their offspring. Aberu who pleased their patrons were permitted to marry abazana. Obviously a number of factors could determine whether a man was redeemed by his own clan, whether he decided to work for his own redemption or whether he remained in a servile position. Other factors were his ambition, how close the relationship between himself and his master grew, whether he desired to return to his own clan—or whether it wished to have him return—and whether servitude was not actually preferable to his previous role.

As the wealthiest Kerebe clan, the royal clan possessed the majority of aberu/abazana. The omukama retained sizable numbers for his own court; the aberu performed numerous menial but necessary tasks there, while the abazana were assigned to serve the omukama's wives. He in turn distributed aberu/abazana to his kinsmen and to other deserving men from nonroyal clans. Through their abilities some aberu gained respected positions under the omukama or other powerful elders. Consequently it was sometimes desirable to remain in a servile state, since factors such as prestige and power could be attained in spite of it. Simultaneously, patrons with obedient, hard-working aberu were anxious to retain their services. They provided a valuable asset to the patron and his clan. Given a favorable reciprocal relationship of this type, the aberu often found it in his best interests to remain with his patron. Furthermore, the aberu realized that the servile status was a gradually diminishing one; by the third generation the offspring were seldom regarded as aberu/abazana. By this time they were recognized as legal participating members of the clan. With such possibilities for redemption and self-improvement within a new clan as incentives to remain in servitude, it is not difficult to discern the confusion that "domestic slavery" caused Europeans of the nineteenth century.[36] In many societies the earlier benign form of servitude continued to function, but altering conditions during the 1800s related to long-distance trade placed considerable stress upon all social institutions, not the least of which was servitude.

Servitude during the Nineteenth Century

Thus far only three categories of aberu/abazana have been discussed: war captives, victims of hunger, and wrongdoers who opted for the servile status. Four other distinct categories are discernible and from information provided by Kerebe oral data it is apparent that these categories are specifically concerned with, if not direct consequences of, the expanding trade opportunities in the nineteenth century. The additional types of aberu/abazana included persons given to the omukama as gifts from other rulers *(aberu* and *abazana w'okulungulwa),* persons who were acquired by barter from inside or outside the chiefdom *(aberu* and *abazana w'okugula),* persons convicted of sorcery or witchcraft *(aberu* and *abazana w'ilogo)* and persons accused but not convicted of sorcery or witchcraft, who placed themselves under the protection of the omukama *(aberu* and *abazana w'ekwitubizya).* While these four categories cannot be related exclusively to conditions emanating from long-distance trade, it can be safely assumed that they were far more significant in the 1800s than any previous era. Sorcery, that is, the conscious but secretive effort to harm someone or their property, is definitely claimed by Kerebe elders to have "commenced" shortly after the death of Mihigo II.[37] Altering social, economic, and political conditions, exacerbated by high mortality rates from diseases such as smallpox and cholera, frequently communicated by coastal traders, enabled sorcery to flourish.[38]

Oral data suggest that depopulation took place within Bukerebe on a significant scale once the chiefdom became actively involved in long-distance trade.[39] Elders cite three conditions to support this assertion, all of which have been discussed at some length in Chapter 2: the devastating effect of the man/beast Butamile, "created" by Mihigo II; expeditions to Buzinza during Mihigo's reign to acquire hoe handles, scarce because there were "too many people" in Bukerebe but yet plentiful by Machunda's reign; and the emigration of people from the interior of the island. The elders do not refer specifically to a decrease in population, but to evidence of substantial former occupation (grinding stones) found in uninhabited areas of the island in the 1920s and '30s. In light of the known effect of new diseases in other communities of the region, disease seems the most probable cause of this particular depopulation.

The elder Buyanza's oral information illustrates this point. In his estimation the royal Silanga clan and other Sese clans on Bukerebe were dying out at the end of the nineteenth century, failing in the struggle to balance births and deaths. Just prior to her drowning at Rukonge's command, Rukonge's sister cursed Rukonge and the entire Silanga clan, declaring that "the family would have few children in the future." This particular "curse" was probably less a prophetic utterance, as implied by Buyanza, than a reflection of current conditons destined, in the wish of the curser, to continue into the future. Although there is no satisfactory comparative evidence available to determine whether mortality rates among all clans were similar or whether the Silanga clan experienced greater mortality, Buyanza supplied valuable information about Nansagate, his father. Nansagate was the brother of Rukonge, a wealthy headman who had married at least twelve wives. When Buyanza was in his early twenties in 1904—his father had been dead some ten years by this time—Nansagate's living children totaled nine. Six wives had borne children that lived at least until the age of ten. Three of these women had one child alive; two others had two alive; and Buyanza's mother had three alive in 1904. Buyanza stated that his mother alone bore a total of nine children. He placed the responsibility for this alarming mortality rate on syphilis, indicating that princes were particularly vulnerable to the disease because they had sexual intercourse with women other than their wives, women exposed to the disease from aliens such as traders.

In addition to health-related deaths, the movement of individuals or even families from one community to another to seek refuge following accusations of sorcery or witchcraft was also responsible for depopulation. People, particularly those of a productive age, became ever more precious and desirable. It is within this milieu that servitude and slavery of the nineteenth century within Bukerebe must be understood. Manpower was at a premium. This altered the role of aberu and abazana, as well as the desire to acquire labor for agricultural work—both to produce a millet surplus and to gain status by avoidance of field work. Seasonal migrant labor alleviated the manpower shortage to a degree, particularly during the latter half of the 1800s. These seasonal migrants came from the neighboring island of Bukara, where the limited geographic area and the dense population combined to encourage men to work as cultivators *(abamilizya)* on Bukerebe in return for a share of the harvest.[40]

The formal penal system of the Kerebe normally functioned to incorporate persons convicted of being sorcerers. Assuming those persons did not flee the chiefdom, they could be fined, placed in servitude (aberu/abazana w'ilogo) or executed. In a few instances, nuclear families or even entire clans were involved in these punishments, but those were exceptional cases in that numerous individuals within the family unit had been accused or convicted earlier. In common with other East African communities, the Kerebe assumed that sorcery or witchcraft (*obulogi*) was a practice consciously passed on from one generation to the next.[41] By ridding itself of the entire family, the community expected that antisocial behavior would cease. Those in authority did not sentence groups of people in this manner merely to exploit their subjects;[42] it was primarily done to cleanse the society of a serious social malady.

The more tragic cases were persons accused or suspected of being sorcerers but not actually convicted. These persons again had the option of fleeing the chiefdom or of seeking the protection of the omukama, which meant placing themselves in his service. These individuals were called aberu/abazana w'ekwitubizya. Oral evidence does not suggest that redemption procedures for those suspected of sorcery were any different for those convicted of sorcery. In practice, however, some aberu/abazana w'ilogo and w'ekwitubizya would seldom be redeemed by their clans because these persons had allegedly harmed others within the family and were no longer desired within the clan. Hence one method of redemption was all but closed for some serviles.

The Kerebe abakama also received a sizable number of abazana, and fewer aberu, as gifts (abazana/aberu w'okulungulwa) from other rulers, a means of abetting diplomatic and commercial relations. Of course this implies that the Kerebe rulers in turn sent abazana and aberu to their fellow rulers. In 1875 the explorer H. M. Stanley noted one such exchange between Mutesa of Buganda and Rukonge of Bukerebe in which he participated. The Kabaka sent Rukonge five tusks of ivory, a "comely virgin of fifteen as wife suitable for a king," trade wire, monkey skins, and a large canoe.[43]

Individual omuzana and omwiru sent from one ruler to another, such as the "comely virgin," tended to be exceptional persons in one fashion or another. Undesirables would never be foisted upon a fellow monarch unless large numbers were involved. In the case of girls, physical attractiveness was a necessary attribute but equally, if not more, important was a quality that can best be described as "social behavior." Relations between persons within the same clan, of different clans, of different ages, of different social strata (in particular the royal clan) were all rigidly defined. Knowing one's place in the social order and acting accordingly was a fundamental characteristic of a well-behaved individual. The Kerebe accordingly judged their abazana and aberu in their social behavior as well as in their response to appointed tasks. "Favorites" manifested qualities approved by the community. Providing such persons were expendable, these were the type of persons frequently given as a gift by a ruler. Some aberu acquired by Rukonge from Mutesa of Buganda, for example, were skilled drum makers who were regarded by the Kerebe as superior to their own craftsmen and were consequently assigned the responsibility of producing royal drums.[44] Abazana and aberu, as well as ivory, were common items of exchange between rulers in the nineteenth century, since, like ivory, they possessed a high value and were easily transported. This exchange was separate from long-distance trade, and the individuals passed along in this manner should not be regarded as victims of slave trading. Economic motives in these exchanges were negligible.

Nonetheless, the extent of diplomatic contacts between rulers increased as cooperation became more important, given the intricacies of long-distance trade. Much of the contact, however, dealt with the problem of how to control unusual or new circumstances that confronted men in authority. They sought successful means, frequently of a magical nature, to gain a greater measure of security. When requesting such knowledge, the inquiring ruler necessarily sent gifts to the possessor of the sought-after information. This same procedure was followed when requesting something more mundane, such as military assistance. Aberu and abazana were instrumental in facilitating these transactions.

Coastal traders apparently practiced the same custom of giving persons in servitude as gifts when establishing a formal relationship with a ruler. The Kerebe evidence for this was the presence of a number of Luo aberu and abazana, also referred to as *abagaya,* in Bukerebe.[45] The presence of these people can scarcely be accounted for except through the trading efforts of Songoro. Besides acting as an agent and facilitator for the Ganda in moving their ivory from Kageyi to Unyanyembe, Songoro acquired substantial numbers of slaves on his own initiative from the eastern shore of the lake, particularly in the Kavirondo Gulf region, for shipment southward.[46] His alliance with Machunda and then with Rukonge enabled him to use their canoes if necessary and their contacts with Ruri elders, who collaborated with Songoro in acquiring captives from their northern Luo neighbors. The only Kerebe who normally traveled that far north were hippopotamus hunters, essentially men of peace desiring to exchange hippo flesh with the Luo for their excellent salt. Songoro's presence could only have disturbed the earlier relationships and thereby curtailed the hunters' activities. While Songoro moved his slaves to the south, he apparently gave many of them to Rukonge as a form of tribute for maintaining a settlement on the island. These slaves essentially became aberu/abazana w'okulungulwa (gifts to the omukama) just as much as those given to him by other rulers. But these Luo aberu/abazana existed under a significantly different set of conditions than any other servile persons discussed: They were a Nilotic speaking people, not Bantu; they were captives and victims of a slave trader; and they were approximately one hundred miles from their home district. This meant that redemption by their clan was a virtual impossibility. In addition, the language and cultural differences between themselves and their Kerebe masters were so great that at least the first generation would have found it more difficult than other servile persons to work for their own redemption.

The final category of servile persons to be discussed reveals major changes in the Kerebe attitude toward their servile population. The earlier institution was a combined welfare and penal system; sorcerers and war captives of the

1800s can be relegated to the same system. Individuals given as gifts by fellow rulers or coastal traders, however, must be placed within a separate category, although they were essentially a byproduct of increased communication stimulated by long-distance trade. All of the various categories of aberu/abazana possess one vital dimension in common: people were not actually sought to fill a servile status; they were placed in it as a means of incorporating dependent persons into the community. By midcentury, during Machunda's reign, aberu/abazana w'okugula are mentioned. These individuals were acquired by outright barter, from either inside or outside Bukerebe, usually the latter. Paralleling local trading developments, these aberu and abazana became the possession of well-to-do Kerebe, seldom the omukama.

Without exception informants describe these individuals as Ruri, although their origins and ethnic identities were diverse. What is clear is that before 1870 men identified as Ruri brought individuals—almost always children—to the chiefdom as an exchange for millet, particularly during one of the not infrequent droughts. The Ruri invariably attempted to kidnap these youngsters from their neighbors; to exchange their own kin for sustenance would have been a definite act of desperation. It is impossible to determine whether slavers such as Songoro initiated such dealings or whether they merely exploited and improved upon a practice already in existence. The latter possibility is the more likely. Climatic factors had produced aberu/abazana in Bukerebe long before 1800 and the intensification of trade. People from Bururi, among other areas, had drifted into Bukerebe, both on an independent and a dependent basis, to seek some form of security. The southward migration of the Luo by the late eighteenth century may have also encouraged others to migrate,[47] but the fact that Kerebe data indicate that aberu/abazana w'okugula were not present until the mid-1800s certainly suggests that internecine struggles between peoples along the eastern lake shore were not as prevalent earlier.[48] As opportunities for trade grew—evidenced in the Kerebe desire for labor—it is likely that the Ruri and Luo engaged in mutually destructive raids upon one another for captives and livestock.

Altered Nature of Servility

The deliberate acquisition of servile persons implies a measure of selectivity on the master's part; this in fact did occur. The Kerebe denounced any form of intentional physical mutilation, whether circumcision, piercing of ears, or filing of teeth, all of which were practiced by various peoples on the eastern side of the Victoria Nyanza. Therefore in acquiring aberu/abazana w'okugula there, Kerebe sought only children who had not been subjected to any physical change. This desire for unmarked children in itself reveals another dimension to Kerebe servitude as it evolved in the nineteenth century. There was little expectation that these particular aberu/abazana would ever be redeemed by their kinsmen. They were virtually destined to remain in lifelong servitude, which in reality meant their eventual incorporation into the clan of their master. It was a procedure for increasing or, more realistically, maintaining numbers within a given homestead while simultaneously providing a source of manpower to perform menial tasks.[49]

The Kerebe became dependent upon this source of aberu/abazana. By the reign of Rukonge during the last quarter of the 1800s, men left Bukerebe explicitly to search for children who could be purchased during drought and famine in Bururi. This initiative was a completely new feature of servitude. Before, the Kerebe had always passively waited for others to approach them. Their dependence upon Songoro's infusion of captives into their society may very well have been instrumental in their taking the initiative once the trader was gone. Nonetheless the Kerebe seldom raided for aberu/abazana, although some instances are mentioned by elders which indicate that kidnapping was performed on occasion.[50] They primarily depended upon climatic conditions to allow them to exchange their surplus millet for children with inhabitants in need of grain.

In summary, the Kerebe institution of servility altered drastically over time. Once a centralized system of government was introduced, and with it a stratified society, aberu/abazana became a feature of Kerebe society. Servility was concomitantly a welfare and a penal institution to care for dependent individuals. Initially, redemption was an accepted and encouraged characteristic of servitude, with unredeemed persons becoming members of their master's clan after two or three generations. Throughout the nineteenth century altering social, economic, and religious values and opportunities provided different sources for servile persons: sorcerers, gifts from other rulers, and individuals acquired by barter. Redemption became less prevalent because kinsmen frequently lived in distant communities and no longer possessed the same opportunities for redeeming persons as earlier, when servitude primarily involved local clans. Depopulation and the desire for labor to cultivate expanded millet plots also served to encourage the permanency of the aberu/abazana status. Yet the absorption of descendants of servile persons in the master's clan remained a constant characteristic. Factors accounting for depopulation served to insure that this feature continued uninterrupted. Bartering for individuals during the latter part of the 1800s also suggests that the Kerebe were increasingly desirous of obtaining servile persons. Only a small minority of Kerebe aberu/abazana were incorporated into the slave trade. The community had adequate sources of agricultural, pastoral, timber, and lake products to exchange for trade goods. It was unnecessary to deplete the servile rank, which was appreciated for its potential contribution to the society, both as a labor source and as an eventual addition to the various clans. Aberu/abazana definitely were not mere "objects or things of property."[51]

Although servitude among the Kerebe was a clearly defined social status, it was a position ameliorated by mobility and covertness. The latter feature explains why elders could speak with authority only about specific aberu/abazana within their own clans. As Buyanza explained, if you walked into another homestead, "it was very difficult to know who was an omwiru or an omuzana and who was not." This type of information was a clan affair not a public one. And as with all forms of good fortune, the Kerebe generally avoided ostentatious display of their aberu/abazana. Only those secure in their social position— such as members of the royal clan, royal advisers, and "friends" of the omukama—dared flaunt their wealth and position. As far as could be determined from the oral data, only about a fourth to a fifth of the population actually aspired to accumulate wealth and thereby acquire higher status; many of this group were members of the royal clan. Only within this segment of Kerebe society could men afford to maintain servile persons. Thus a majority of the population had little actual contact with the servile rank. Strong clans or segments of clans meant numerous members. Whether this was achieved through natural increase or by incorporating outsiders into the clan was relatively unimportant and certainly not the affair of other clans.

Status and Rights

The royal clan possessed the most absorbative tendency. Most Sese clans living in the chiefdom had rigid restrictions regarding breach births or the cutting of upper before lower teeth or the birth of twins; all such children had to be abandoned. Members of the royal clan had no such restriction and would frequently rescue such infants abandoned by others, rearing them as their own. The royal clan also absorbed by far the greatest number of aberu/abazana descendants into its ranks, the assumption being that a numerically large royal clan was strong. The mother of the fourth omukama, Mihigo I, who ruled in the early 1700s, was an omuzana. This is the only example, however, of a man with this particular heritage becoming a ruler until Mukaka's reign (1895-1907). But Mukaka's case is unique; he was placed in office by the German authorities. While sons of an omukama by a former omuzana could be appointed as *abakungu* (headmen) or otherwise form a portion of the privileged princes *(abahinda)*, descendants of aberu and abazana who became Silanga (the royal clan) after two or three generations normally would not be considered for an appointed position.

This same pattern was evident in other clans. If the master married an omuzana, or if another Kerebe redeemed her and then married her, the offspring were accepted as members of the father's clan with full inheritance rights. Only when an omwiru married an omuzana, and this was virtually the only alternative for an omwiru unless he was redeemed, did the children inherit servile status, a status that only time and the proper social etiquette could obliterate. The one exception to this condition of slower mobility for men mentioned by elders was if an omwiru married the wife of his deceased master and she bore the omwiru's children. The omwiru was then accepted as a free man, but with his clan membership altered to that of his master. Hence the former omwiru's children were also members of the former master's clan.[52]

Since the Kerebe themselves were unable without effort to determine who was in a servile position and who was not, the day-to-day treatment of servile persons did not vary significantly from the treatment accorded other members of the homestead. The major barriers for aberu/abazana were of a legal nature. Inheritance rights were practically nonexistent for their descendants. Marriage, of course, was arranged by the master, not by the servile parents. The relative insecurity of aberu/abazana is most apparent in elders' descriptions of the treatment accorded to persons committing serious crimes. For example, in sorcery proceedings free men or women could appeal the decision of an *omufumu* (medicine man) concerning their guilt. The more influential the accused, the longer the appeals could go on. An omwiru or omuzana, though seldom accused of sorcery, was executed forthwith. This practice underscores the fundamental dependent status of servile persons having no clan to uphold their rights. It was alleged by some informants, but also denied by others, that some aberu/abazana were brutally killed by having a sharpened stick driven into the top of their heads and through their bodies.[53] While the allegation may not be correct, it is significant that this was mentioned only in relation to servile persons, suggesting that their treatment in extreme instances varied from that of nonservile persons.

Servile persons also possessed rights which could be increased in rare instances to the extent of redemption, providing they pleased their masters. They could marry, request land to cultivate their own millet, and accumulate possessions such as goats to redeem themselves. One of their most significant rights, probably depending on their own behavior and certainly that of their master, was the privilege of leaving a master who ill-treated them and subsequently seeking an alternative master within the chiefdom. Thus aberu/abazana had a right to humane treatment. If they did not receive it, it was their privilege to exchange masters. Their status was unaffected by this action. The original master represented the sole losing party. He was not compensated for his loss by the second master. Undoubtedly this procedure was extremely complex because the omwiru would have had to insure that another master would accept him prior to leaving the first. The move could also have meant ill will between the two masters involved.

Services performed by aberu were primarily menial tasks—those involving drudgery, including cultivation. With aberu at their disposal, masters had the option of working alongside them in the fields or of relegating all such tasks to them. Abazana concomitantly relieved the master's wife or wives of chores such as cultivation, collection of firewood, and carrying water. Only the wealthy—the royal advisers and many men of the royal clan, particularly the sons and grandsons of an omukama—possessed aberu/abazana, and the vast majority were actually distributed by the omukama to his relatives.

In particular, those aberu at the royal residence had an opportunity to become influential and occupy positions of trust and responsibility. Some of these men had considerable wealth in addition to possessing aberu/abazana of their own. These successful aberu were apparently as plagued by sorcerers as the successful Kerebe.

The former legal status of aberu/abazana in Bukerebe is evident today when attempting to acquire information from elders. Persons whose ancestry is Sese freely speak of the institution, while descendants of servile persons are unwilling to discuss it except in general terms. The history of their parentage is not open for discussion. Yet only one Kerebe elder readily supported Stanley's assertion that the Kerebe trafficked in the slave trade with coastal traders.[54] That practice is not presently condoned by elders, although the historical institution of servitude itself is not considered a subject to be concealed. Since servitude was originally conceived as a welfare and penal institution, few observers would disagree with them. The evolution of the system in the late 1800s, however, reveals the transition from the earlier form into a more rigid institution designed to augment both the labor supply and depleted lineages, although it was still substantially tempered by mobility.

Summary

Individual Kerebe exerted a concerted effort to increase their participation in regional trade during the 1800s, a development paralleling long-distance trading. By 1875 Stanley characterized the Kerebe as "an enterprising and commercial people." He observed their canoes in the far northeastern part of the lake—in the vicinity of Kavirondo Gulf—as well as on the opposite shore north of the present city of Bukoba and along the shores of Buzinza in the south.[55] There is no evidence that the omukama ever systematically inhibited this activity, contrary to the hypothesis advocated by Meillassoux. Trading in local commodities was a prerogative of his subjects and he gained indirectly from their imports by receiving a share through the normal tribute system. Yet a market-oriented economy had

not appeared by the end of the century, in spite of the growing concern for wealth—whether beads, cloth, hoes, people,
or cattle. Both the omukama and his subjects continued to
channel the goods into pre-existing social categories, a
seemingly inevitable situation given the restricted opportunities to do otherwise. Once it is apparent that the Kerebe
manifested a desire to increase their wealth, the more
significant question to raise is why this was the case, a question further analyzed in the two subsequent chapters.

The altering role of serviles and the concomitant increase
in the production of grain partially reveal the answer.
Perhaps by referring to the question posed at the beginning
of this chapter, based upon servile categories noted by
Meillassoux, the function of local trade for the Kerebe can
be clarified: Were servile people only a means of social
reproduction or were they actual producers?[56] The original
Kerebe concept of servitude conforms to neither of these
categories; it was basically a welfare/penal relationship
with redemption a real possibility. During the nineteenth
century serviles emerged both as a means of social reproduction, that is, increasing the clan's numbers, as well as
agricultural producers. Nonetheless the Kerebe no doubt
regarded the aberu and abazana as more important for
social reproduction than for labor purposes, which reflects
both the continuing subsistence-oriented economy and the
concern about high mortality and subsequent depopulation.
Both serviles and surplus grain were vital components in
what Kerebe commoners considered to be wealth. To be
sure, they sought wealth to enhance their social status; but
more significantly, they were consciously seeking an intangible goal, what we call security. I submit that it was this
concern that motivated the "enterprising and commercial"
Kerebe, since their very survival was at stake.

Notes

1. Gray and Birmingham, *Pre-Colonial African Trade,* 22.

2. *Ibid.,* 11.

3. C. Meillassoux, "Introduction," *The Development of Indigenous Trade and Markets in West Africa,* ed., Claude Meillassoux (London, 1971), 60-64

4. *Ibid.,* 61.

5. *Ibid.,* 60-61.

6. See Stanley, *Through the Dark Continent,* I, 200. The explorer's assertion was that twelve goats, equal to one cow, and three hoes were required for bridewealth. The items themselves varied from different species of livestock to hoes. However, hoes were significant, a constant item, even though their quantity was not set.

7. David N. McMaster, *A Subsistence Crop Geography of Uganda* (Bude, England, 1962), 88.

8. Kaliga s/o Lwambali, Kazimili s/o Mazige and Mfaume s/o Gatalya also contributed information on this subject.

9. The same options for obtaining salt have been noted by J. E. G. Sutton and A. D. Roberts in "Uvinza and Its Salt Industry," *Azania,* III (1968), 61, 69-70.

10. Charles F. Holmes, "A History of the Bakwimba of Usukuma, Tanzania, From Earliest Times to 1945 " (unpublished Ph. D. dissertation, Boston University, 1969), 146.

11. See A. Schynse, *A travers l'Afrique avec Stanley et Emin Pasha* (Paris, 1890), 77; C. Waldemar Werther, *Zum Victoria Nyanza* (Berlin, n.d.), 183.

12. Buyanza, Makene s/o Ikongolero, Mpehi s/o Magesa and Mfaume s/o Gatalya.

13. See H. A. Fosbrooke, "Some Aspects of the Kimwani Fishing Culture, with Comparative Notes on Alien Methods," *Journal of the Royal Anthropological Institute,* 64 (1934), 1-2, 19-22. Fosbrooke describes Kerebe fishing voyages and practices in the present century.

14. Mpehi s/o Magesa.

15. Speke, *Journal of the Discovery of the Source of the Nile,* 401; John Roscoe, *The Baganda* (London, 1911), 438.

16. Bahitwa, Buyanza, Kaliga s/o Lwambali, and Mfaume s/o Gatalya.

17. See H. S. Senior, "Sukuma Salt Caravans to Lake Eyasi," *Tanganyika Notes and Records,* 6 (1938), 87-90.

18. All informants mentioned in footnotes 12 and 16 implied the same increase.

19. Brief but pertinent comments on the Ziba and other people dwelling around the lake are found in "Rapport du P. Brard sur les tribus insulaires du Nyanza Meridional," *Chronique trimestrielle de la Société des missionnaires d'Afrique,* 73 (1897), 152-57. Buyanza provided the detailed information on this trade.

20. Aniceti Kitereza, "Omwanzuro gw'Abakama ba Bukerebe," unpublished Kikerebe manuscript, Kagunguli Parish, Ukerewe, Tanzania.

21. This is discussed at greater length in Hartwig, "Oral Traditions Concerning the Early Iron Age," 101, 109. Oral information was contributed by Buyanza, Bahitwa and Zumbula s/o Gilolo.

22. Numerous comments by observers in other East African communities suggest that being relieved from most agricultural work was considered a worthy aspiration: Burton, *The Lake Regions of Central Africa,* 521; Grant, "Summary of Observations," 250; Felkin, "Notes on the Waganda," 746; C. T. Wilson and R. W. Felkin, *Uganda and the Egyptian Soudan* (London, 1882), I, 186; Capitaine Storms, "L'esclavage entre le Tanganika et la côte est," *Le Mouvement Antisclavagiste,* I (1888-89), 16-17; Adolphe Burdo, *Les Belges dan l'Afrique Centrale; De Zanzibar an Lac Tanganika* (Bruxelles, 1886), 24; V. L. Cameron, *Across Africa* (New York, 1877), 281; Jerome Becker, *La Vie en Afrique* (Paris, 1887), II 339.

23. Arthur Tuden and Leonard Ploticov, eds., "Introduction," *Social Stratification in Africa* (New York, 1970), 11-12.

24. Information on servility is based upon contributions by Buyanza, Bahitwa, Kaliga and Simeo Rubuzi.

25. John S. Mbiti, *African Religions and Philosophy* (London, 1969), 104-09.

26. *Pre-Colonial African Trade*, 18.

27. Allen Isaacman notes the existence of the same phenomenon in Mozambique: "The Origin, Formation and Early History of the Chikunda of South Central Africa," *Journal of African History*, XIII, 3 (1972), 450-51.

28. Chavery Wanzura, Jeremi Mukama Baruza, Manumbi, Musumali, Bahitwa and Buyanza.

29. Bahitwa, Buyanza, Magoma, Bundala Kakenki, Kammando Mzinza, Makene s/o Ikongolero, and Palapala s/o Kazwegulu.

30. See Emin Pasha, "On Trade and Commerce among the Waganda and Wanyoro," *Emin Pasha in Central Africa*, eds., G. Schweinfurth et al. (London, 1888), 117; Speke, *Journal of the Discovery of the Source of the Nile*, 251.

31. For comparative Nyamwezi data see E.J. Southon, Journal, 12 August 1880, London Missionary Society Archives; Norman R. Bennett, *Mirambo of Tanzania* (New York, 1971), 133.

32. Grant, "Summary of Observations," 250.

33. Felkin, "Notes on the Waganda Tribe," 746.

34. S. Tristram Pruen, *The Arab and the African* (London, 1891), 209.

35. Bahitwa and Buyanza.

36. See Tuden and Plotnicov, *Social Stratification in Africa*, 12-13.

37. Buyanza, Bahitwa, and Kaliga.

38. Wilson and Felkin, *Uganda and the Egyptian Soudan*, I, 183. Wilson stated that "diseases to which the Baganda are subject make a formidable list; smallpox is one of the most fatal, coming

at intervals in epidemics, and carrying off thousands of victims; few attacked ever recover. . . ." Also note Felkin's comments in *ibid.*, II, 48; Cameron, *Across Africa*, 85; Burton, "The Lake Regions of Central Equatorial Africa," 387; E.J. Southon, "The History, Country and People of Unyamwezi," London Missionary Society Archives.

39. Buyanza, Bahitwa, Kaliga, Magoma, and Alipyo Mnyaga.

40. Simeo Rubuzi, Kammando Mzinza, Kaliga, Bahitwa, and Buyanza.

41. This is a common belief held by numerous people in eastern Africa. See T.O. Beidelman, "Witchcraft in Ukaguru," *Witchcraft and Sorcery in East Africa,* eds., John Middleton and E. H. Winter (London, 1963), 67-68; Robert F. Gray, "Structural Aspects of Mbugwe Witchcraft," *Witchcraft and Sorcery in East Africa,* eds., John Middleton and E. H. Winter (London, 1963), 168-70; Robert LeVine, "Witchcraft and Sorcery in a Gusii Community," *Witchcraft and Sorcery in East Africa,* eds., John Middleton and E. H. Winter (London, 1963), 228-29.

42. Edward A. Alpers, "The East African Slave Trade," Historical Association of Tanzania Paper No. 3 (Nairobi, 1967), 19.

43. Stanley, *Through the Dark Continent,* I, 329.

44. Buyanza, Bahitwa, Makene s/o Ikongolero, Matuli, and Mongelele Bulolima. See Hartwig, "The Historical and Social Role of Kerebe Music," 47.

45. Buyanza claimed that these Luo were aberu and abazana, although Alexander Mackay of the Church Missionary Society inferred in 1878 that the Luo he saw at Rukonge's court were freemen: "I was quartered in the largest hut in the place except that of a native of Ugaya [the region of Kavirondo Gulf], a small colony of people from that country having settled in Ukerewe." Mackay to Wright, 28 July 1878, C. A6/O 16, Church Missionary Society Archives. None of the other C.M.S. representatives visiting Bukerebe at this time apparently realized that some individuals were in a servile state.

46. Stanley was extremely critical of Songoro; he stated that "nothing would have pleased me better than to have been commissioned by some government to hang all such wretches [slavers] wherever found; and, if ever a pirate deserved death for inhuman crimes, Sungoro [Songoro], the slave trader, deserves death. Kagehyi, in Usukuma, has become the seat of the inhuman slave trade. To this port they are collected from Sima, Magu, Ukerewe [Bukerebe], Ururu and Ugeyeya [Bugaya, i.e., the entire eastern lake shore]; and when Sungoro has floated his dhow and hoisted his blood-stained ensign the great sin will increase tenfold, and the caravan road to Unyanyembe will become hell's highway." Cited in Norman R. Bennett, ed., *Stanley's Despatches to the New York Herald, 1871-1872, 1874-1877* (Boston, 1970), 214. In *Through the Dark Continent* the explorer's remarks about Songoro were less emotional.

47. See Ogot, *History of the Southern Luo,* 206-10.

48. Buyanza and Kaliga.

49. See Monica Wilson, "Changes in Social Structure in Southern Africa: the Relevance of Kinship Studies to the Historian," *African Studies in Southern Africa,* ed., Leonard Thompson (New York, 1969), 79.

50. Buyanza, Bahitwa, Kaliga, and Simeo Rubuzi.

51. Tuden and Plotnicov, *Social Stratification in Africa,* 12.

52. Bahitwa and Buyanza.

53. The most adamant elder, Simeo Rubuzi, is of Kara descent with a probable—though not admitted by him—servile heritage; Josephat Mdono held a similar view. Buyanza would not entertain such an idea.

54. Kaliga s/o Lwambali had no qualms about accepting Stanley's allegation whereas Buyanza and Bahitwa consistently denied any such activity.

55. Bennett, *Stanley's Despatches to the New York Herald,* 232.

56. Meillassoux, *Indigenous Trade and Markets in West Africa,* 63-65.

4 Altering Political Authority and Social Roles

Changes in political institutions and political relationships in eastern Africa during the nineteenth century have attracted considerable attention from historians. Andrew Roberts has summarized the major conclusions of numerous intensive studies in his article "Political Change in the Nineteenth Century."[1] He suggests that the main political change "consisted of a shift from religious to military power as a basis for political authority."[2] The increased reliance on military power was a direct response to mounting external pressures, pressures that could not be met by the political structures and values of an earlier age. Roberts contends that the scale of political organization in Eastern Africa was enlarged, while social and political life simultaneously became more specialized. The specialists to which he refers included mercenary soldiers, blacksmiths, ivory porters, and administrative officials.

Leaders who effectively enlarged their political base had to insure their superiority over subordinates. This meant the establishment of military supremacy, the development of administrative control to maintain authority, and the creation of a political organization that would outlast the death of the ruler.[3] As is apparent from the previous chapters on long-distance and local trade, rulers were confronted by a new range of goods as well as of weapons. Roberts contends that this in turn "increased the opportunities of chiefs and their subjects to make themselves richer and more powerful."[4]

The forces unleashed by the presence of imported goods were monumental, complex, and contradictory. As Roberts states, the opportunities for rulers and subjects alike increased, setting in motion social and economic developments beyond the direct control of any single individual or group. Leaders such as Mirambo of Unyamwezi and Mutesa of Buganda managed to remain abreast of these developments, thereby becoming excellent examples of leaders exploiting the changes indicated by Roberts. But what is frequently ignored is the response to these developments by the rulers' subjects. They too experienced change, and their responses had to be met by rulers. The increased use of force as the century waned reflected the unrest within chiefdoms as much as the conflict between political entities.

Political developments within Bukerebe during the 1800s cannot be satisfactorily compared with large militaristic societies such as the Nyamwezi, Kimbu, or Ganda.[5] Bukerebe was always a small political unit and was never obsessed by military expansion, a fact best explained by the chiefdom's isolated geographical character. Thus the problems of military superiority, administrative control, and organizational continuity did not dominate Kerebe political life to the degree found in societies discussed by Roberts. Nonetheless, the Kerebe experience reveals substantial insights into the problem of shifting political relationships as a consequence of developments stimulated by external factors. Analysis of the role of the omukama and of the *enfura* (friends of the omukama) clarifies the nature of political change in Bukerebe. To understand these roles it is necessary to survey the political institutions of the eighteenth century and to discuss the friction between the two major royal clans of Bukerebe and the fissure of the royal clan.

Authority of the Omukama

The royal Silanga clan established a chiefdom on Bukerebe during the seventeenth century when they and their followers fled from the chiefdom of Ihangiro on the southwestern shores of the lake after a political upheaval. The Bantu-speaking inhabitants of Bukerebe resisted strongly, until guile and force eventually won the day for the Silanga. This entrenchment of the Silanga meant that the customs and language of the interlacustrine region from which they had come were henceforth prevalent in Bukerebe.[6] However, not all sections of the island/peninsula came under Silanga control.[7] The southern area remained under the jurisdiction of the Kula clan, a cattle-keeping Bantu family which originated in Buzinza and whose ancestors emanated from the Longo smiths. Friction between the Silanga and Kula is a constant theme in Kerebe historical accounts.[8]

The Silanga introduced a new political system into Bukerebe. The omukama represented the ultimate source of power within the new order. His functions were broad, incorporating judicial, administrative, and legislative duties, which were discharged in close collaboration with his council of elders. This was the system which underwent change in the 1800s. What were its characteristics?

The omukama was assumed to be the intercessor between his people and the spiritual realm. Hence he was in a position to assist the Kerebe during their time of need. In contrast to the neighboring Kara to the north and the Jita/Kwaya and Shashi to the east, the Kerebe omukama possessed more concentrated power than any individual in those chiefless societies. Even the Sukuma chiefdoms south of Speke Gulf regarded the omukama with considerable respect for his reputed rainmaking powers.[9] Throughout the southeastern lake region there was no more consistently successful rainmaker than the omukama, a factor that added significantly to his prestige among other communities. Rainmakers *(abagimba)* always held a significant position of power in Kerebe society, even before the arrival of the royal Silanga clan. Hence by merely professing rainmaking powers, the Silanga could hardly convince the inhabitants that their existing practitioners should be replaced by new-comers. In fact, the Silanga rulers did not displace the ex-isting abagimba, even though theoretically their rain-making powers were supreme. Each clan retained its own rainmaker; the omukama was approached by a clan only when it was seriously threatened by drought.

Similarly, the appeal by each clan to its ancestors re-mained a family affair; that is, a particular form of spiritual worship existed before the Silanga arrived, and no alterations were made in the basic institution just because an omukama was present. Yet the royal clan's presence con-tributed an additional dimension to the prevailing means of invoking the assistance of the spiritual realm. Because the Silanga displayed a more varied and complex set of relationships to the secular realm, one based on their lacustrine cultural base, it was assumed that their access to the spiritual domain was superior. Consequently, nonroyal clans respected the omukama's superior powers, although they would request his assistance only when their own ef-forts proved unsuccessful. Clan responsibilities such as rain-making and appealing to the spirits of their ancestors con-tinued after the chiefdom came into being; henceforth, the Kerebe possessed two mutually compatible avenues to ap-proach the awesome spiritual world.

Theory and practice operated in an intriguing manner among the Kerebe. While theoretically supreme, in practice the omukama proved his excellence as a leader by attracting to his court those specialists from nonroyal clans who were acknowledged as the best within the chiefdom. If people were experiencing drought, for example, they would inform the omukama of their dilemma and the ineffectiveness of their own efforts to provide rain. He in turn would call the most highly regarded rainmaker in the chiefdom to the court and direct him to use the omukama's rainpot, stones, and medicine to provide rain.[10] In the case of an invasion by locusts, the representative of a particular clan which claimed power to drive the holocaust away was summoned by the omukama to perform this service for the chiefdom. Specialists were well rewarded for their assistance and acquired considerable social recognition for their association with the omukama. Failure had the contrary result. The system as practiced made the omukama less vulnerable to criticism.

Rainmaking can be placed in a category of intangible powers, along with other attributed powers, that helped to strengthen the position of the omukama. Appeals directed by him to his ancestors, to Namuhanga the creator, and to lesser intermediary deities in time of affliction tested the ultimate authority of the ruler. Inability to conform to these expectations over an extended period of time was a major reason for deposing an omukama. Thus one of the concerted efforts by rulers such as the Kerebe abakama in the nineteenth century—and presumably this would have been equally true earlier—was to seek knowledge or power to bolster the position of men threatened by increasing pressure from alien forces.[11] Much of this knowledge came in the form of "medicine"—some that was credited with supernatural power to enable the leader to overcome an unprecedented situation, some that was harmful for use against enemies, and some that was useful in curing new diseases. Because of the continual growth of these intangible powers, the functions and role of the omukama were dynamic and increased in complexity with each new development. When viewed from this perspective, it is misleading to refer to the Kerebe as a "traditional" society. The Kerebe social system was never static; an increasingly complex role is a marked characteristic of the omukama's office as well as of the conditions under which Kerebe society evolved.

Selection of the Omukama

The Kerebe system for selecting an omukama minimized the opportunities for strife that could lead to dynastic con-

flicts.[12] Sons of a ruler were theoretically eligible for the
position of omukama.[13] Flaws in their pedigree, however,
precluded numerous sons from candidacy. A son whose
mother was a member of the Kula clan, for example, or
whose mother was a Jita, or the son of a woman whose clan
resided outside the community was not considered a suitable
heir to the office. The rationale was that if an omukama encountered serious difficulties within the chiefdom he would
be unable to call upon his uncles (his mother's brothers) for
assistance, since they lived outside the chiefdom. A second
restriction was the age factor. Before the twentieth century,
an immature boy was not accepted as a candidate. If a lad
was chosen, a regent would be necessary and the Kerebe
feared placing their trust in a man to act on behalf of the
rightful ruler. Reluctance to select a youngster as omukama
was evident when Ibanda was deposed in favor of Machunda
in the early nineteenth century. The latter, in his teens, was
living in exile to the east of Bukerebe when an elder visited
him with the specific intention of measuring his height. Apparently the plotters were not satisfied with Machunda's
size and a second trip was taken later, by which time
Machunda had achieved sufficient stature and maturity to
allow the deposition of Ibanda to take place. Thirdly, a candidate could in no way be deformed or physically marred. In
practice this meant that he could not be circumcised, have
pierced ear lobes, or front teeth extracted—all practices of
various people living to the east of the Kerebe. Conversely,
if a newly appointed ruler wanted to disqualify any of his
ambitious brothers from office, he merely had to pierce
their ears or extract some of their teeth to achieve his objec-
tive.[14] This procedure tended to reduce fratricide by the
ruler.

Beyond the restrictions imposed by the mother's clan,
age, and physical attributes, the eldest son generally received first appraisal and under normal circumstances could
expect selection. But candidates were not at liberty to act
irresponsibly, even though their privileges as sons of the
omukama *(abalanzi)* were numerous. They had to convey a
sense of responsibility and respect to the elders who would

ultimately determine the next omukama. Acceptable behavior, then, was the fourth qualification.

The selection of an omukama was theoretically limited to the elders of a single nonroyal clan, the Sita, although in practice a few valued advisers of the Sita may also have participated.[15] The role of this particular clan in the selection of a ruler was unprecedented in other interlacustrine societies where the usual selection procedure was restricted to the royal clan itself.[16] The Sita are representatives of an old and powerful clan that had possessed political power in various communities within the interlacustrine zone prior to 1500, that is, before the appearance of the Hinda (Karagwe) and Bito (Bunyoro) ruling clans. Kerebe accounts, however, do not impute any unusual authority to the Sita during the seventeenth century or before. Informants from various clans explain that the special powers and privileges of the Sita are a result of the unique relationship that developed between the founder of the Silanga clan and Buniri, the first member of the Sita remembered by name, when they departed as hunters from Isene centuries ago. Buniri appears in oral accounts subservient to the forebear of the Silanga, not as his equal.

The Sita had a number of days at their disposal during which they agreed upon a replacement for a deceased ruler. The time for selection occurred between the death of the incumbent and his burial some two to four weeks later. Major variables determining when burial took place included the time of the omukama's death in relationship to the next appearance of the new moon, and the prolonged process of severing the head from the deceased's body.[17] When the body was prepared for burial and the new moon appeared, the death of the ruler was formally announced by striking the symbolic drum of the chiefdom, the *matwigacharo*. Only a few individuals—the Sita, councilors, and some persons working within the court—would previously know, officially at least, of the omukama's death.

The elders of the Sita clan would decide on a successor during the brief interregnum, unannounced to isolate the

Sita from pressure. Secrecy discouraged potential candidates and their uncles from influencing the selectors' decision and decreased the possibility of internecine struggles. Although the Sita married only members of the Silanga clan, the creation of vested interests was avoided since intermarriage could only be with Silanga who were ineligible for the position of omukama. Likewise, Sita women could not be married to eligible sons or grandsons of an omukama.

The actual discretionary power of the Sita in selecting an omukama was theoretically broad, since Kerebe elders primarily emphasized "behavior" as the significant determinant. The extent of pressure exerted by candidates upon the Sita before the death of an incumbent is problematical. The most acceptable form of lobbying was overt respect or periodic visits to the Sita elders. Since they were fundamentally concerned about the "behavior" of a candidate, the elders desired an individual who would provide a stable, auspicious set of conditions in which they and society in general could flourish. They distrusted any individual who flaunted his privileges in a callous manner. Such arrogance of office would ultimately infringe upon the privileges of themselves and others.

Deposing an Omukama

An equally important function of the Sita clan was the responsibility of deposing an incumbent who did not fulfill the demanding expectations of his office. Drought over an extended period of time, sometimes of more than a year's duration, was a serious condition for an agricultural community and the omukama was held directly accountable for it. In the 1830s, Ibanda was deposed for this reason. On the other hand, Ruhinda, Ibanda's predecessor, was allegedly deposed for failure to control an excessive amount of rainfall.[18] The "behavior" expected of an omukama in a different situation is illustrated in the case of an eighteenth-century ruler, Lutana Mumanza. His reign commenced auspiciously when he generously shared a large number of

his cattle with his subjects. Sometime later, however, he un-
wisely demanded the cattle back, a decision that prompted
his removal. Nago, in remembered contrast to Lutana
Mumanza, followed his predecessor's lead in generosity, but
avoided the wrath of his people and simultaneously earned
their gratitude by his continuing generous policy.

Discontent with the abakama ruling between approximately 1820 and 1835 is reflected in the number of
deposed abakama. This political instability was only
brought under control by Omukama Machunda, who
successfully checked the probable abuse of power by the Sita
elders. Though this period is remembered as having unusual climatic conditions, the Sita were undoubtedly dis-
tressed by other factors, primarily the introduction of diseases that placed a new stress on the social fabric. The
abakama did not resolve this stress satisfactorily for some
time.

Considerable preparation characterized an attempted
deposition of an incumbent, if the reported details of Ibanda's removal in the early 1800s are any indication.[19] As
previously mentioned, a representative of the Sita visited
Machunda to determine whether he was sufficiently mature
to replace Ibanda, who was confounded by an extended
drought. Not until after the second visit to Machunda did
the Sita make their decision to depose Ibanda. Hence the
amount of time consumed while plotting the deposition
may have extended over three years, particularly since the
physical maturity of Machunda assumed an important place
in the final decision.

The omukama continually gauged the political climate of
his chiefdom by means of the council of elders, the visiting
enfura (friends of the omukama), the abakungu (headmen),
and the abazuma (messengers). The Sita held numerous of-
fices at court and consequently were in a position to hear the
reports coming in from the villages. If serious issues
remained unresolved for a prolonged length of time, the
omukama—and the Sita—were well aware of it. The resultant stress between the Sita, representing the concerned

populace, and the omukama, together with his uncles and other supporters, during periods of tension would surface in daily affairs. As a general rule the Sita could attempt a deposition only when an omukama's apparent support dwindled to a low ebb. Until such time the Sita had to limit themselves to a period of watchful waiting. In this sense the Sita did not possess unusually significant political prerogatives, but rather were an institutionalized means of ridding the chiefdom of a ruler who had lost the support of his people. Certainly in the late nineteenth century, the Sita openly resented Rukonge, who is generally regarded as a cruel and tyrannical omukama during a very disturbed era. Yet the Sita could not depose him. Rukonge had fortified his position by an alliance with the Ganda, in addition to attaching numerous dependable men to his court. Some of these men were Ganda migrants who had settled on Bukerebe and owed personal allegiance to Rukonge. Given the restrictions on the Sita's role, the chiefdom benefited from a relatively stable political system in which the omukama either satisfactorily fulfilled his responsibilities or faced expulsion.

Administrative Positions

The Silanga forcibly introduced the hierarchical Kerebe political system. Oral information implies that the royal clan evolved a system of government over a period of time; the various officials and representatives of the omukama in the 1700s were not immediately appointed when the Silanga assumed power in the 1600s.

The omukama and his councilors formed the powerful and prestigious center of the political system. The Silanga found councils composed of clan elders already in existence in the 1600s. This system was modified by the royal clan to the extent that an omukama ruled in conjunction with a council composed of elders from nonroyal clans. The council retained the prerogative of controlling its own number as well as of electing its own membership, thereby maintaining a degree of independence. All clans were not necessarily represented on the council, the only official body that influenced the decision-making process.

Introduction of the chiefdom brought with it greater territory, original boundaries including the northern portion of the island peninsula and numerous islands in the vicinity. Representatives of the omukama were needed to control the various villages. Essentially the administration of village matters was delegated to *abakungu* (singular, *omukungu)* or headmen, who resided in the villages. Unlike the councilors, the abakungu were members of the royal clan or a subclan of the Silanga or had married into the royal clan. The majority of headmen were in fact brothers or uncles of the omukama, although it was possible for the ruler to designate a sister or daughter as an omukungu, in which case the woman's husband could perform the daily tasks of the office.

Abakungu were present from the inception of the chiefdom. By means of these officials the Silanga royal clan subjected the population to the rule and administration of a single family. Although most abakungu were descendants of an omukama and consequently had a vested interest in the chiefdom, they were concomitantly the most potentially disruptive group in society. From their ranks came men who could encourage the Sita to depose an omukama, but they themselves could in turn be disqualified for the royal position by swift royal action.

Abahinda (princes) comprised the privileged portion of Kerebe society. It is from this group that the omukama selected his headmen and other officials. The abahinda were second- and third-generation descendants of abakama. Being members of the royal clan they were given considerable license as befit their position. No one, including the omukama himself, could physically attack them, although there are numerous accusations about Rukonge's violation of this principle in the late 1800s. The abahinda were not entirely above the law. An omuhinda who abused his privileges and harassed people was a social nuisance. These particular abahinda were usually men who did not hold official positions, men who were not trustworthy or useful to the omukama. One successful means of getting rid of an abusive omuhinda was for prominent men to insinuate to the omukama that the individual in question was plotting to depose him. The abusive omuhinda was then expelled or forced into exile, the most common means of removing potentially troublesome relatives from the chiefdom.

An omukungu had numerous duties within his village or villages. Minor civil and criminal cases came under his jurisdiction, as did the disposal of unoccupied land within the village. Immigrants to the chiefdom who desired land approached the abakungu directly for it, or, in some cases, the omukama himself directed an omukungu to provide land for newcomers. The assessment and collection of taxes was also a major annual task. The Kerebe royal clan levied two substantial taxes: The *omuseku* was based upon the total possessions of a man, such as goats, cattle, and hoes, while the *omusoro* was a millet tax. In each case the omukungu determined the amount payable by each householder. As tax assessor, the omukungu retained a portion of the tax as a fee of office. If a man in the village needed temporary aid, however, the omukungu was expected to provide it from his stores, while the remainder was forwarded to the omukama. One check on the omukungu's discretionary powers was that any prominent man could report oppressive taxing to the omukama.[20]

The omukama possessed land within each village on a portion of which the omukungu had rights of cultivation while he held his position in the village. When he was replaced, his successor used the same plots. This was an efficient and practical system for the omukama. It also placed the headmen in a dependent, landless category which could be offset by independently acquiring an *obusi* (land which "belonged" to the family concerned) to which abakungu could move if they lost their appointed position. Once land was cleared it became an obusi of the family, a possession retained as long as it was used.

There were a few abakungu whose responsibilities included two or more villages. A headman could name assistants to help with his duties, providing the villages contained a substantial population. He often selected an *entwalilizya* (subheadman) from among relatives or friends, not necessarily Silanga. The entwalilizya, as in the case of his superior, assessed taxes and retained a modest share of those collected.

In addition to headmen, the Silanga created a separate administrative echelon composed of *abasiba* (watchmen), who outranked the abakungu.[21] The abasiba were created because of Silanga concern about potential threats to the chiefdom from external sources. The omukama delegated considerable authority to the abasiba, who presumably represent an eighteenth-century administrative development that accompanied the expanding territorial limits of the chiefdom. There were only four remembered posts for abasiba in the late nineteenth century, the primary duties of which consisted of warning the omukama of approaching strangers and determining the nature of their presence or business. To fulfill these duties, the abasiba lived at strategic locations around the chiefdom, frequently on capes. The most influential omusiba lived at Ngoma, where he was in a position to observe any hostile force approaching from the mainland. His role in welcoming trading caravans in the nineteenth century also enhanced the importance of the position. Traders approaching from the east by land passed his residence as well as those who arrived by water from Kageyi or Mwanza.[22]

Abasiba normally did not perform functions of headmen, but occasionally they were summoned to court to assist the omukama in judging difficult cases. The abasiba, as royal appointees, were also members of the Silanga clan, but they could not be a candidate for the office of omukama. Since only the sons of an omukama were serious contenders for the royal position, many of the Silanga clan, grandsons of former rulers for example, were outside the select circle of prime candidates. Another distinction between abakungu and abasiba was that the former normally did not possess their own obusi within the village as did the abasiba.

Possessing obusi meant more permanence for abasiba in their appointment.

The abasiba possessed large drums symbolic of their important position in relation to the omukama. The omukama's set of drums, collectively referred to as *emilango,* was a symbolic aspect of royal power; only his representatives—abasiba and a few of the important abakungu—had any reason to use a drum. An exception to this general rule was a small replica of the royal drum used by some clan elders and medicine men for ritual purposes. Only after a different style of drum appeared around the beginning of the nineteenth century were drums of any sort used for entertainment outside the royal court.[23]

Near the royal residence, the *abazuma,* the messengers of the omukama, lived in close proximity to the elders of the council. The abazuma were a collection of men who gravitated to the court and acquired positions of responsibility there. While relaying messages and performing errands were the daily tasks of the abazuma, they also assisted in tax collection by assuring that the abakungu sent their quota to the omukama on time. Occasionally some of these men, who came from nonroyal clans, could rise to prestigious positions. Some of the abazuma were in fact boys who were sent by their families to the court to serve the omukama. Not all clans chose to send their sons; it was not a mandatory service. Compensation for an omuzuma was proximity to the source of political and social power, in itself an awesome opportunity for the average subject. He might eat somewhat better than others, but according to informants, his position was not highly respected and therefore it was actively sought only by individuals from the lower social ranks who would gain from the post.[24] If the omukama had developed a standing army in the nineteenth century similar to those of the Ganda and Nyamwezi, the abazuma would have most likely formed the core of it.

Silanga Rivalry with the Kula

Long-distance trade had pronounced and predictable effects upon relations between the rival Silanga and Kula clans. Alterations in the Silanga political system were not necessary for this type of change to occur. Nonetheless the trading aspirations of the Silanga required them to remove the Kula from the strategic position they occupied in the eighteenth century, a position deterring easy access to the Sukuma chiefdoms to the south.

As Map VI indicates, the early occupation of the island/peninsula found the Kula situated in the southern confines of the peninsula. They were primarily herders and hunters at the time the Silanga arrived and did not then claim chiefly powers. The Kula elders gradually developed royal aspirations and institutions, no doubt as a response to the Silanga. The peninsula itself provided a natural buffer to separate the Kula and Silanga. The latter group concentrated more on fishing and agriculture and therefore lived along the northern shores. The interior of the peninsula was relatively dry with unreliable rainfall, excellent for

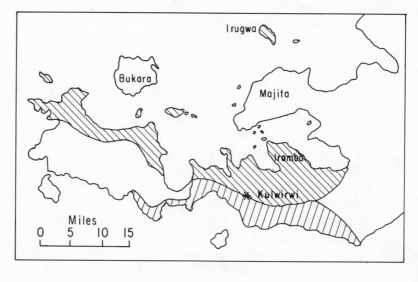

MAP VI. APPROXIMATE EXTENT OF CHIEFDOMS IN 1700

herding and hunting. By keeping to the south of the peninsula the Kula managed to avoid intensive contact with their stronger northern neighbors. But the Kula herds attracted attention.[25]

Cattle raiding therefore characterized the periodic conflicts between the Kula and Silanga during the seventeenth and eighteenth centuries. In both Silanga and Kula oral accounts the Silanga emerged as the inevitable victor, no doubt a result of more manpower. Although efforts to stabilize relations are suggested by numerous marriage alliances between the rivals, the major consequence of the conflict was the Kula's continual shift westward in an effort to decrease pressure from their opponents. But the Silanga themselves experienced a major setback from the pastoral Tatog in the mid-1700s. Iramba had been the site of the Silanga court on the northern peninsula. It was abandoned after their defeat by the Tatog and the Silanga and their subjects fled westward to join the Kula on what was to become the island of Bukerebe.

By the beginning of the nineteenth century, during the reign of Mihigo II, the Silanga and Kula lived side by side on the island, both having left the peninsula to the pastoralists. A significant result of this move was the abandonment of Kulwirwi, a massif that had supplied the subjects of the Silanga with iron ore. Dependency upon hoes from the Longo smiths of Buzinza originates from this period although Silanga conflict with the Gabe clan brought about the Gabe dispersal.

With long-distance trade becoming a factor under Mihigo II, the Silanga began to encroach on Kula territory. Mihigo and his successors desired direct access to caravans coming from the east and better access by water to the major Sukuma trading base at Kageyi. To permit the Kula to occupy the strategic village of Ngoma, which overlooked the strait "separating" the island from the peninsula, was intolerable for the Silanga. Yet it was not until the early years of Machunda's reign, ca. 1840, that the Silanga completely eliminated the Kula from the eastern end of the island.

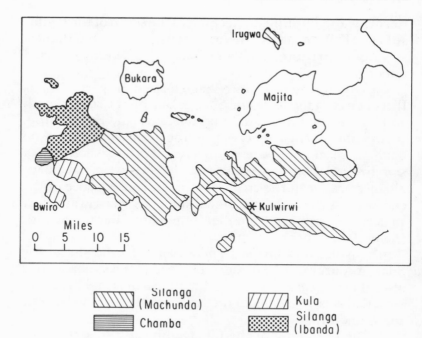

⬛ Silanga (Machunda)	⬛ Kula	
⬛ Chamba	⬛ Silanga (Ibanda)	

MAP VII. APPROXIMATE BOUNDARIES OF CHIEFDOMS IN 1850

Thereafter the Silanga omusiba resided at Ngoma and fulfilled his functions as watchman for hostile invaders and intermediary between the omukama and approaching traders.

As illustrated on Map VII, the Kula fled to the southwestern corner of the island where they lived a rather precarious existence. Gone were the days of substantial hunting and herding; they now devoted more energy to agricultural pursuits in their effort to remain independent of Silanga control. The Silanga, on the other hand, once again ventured onto the peninsula, claiming control by appointing headmen to various villages along the shore line. The center of the peninsula remained the preserve of the Tatog. Henceforth the Silanga virtually monopolized the long-distance trade to Bukerebe.

Silanga-Kula Rivalry and the Traders

Relations between African rulers of course had important ramifications for alien travelers. The latter simply could not be aware of all political problems existing between neighboring rulers as they passed through a given district. A case in point was Bukerebe's Silanga-Kula enmity, which inconvenienced John Speke when he visited the southern shores of the Victoria Nyanza in 1858. Although Speke never reached the island chiefdom to make his desired geographical observations, he eventually realized that he had erred in visiting the chiefdom of Mwanza rather than Busukuma.

> As regards the collection of boats taking a long time, these arguments are very fair . . . ; but the only danger would consist in the circumstance of the two sultans [the rulers of Mwanza and Busukuma] being at enmity with each other, as in this land anyone coming direct from an enemy's country is suspected and treated as an enemy. This difficulty I should have avoided by going straight to Sukuma Kageyi (where the boats, I am inclined to think, usually do start from, though all concur in stating that this [Mwanza] is their point of departure), and there obtaining boats direct.[26]

Speke seems to have known, or certainly learned upon his return to Unyanyembe (Tabora), that strained relations existed between the chiefdoms of Mwanza and Busukuma. What was not clear to him or to Richard Burton was that Machunda, the significant Silanga ruler (his brother Ibanda then ruled Ilangala on the western end of the island), had a diplomatic marriage agreement with the ruler of Busukuma.[27] Consequently the Arab and Swahili traders had to visit Busukuma and its port village of Kageyi to obtain canoes for visiting Machunda on Bukerebe. To ally oneself with the ruler of Mwanza, as Speke did—to his regret—was to ally oneself with friends of the Kula chief-dom and of the breakaway Silanga ruler, Ibanda. Speke did not take the time to unravel the complex diplomatic alignments that forestalled his acquisition of canoes and hence his voyage to Bukerebe, but he did display wisdom in not forcing the situation. He had simply ended up in the wrong chiefdom. There was ample reason for the Arab community at Unyanyembe to avoid Mwanza when trading with Machunda, although Speke never completely understood what the reason was: "These negroes' manoeuvres are quite incomprehensible."[28] But by visiting Mwanza, Speke learned that two other rulers existed on Bukerebe in addition to Machunda, revealing that his hosts attempted to provide him with information about the realities of Kerebe politics, information which was either incomplete or poorly understood by Speke.[29]

What Speke's information aids us in understanding is the forthright manner in which Machunda thwarted traders who might in any way deprive him of trade goods and simultaneously assist his opponents. Speke found an impoverished trader, Mansur bin Salim, in Mwanza. He was an unfortunate individual, described by Burton as "a half-caste Arab, who had been flogged out of Kazeh [Tabora] by his compatriots."[30] Thus he was not welcome to trade with his compatriots in Busukuma. Nonetheless, he tried to evade their animosity toward him by going to Mwanza and there attempting to trade with Machunda. The poor man was so intimidated by everyone that he took the advice of Mahaya, ruler of Mwanza, and did not accompany his goods to Bukerebe. He merely sent "fifteen loads of cloth and 250 jembis or hoes" to Machunda with a message that he wished ivory in return. When Speke arrived nine months later Mansur was still waiting for the ivory and living "like the slaves of the country."[31] Machunda knew full well where Mansur was residing and why. This information necessarily accompanied Mansur's trade goods since they were transported in canoes from Kageyi. Machunda, of course, did not have to listen to advice from Mansur's hostile compatriots to rob the "scroundrel." He may simply have followed his own design to punish anyone consorting with an ally of his enemies or who did not follow the established trading network which was specifically created to enhance his position.

An Interlude of Instability

During the nineteenth century four Silanga abakama dominated the political scene on Bukerebe. Mihigo II's role has been discussed. He led the community as it began to participate in long-distance trade at the turn of the century. After Mihigo's death the chiefdom experienced significant political changes for a variety of reasons, some associated with the intrusion of alien forces, others emanating from local conditions. These changes revolved around the personalities of Ibanda, Machunda, and Rukonge. Each of these men left an indelible mark upon the chiefdom and its political institutions. Their relationship to Mihigo II, the eighth ruler in the Silanga line, and their approximate period of rule, as well as that of less important abakama is illustrated in the genealogy.

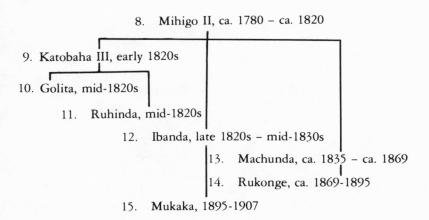

8.   Mihigo II, ca. 1780 – ca. 1820

9. Katobaha III, early 1820s

10. Golita, mid-1820s

11.   Ruhinda, mid-1820s

12.   Ibanda, late 1820s – mid-1830s

13.   Machunda, ca. 1835 – ca. 1869

14.   Rukonge, ca. 1869-1895

15.   Mukaka, 1895-1907

Under normal circumstances, that is, circumstances experienced by the royal clan for the preceding century and a half, neither Ibanda nor his brother Machunda would have had the opportunity to rule. They were both younger sons of Mihigo II. But the early 1800s witnessed numerous novel developments in the lake region which taken together account for the presence of Ibanda and Machunda as rulers.

There are hints that ecological and climatic alterations occurred within and around Bukerebe during the early part of the nineteenth century. The supply of hardwood hoe handles is a clue offered by oral data. The Kerebe were as dependent upon the importation of hoe handles as upon hoes while Mihigo II reigned. These handles are often mentioned in oral accounts since they were a frequently borrowed object in the early 1800s and thus became a source of obligation on the debtor's part.[32] Minor social infractions were also punished by confiscating a man's hoe handle. By midcentury, handles were no longer a scarce commodity. People were then able to obtain sufficient supplies at home without having to make a canoe trip to Buzinza.

Elders offered various explanations for this change. Perhaps the most ingenious came from Bahitwa, the Kerebe historian:

> During Mihigo's time there were no trees; people went to cut their hoe handles at Nassa, Rwondo, Kome and Mesome [Usukuma and Buzinza]. If someone had a debt and he did not pay it back the lender took the debtor's hoe handle to settle the debt. This means that there were no trees anywhere in Bukerebe, even at Ilangala [this is now a densely wooded portion of the island]. Trees started growing after locusts invaded the chiefdom because seeds of trees were in the excrement of the locusts and the seeds grew. The locusts came from the north. After their appearance in Mihigo's time there was no longer trouble with hoe handles.

While the eastern end of the island is well stocked with trees today, the vast majority are fruit trees, such as mango trees, and have been planted within the past eighty years. On the other hand, the western end of the island was well wooded at the turn of the present century.[33] It is possible that a particular species of vegetation was absent around 1800, or, as Buyanza explained it, there may have been too many people about during Mihigo's time, hence the shortage. Regardless of the actual cause-effect circumstances, around 1800 hoe handles were in short supply and therefore highly desired. But within a generation a balance between local supply and demand developed. This was a beneficial change during years of political instability, although depopulation may have been a significant factor in accounting for the balance.

While political conditions were not adversely affected by the supply of hoe handles they were influenced by either an overabundance of rain or by drought, both of which occurred during the period following Mihigo's death. Bahitwa contended that between approximately 1825 and 1830, during the brief reign of Ruhinda, the lake level rose appreciably, thereby forming islands where none had existed before. Bukerebe became an island at this time. As indicated above, the increase in the water level did not have to be great to create the island of Bukerebe. It was no easy task for Stanley to force his small boat through Rugezi channel in 1875 illustrating that Bukerebe was then an island in technical terms only.[34] A drop in the lake level would have rendered Bukerebe a peninsula during the 1870s. Bahitwa stated that the major rise in the lake level during Ruhinda's time prevented people from "walking," or wading, to nearby previously accessible islands. Interestingly, his information complements a Sukuma tradition that refers to an unspecified time when Mwanza Gulf (or a major portion of it) did not exist.[35] When the Sukuma and Bahitwa traditions are compared it becomes reasonably well established that a significant—to the degree that it affected human habitation—increase in the water level occurred at some

historically recent time. Whether Bahitwa's association of
the event with Ruhinda in the 1820s is correct is another
matter. An occurrence of this nature, of course, would have
forced people living along the shore to move inland.
Ramifications within the political sphere would follow
since the omukama was responsible for rainfall.

While Bukerebe experienced ecological and climatic
modifications, the political system of the Silanga encountered difficulties never before experienced. A brief
period of short reigns occurred. Four abakama were selected
between Mihigo's death and Machunda's accession to office
in the mid-1830s and each ruled for a relatively short time.
Why? Because of their inability to control their environment:[36] Two may have been killed by diseases and two
others could not satisfactorily control the rainfall. Following Mihigo II's death ca. 1820, his son Katobaha III reigned
briefly as his successor. Katobaha died in office in the early
1820s and his son Golita was in turn selected omukama by
the Sita. Golita died in office after a short time without eligible issue so his brother Ruhinda succeeded him. Ruhinda
was deposed a short time later by the Sita for failure to stop
the heavy rainfall, according to Bahitwa, and he fled to
Bukara and then on to Bururi. The Sita ignored Katobaha
III's descendants, assuming some remained, and made their
next selection from among the sons of Mihigo II. They
chose Ibanda, only to depose him also after a few years
because of an exceedingly severe drought. The next
omukama, the fifth in approximately fifteen years, was
Machunda, yet another son of Mihigo II. The Sita had
checked twice on Machunda's "height" or maturity while he
lived in exile, as mentioned above; hence it is assumed that
he was in his teens when installed and must also have been
one of the last born of Mihigo II's sons. The four abakama
who reigned prior to Machunda may have had an average
reign of some four years. Of the four men, Ibanda and
possibly Katobaha III ruled for longer periods than Golita
and Ruhinda, based on the fact that so little is mentioned in
oral sources about the latter two men.

Ibanda's tenure as omukama was by no means pleasant. The powerful Sita were extremely disturbed about a very severe drought that Ibanda was unable to end. Ibanda is remembered by the Kerebe as Omukama Chomya (hunger) because of widespread starvation. Stalks of banana plants as well as roots of other shrubs and plants were utilized as food. Children born during the extended drought, which lasted for more than two years, were named after the various "hunger" foods. The intensity of the suffering made a deep impression upon the survivors, who spoke of their ordeal with such fervor that their descendants, three to four generations removed, recall Ibanda's drought as the most severe of that century.

Machunda, accompanied by his uncle as well as by a brother and a sister, went into exile shortly after the beginning of the drought which reflected Ibanda's insecure position. There was talk that Machunda was "causing" the absence of rain, and his uncle therefore decided that exile was the only solution to protect his nephew's chances of ever becoming omukama. The Sita were also in an awkward predicament. They had selected four leaders within a decade and, although their power undoubtedly increased by this development, they were unsuccessful in selecting a ruler capable of resolving the increasing difficulties experienced by the Kerebe. Chief among these problems was the continued presence of diseases such as smallpox and cholera.[37] Ibanda did his best to alleviate the suffering by seeking "medicine" from both the Jita and Zinza to counteract the killers.

Machunda's Selection as Omukama

Ibanda, no less than any other Kerebe ruler, was aware that his days as omukama were limited as long as the drought continued. The extended duration of the drought before Ibanda's deposition indicates that he employed every means at his disposal to retain his position as omukama.

Although oral accounts preserve only the exile of Machunda, Ibanda had probably taken the precaution of ridding the chiefdom of other potential rivals to his position. The Sita patiently endured before commencing intrigues to locate and eventually return the exiled Machunda to Bukerebe. Given the inability of Ibanda to produce rain, they had little choice. Time and suffering gave them the upper hand, as Ibanda continually lost support in spite of his efforts.

That Machunda's place of refuge was among the pastoral Tatog was most unusual. Exiled Kerebe princes were certainly no novelty in this region of the lake, although in the latter part of the 1800s it seemed to be more common for brothers of the omukama to leave the chiefdom. Princes usually cast their lot with one of the Sukuma chiefdoms along the lake shore, chiefdoms such as Nassa, Busukuma, and Mwanza, while a few went northward to find solace among the Jita or others. A prince's country of exile probably depended upon his mother's family. For example, if members of her clan were found in a particular area, such as Bururi, Majita, or Nassa, then he could seek a home there. Yet Machunda went to live with the pastoral Tatog, although his mother's clan was Yango, a group with no indicated relationship on the male side with the Tatog.

Machunda established a lasting friendship with these people even though he encountered some difficulties while living with them. The duration of Machunda's exile probably did not exceed two or three years, but during this time a brother who had accompanied him was allegedly killed by the Tatog and his sister died shortly thereafter. The Tatog assumed that Machunda, since he was a lad in his teens, would be circumcised and thus become one of them. But Mugangi, Machunda's uncle, refused to grant permission as this would disqualify his nephew from becoming an omukama, an option that he wanted to keep open. Consequently Mugangi offered to submit himself to the rite in place of his nephew. This was an acceptable arrangement.[38]

The Sita could not overthrow Ibanda without thoroughly preparing for his successor's assumption of authority.

Simply killing an undesirable ruler was not possible. To kill a member of the royal family was to invite disaster to the participants. The mastermind behind the Sita conspiracy was Chehaga, guardian of *enzu ya menzi,* the storehouse of the ruler's most powerful magical and ritual possessions, including his predecessor's head. It was Chehaga who had dispatched messengers on two occasions to visit Machunda among the Tatog. Machunda secretly returned on the second journey so that he could step into the position when it was declared vacant at an auspicious time. Once Machunda was available, Chehaga had to remove Ibanda from the palace area so that he would be vulnerable. This was accomplished by arranging for an elaborate hunt in which Ibanda was enthusiastically encouraged to participate. Ibanda agreed to accompany the hunters and on the second day of the hunt the *coup d'etat* took place. The hunters heard the sound of the chiefdom's symbolic drum, *matwigacharo,* at the royal residence Bukindo and they informed Ibanda that a new omukama had taken possession of the vacated royal residence. Ibanda made a futile attempt to arouse support for his cause, but his inability to end the drought had convinced the vast majority of Kerebe that he was an inadequate ruler. He and a few followers were quite easily sent on their way to seek a life outside Bukerebe. Ibanda, temporarily powerless, sought refuge first in Mwanza chiefdom and later in Buzinza.

Machunda's ascendency to authority was marked by an end of the drought. Nonetheless, his right to remain in office was quickly challenged by Chehaga himself who became disenchanted with his clan's most recent choice of omukama. Chehaga charged that Machunda had lived among the Kangara (Tatog) too long and when eating he licked his fingers, considered poor etiquette by the Kerebe.[39] Chehaga and other elders were sufficiently dissatisfied for some reason to attempt their third deposition of an incumbent within two decades. Whatever his motives, Chehaga seriously miscalculated his strength in relation to that of Machunda. Any deposition required substantial support, or at least neutrality, from the populace to achieve success. In this case the incumbent had powerful uncles who in turn had Kwaya (Jita) allies. The tables were turned on Chehaga, who was forced to flee to Buzinza a beaten man. Having survived this threat to his position, Machunda went on to reign for some thirty-five years, until the late 1860s. The unstable political era came to a close.

Establishment of a Rival Chiefdom—Ilangala

As one of the youngest sons of Mihigo II, Machunda's selection to the office of omukama was highly unusual. It was necessary for two predecessors to die early in office and two others to be deposed before he was considered. Depositions themselves had been uncommon earlier. Only one of eight incumbents prior to 1820 was forced out of office. Because of these unusual circumstances the Kerebe attitude toward political authority altered, transforming the system as practiced under Mihigo II and his predecessors.

Fragmentation of the royal Silanga clan was an obvious consequence. The man responsible for this development was the deposed Ibanda. Although he found temporary refuge in the Mwanza chiefdom, Ibanda did not find the type of support he desired in this ally of the Kula clan. He moved on to Buzinza, where he schemed a successful return as omukama. He did not, however, possess the necessary strength to confront Machunda. He established himself instead at Ilangala, a sparsely populated area on the northwestern side of Bukerebe. He no doubt had intentions of eventually returning to Bukindo, his former residence, but this was denied him. Instead he spent the remainder of his life outside the mainstream of trade, effectively stymied by Machunda's astute dealings with Arab and Swahili traders. The latter could deal with only one of the Silanga rulers and they naturally remained with the man who provided them with ivory or the wherewithal to obtain it.

Ibanda's decision to return to Bukerebe rather than live in enforced retirement was very likely related to the ivory trade. Traders from the Indian Ocean coast had probably visited his court. He had received their trade goods through the monopolistic system practiced by his father, Mihigo II. He in turn was known by name to the Arab traders at Unyanyembe who told Burton about the rival brothers on Bukerebe.[40] By locating independently at Ilangala, Ibanda still had access to limited quantities of ivory tusks, since elephants inhabited the western part of the island. By taking his own ivory to Mwanza chiefdom or further south, Ibanda obtained trade goods. In this way he maintained contact with the traders of Unyanyembe.

Trade was necessary for Ibanda. When he established himself in Ilangala, it was sparsely populated. His greatest need was for people who would live under his jurisdiction. How was he to entice people to live in his newly established chiefdom? Where would they come from? Trade assisted Ibanda in overcoming this problem. With beads and other items to redistribute, Ibanda could establish himself as a generous ruler. A reputation for generosity was highly desirable for a ruler like Ibanda who wished to attract dissatisfied people. And the region was not lacking in them. Movement of individuals, nuclear family units, or bands of three or four persons has always characterized Bantu Africa, and the nineteenth century witnessed an increase in this phenomenon, a condition related to increased accusations of sorcery and witchcraft. Ibanda gradually enticed people, particularly from the comparatively densely populated island of Bukara, to settle in Ilangala. Oral accounts today refer to Ibanda's chiefdom as a haven for social outcasts from Bukara and Majita, with a liberal sprinkling of others from Machunda's chiefdom. Ibanda was only too pleased to have these particular migrants.[41] They helped him construct a viable chiefdom over a period of time and he, simultaneously, had to make his realm attractive by creating an impression of generosity.

Ibanda's chiefdom did not evolve sufficiently, however, to threaten Machunda directly, and both men died about the same time. Yet one of Ibanda's sons lived to revenge his father's deposition. He was Mukaka, the physically marred son of a Jita woman, two conditions which normally would disqualify him from the office of omukama. With the assistance of German authorities in 1895 he succeeded the German-deposed Rukonge as omukama. And it was his son and grandson who succeeded him in the twentieth century. Thus Ibanda's descendants, not those of his rival, Machunda, ruled Bukerebe during the colonial period.

Factors Affecting the Political System

Political fragmentation of ruling clans was common during the 1800s, a phenomenon closely associated with the opportunities offered by long-distance trade. It has been noted, for example, among the Sukuma, Nyamwezi and Kimbu,[42] and Pare.[43] The process of political fission of ruling clans certainly encouraged competition between rival factions for trade goods, but that was only one manifestation of the pressures at work. A more significant manifestation was the rivalry for subjects, as illustrated by Ibanda's necessity to attract people to his new chiefdom. He was, in fact, competing with Machunda for many of the same people from Bukara and Majita. Machunda was experiencing his own problems with depopulation, a consequence of disease and emigration due to accusations of sorcery. He went so far as to provide transportation in his personal canoe to immigrants from Majita and Buzinza, usually freemen experiencing problems within their own community. In at least one instance Machunda asked a Zinza ruler for Longo smiths to immigrate to Bukerebe, thereby revealing a shortage of these necessary craftsmen in his chiefdom. The search for subjects was one aspect of the dramatic shift in the nature of political authority during the century.

When Roberts refers to the change from "religious to military power as a basis for political authority," he implies that the ruler began using active, secular means to achieve his purposes.[44] Staying abreast of developments required initiative. Rather than rely upon spiritual means to overcome the problems, the rulers found practical means to ex-

pedite their needs. Men like Machunda and Ibanda required
immigrants. Previously immigrants had been welcomed if
they happened to come to Bukerebe, but by midcentury both
Machunda and Ibanda actively sought these people. This
parallels the development among Machunda's subjects by
which they first welcomed, then became dependent upon
and actively sought servile labor to facilitate increased
agricultural production.

The process of fragmentation was less significant to basic
political changes than the actual role of the ruler who acquired new functions and simultaneously loses authority in
the spiritual realm. This aspect is discussed in the following
chapter. Fragmentation merely exposed the weakness of
the administrative authority and structure of the earlier
system. With new opportunities rulers frequently lost control over their kinsmen on the periphery. Political units of a
manageable size emerged. In many instances this meant a
proliferation of political units and in a few cases the con-
solidation of a number of units into one. But what happened
to the functions of the rulers?

The act of seeking migrants itself indicated that the
omukama was desirous of strengthening his realm. The extent to which the prestigious council of elders and advisers
with ascriptive positions participated in encouraging im-
migration is problematical. Nonetheless, the nature of im-
migration was sufficiently related to the nature of long-
distance trade to suggest that it was the omukama who took
the initiative. Both developments deal basically with people
outside the chiefdom. The council had no specific authority
in this sphere, although it certainly could give advice. Concomitantly, when trade goods entered the chiefdom it was
the omukama who distributed the largess. This would obviously be done with an eye to rewarding those who most
enthusiastically supported the omukama. Likewise, arriving
immigrants were dispersed and settled in the chiefdom in
compliance with immediate concerns. This was not a new
development. The omukama had normally settled newcomers on the periphery of the chiefdom, to bolster the
population along sensitive borders. Under Machunda the

placement of immigrants was particularly critical. Families residing along the borders of the Kula chiefdom and of Ibanda's Ilangala dwelt along a hostile buffer zone. Clan elders from villages near the buffer zones did all in their power to persuade the omukama to place immigrants in their districts. Practical problems of this nature enabled the omukama to use means at his disposal to buttress his position in office.

The ascriptively powerful role of the Sita clan under the pre-1800 system altered with events following Mihigo's death. The Sita role of selecting and deposing abakama functioned well until new forces disrupted political relations. As long as the omukama's primary concerns focused on internal affairs, the Sita and the council of elders had a powerful voice in governing the chiefdom, comprising the dynamic elite within a socially hierarchical system. But the omukama's ability to control trade goods, for example, helped reduce their position from that of virtual co-equals to the omukama, given their ascribed positions, to definite subordinates. They were then placed in a position of competing among themselves for favors from the omukama. During the period of short reigns, there is no indication that the Sita exceeded their normal functions. Unexpected deaths and adverse climatic conditions required them to act as they did. But in their attempt to depose Machunda, it is clear that the Sita, and their spokesman Chehaga in particular, had acquired an abnormal conception of their role. Their dissatisfaction with Machunda was not based upon his inability to control rainfall or upon his abuse of subjects, either of which would have been legitimate reasons for his removal. And Machunda's display of poor etiquette was assuredly not the primary reason for Chehaga's attempt to depose him. The crux of the matter was probably one of two possibilities: either Chehaga wanted to become omukama himself or he was acting on behalf of Ibanda.[45] Regardless of the actual reason or reasons, Chehaga and his Sita kinsmen acted in an arbitrary manner. The fact that they were unsuccessful further damaged their relationship to Machunda. They had to heal this breach over time to regain royal favor. Their subordination to Machunda, a forceful and resourceful man, was evident to all.

Why had the Sita acted in this manner? As will be discussed in more detail below, the immediate predecessors of Machunda had lost the aura of office that had been assumed before and during the reign of Mihigo II. Therefore, rulers did not simply opt to use more secular manifestations of governing. They actually had lost powers and authority previously assumed by abakama, the basis of which had been primarily ritual. Or it may be more realistic to assume that the omukama's spiritual powers did not increase to enable him to control disturbing new factors such as disease. This shortcoming was readily acknowledged by Machunda and his successor Rukonge, since they openly sought knowledge of both a sacred/magical and a secular nature from fellow rulers or other renowned individuals to improve their ability to control a particular problem. The omukama's office continued to be regarded with awe by the Kerebe throughout the century, but that awe was tempered by an increasing concern for what the omukama could do to or for the individual. The image of the beneficent father figure of the entire community became tarnished during the nineteenth century. The omukama's expected ritual powers fell short in protecting the community and even his own person. As he began to reward those who supported him with important luxury items, rivals within his own clan and members of the Sita clan came to regard the man in office as more important than the office itself.

The New Men—the Enfura

As the apparent and actual powers of the omukama altered, his need to insure stability for his own position increased. This need gave rise to individuals referred to by the Kerebe as *enfura,* that is, friends of the omukama. The enfura were men whose relationship to the omukama—

essentially civil rather than military—was based upon personal loyalty and service to him, whose achievements contributed more to their position than kinship or ascriptive status. This type of individual is well described in the literature, since it was particularly vital to large expanding states.[46] Even for a small political entity such as Machunda's chiefdom, enfura were indispensable.[47]

The unofficial position of enfura no doubt existed before 1800. The word itself is part of the interlacustrine vocabulary, although among the Haya it refers to high-status clans, whereas the Kerebe use it to describe high-status individuals.[48] The composition of the council of elders during the Silanga era had never been representative of all clans. Enfura came from any clan, hence clans not represented on the council of elders could aspire to have one of their elders become an enfura. This was obviously in the interest of an unrepresented clan, since the problems and ambitions of persons near the center of authority usually received sympathetic consideration. As political relationships shifted during the 1800s the position of enfura became increasingly important for the omukama and for the enfura themselves.

How did one become a friend of the omukama? Men outside the royal clan and without ascriptive positions could normally become known to the omukama only by periodic visits to the court. Such a visit was always accompanied by a gift, such as beer, livestock, honey, fish, or hoes, as a token of respect. Obviously this social requirement disqualified men or clans of limited means. Mere visits to the royal court by no means assured a man of recognition as one of the enfura. His intelligence, wit, and general demeanor were important characteristics. Recognition of enfura was based upon the value of the man to the omukama, upon his wisdom, his advice, and, not least of all, his loyalty. The omukama benefited from the enfura by having trustworthy ambitious men about him, men who were in touch with village affairs, thereby ensuring an unofficial source of intelligence from the chiefdom's villages. (Primary responsibility for reporting on affairs of the villages remained with the headmen, however, who continued to be the omukama's kinsmen throughout the century.)

The importance of the enfura to the omukama is easily discernible. He increasingly needed to insure the loyalty of his kinsmen and other men with ascriptive positions. If such men became overtly ambitious for deposing the omukama, he could be assured of hearing about it from the enfura. Yet the omukama could not always be assured of absolute loyalty from the enfura. In particular, there is every reason to believe that a severe drought could have caused the deposition of Machunda. The enfura had their own welfare to look after as well. Rukonge dealt with this fact by becoming less reliant upon the enfura while expanding the ranks of the abazuma—the messengers—with servile people and men from Buganda. The abazuma then became the faction whose loyalty to the omukama was definitely of a personal nature. Nonetheless, Rukonge's enfura provided him with an additional and sorely needed source of support during the 1880s and until his removal by the Germans in 1895, a period of exceedingly difficult problems for a ruler and his subjects.

What motivated individuals to become enfura? What was their gain? The answer to both questions is basically simple: security. True, these men gained materially from their close social and political relationship to the omukama. Redistribution of trade goods or the granting of gifts such as cattle by the ruler assuredly went to those men who assisted him. But gift giving was reciprocal. When enfura visited the court, they continually brought the types of wealth available to them. It necessarily follows that a characteristic of the enfura was their respected position in the community—which included being men with considerable means—even before making periodic visits to the court. As discussed in the previous chapter, approximately a fourth of heads of nuclear families participated in the conscious process of increasing their millet production to enable them to participate actively in local trading opportunities. Enfura came from this group of men. The deliberate decision to take advantage of an existing opportunity, in this instance among nonroyal groups, again illustrates the secularization process. But the goal was not the simple accumulation of hoes or cattle or a servile population. It was to acquire these items which could then be used to improve their status with the omukama. An accumulation of wealth for the sole purpose of improving one's social status, or that of the nuclear family, could not occur. Personal or family status was linked to that of the omukama, who of course could confiscate one's property at any time.

In his story, Aniceti Kitereza recognized this rather tenuous aspect of Kerebe life in the 1800s when he gave one of his characters the name Bulihwali. According to Kitereza, the meaning of the name is as follows: "One day a man may have wealth; he has strength in his body and joy in his heart. But tomorrow his wealth may vanish and he is once again a poor man without even a skin to cover himself; and he has grief beyond measure."[49]

Survival was an overriding concern for the Kerebe, and this concern by no means diminished as the century wore on. The men who sought to become enfura attempted to confront unseen forces in an aggressive, active manner. The majority of the Kerebe, on the other hand, remained relatively passive, drawing as little attention to themselves as possible. This meant no avoidable visits to the omukama, no acquisition of excess material wealth, and a reliance upon earlier established procedures for dealing with daily pressures. They too, in their less obvious way, combatted unseen forces to survive. But efforts of men to gain the status of enfura and thereby the recognition of the omukama displayed atypical features and best illustrate the difficulties and insecurity of the nineteenth century.

While their relationship to the omukama definitely can be characterized as patron-client, the enfura did not receive official administrative positions for their loyalty. Their gain was certainly an improved socio-economic status, but they were still totally dependent upon the omukama's continued approbation and remained so, in spite of the omukama's increasing inability to control threatening internal and external forces. Although his powers were no longer regarded as omnipotent, no other figure in the community had more power at his disposal, and the enfura consequently sought refuge and security with him.

A final relationship meriting examination is that of the ascriptive officials, such as the council of elders, the Sita, and the royal kinsmen, to the new men, the enfura. The latter did not formally displace the ascriptive officials. Only the Sita could perform vital ritual functions for the omukama, and these functions remained their prerogative. But after Machunda successfully frustrated the Sita-inspired effort to depose him, Sita importance in selecting future abakama was forever reduced. The colonial regime guaranteed this, beginning with Mukaka's accession in 1895. But even Rukonge's emergence as omukama following Machunda's death bears the imprint of an upstart who took matters into his own hands. Oral accounts indicate that Lutami was the assumed successor to Machunda.[50] Rukonge, however, connived with a faction of the Sita to have himself, rather than Lutami, installed. Rukonge was successful. He had tampered with the established procedures for selecting an omukama and the Sita had been vulnerable to his machinations—another example of former relationships undergoing stress and alteration. The Silanga continued to exert ever greater secular control over their subjects, ascriptive officials being no exception.

The advisory role of the council of elders also diminished with Machunda's accession to office in the 1830s. Greater reliance was placed upon the enfura. This was essentially a matter of shifting priorities rather than preference for the new men at the expense of established officials. With externally oriented affairs demanding greater concern, the enfura were selected for their knowledge in this realm; for example, they were generally active in local trade. The council, on the other hand, was primarily concerned with internal matters. Its members may or may not have had useful knowledge on external developments. The council remained in existence as an official body, but as an institution with attenuated functions.

The tendency toward fragmentation within the royal clan created problems of its own. Machunda relied upon enfura to insure the continued support of his kinsmen in official capacities. Fortunately for both Machunda and Rukonge, the stigma of physical imperfection prevented a man from being considered for the position of omukama until the end of the century. Therefore known plotters for royal power could be rendered impotent by knocking out a few teeth or piercing their ears. Royal kinsmen with poor relationships to the omukama went into voluntary exile to prevent disfigurement.

Rukonge was a most unusual omukama in many respects, partially explained by the very disturbed period when he reigned. He ordered the death of two or three of his kinsmen, as well as of one member of the Sita clan. There was a time-honored restriction, that is, taboo, against killing either a Sita or a Silanga, even by the omukama. Rukonge also broke another precedent; he was extremely reluctant to claim parentage to any sons born to his wives. Both Mihigo II and Machunda are proudly remembered as men with many sons: Machunda's sons are estimated at 80. Because of this contribution to clan numbers, and hence clan strength, they are now highly praised. Yet Rukonge steadfastly declined to recognize his sons. His usual ploy was to declare his wife's infidelity, thereby refusing to acknowledge an heir. The present explanation given by informants is that he feared being deposed, a very real possibility since he allegedly abused his powers.[51] Oral sources uniformly categorize him as a "bad" omukama.[52] Rukonge's efforts to insure his position included this unusual attitude toward male offspring as well as his use of foreign—primarily Ganda abazuma and local enfura to support his incumbency.

The enfura represented a new type of individual in Kerebe society, men who participated in expanded local trading activities to accumulate wealth that was in turn used to establish a close social-political relationship to the omukama for their own security. The omukama's power and authority were also undergoing modification, and he welcomed the enfura as a source of additional support for his position. Against the background of significant change, as exemplified by the new importance of external forces, the omukama had to become active in seeking solutions to externally stimulated problems. As his former role altered, those of ascriptive officials and royal kinsmen decreased in significance. These elite of the eighteenth century were also required to adapt to new situations if they were to retain important positions in the nineteenth century.

This political analysis of Kerebe life has purposely avoided perhaps the major issue of the 1800s—the higher death rate. Death and the Kerebe response should complete the picture of long-distance trade's impact upon Bukerebe.

Notes

1. Andrew Roberts, "Political Change in the Nineteenth Century," *A History of Tanzania,* eds., I.N. Kimambo and A.J. Temu (Nairobi, 1969), 57-84.

2. *Ibid.,* 83.

3. *Ibid.,* 59.

4. *Ibid.,* 72.

5. See Bennett, *Mirambo of Tanzania;* Shorter, *Chiefship in Western Tanzania;* and Kiwanuka, *A History of Buganda.*

6. The Silanga clan had political power in Ihangiro, undoubtedly as subchiefs, under the Hinda rulers. While the Silanga still identified closely with the Hinda clan, the only possible relationship was through marriage, which was simply a political maneuver by the Hinda to ensure the loyalty of the subordinate Silanga. The Silanga claim that they were directly related to the Hinda was accepted literally and recorded by administrators in the 1920s; this view is found in Roland Oliver, "Discernible Developments in the Interior," 186.

7. Bukerebe was only technically an island in 1858. John H. Speke's observation at that time is substantially correct: " . . . instead of its being an actual island, it is a connected tongue of land

. . . which, being a wash, affords a passage to the mainland during the fine [dry] season, but during the wet becomes submerged, and thus makes Ukéréwé [Bukerebe] temporarily an island." *What Led to the Discovery of the Source of the Nile,* 310. Stanley experienced difficulty in getting his small vessel through the channel that "created" the island; it was only "six feet wide in some places." *Through the Dark Continent,* I, 248.

8. Bahitwa, Buyanza, Magoma, Kammando Mzinza, and Makene.

9. Masalu Kapongo of Nassa, Usukuma.

10. Kaliga, Bahitwa, Buyanza, and Makene.

11. See Terence Ranger, "The Movement of Ideas," 162-63.

12. For comparisons with other lacustrine societies see D.J. Stenning, "The Nyankole," *East African Chiefs,* ed., Audrey I. Richards (London, 1960), 148; in the same volume also see J. LaFontaine and A.I. Richards, "The Haya," 178-79, and LaFontaine, "The Zinza," 197.

13. Informants contributing to the general subject of government include Bahitwa, Buyanza, Magoma, Kaliga, Makene, Alphonce Golita, Alipyo Mnyaga, and Simeo Rubuzi.

14. The introduction of colonial rule upset the prevailing system. In 1895 the German administration enthroned Mukaka, who had the distinction of possessing two restrictions that normally barred a man from consideration as a candidate for the position of omukama: his mother was a Jita, and very likely an omuzana at that, and his ear lobes were pierced. Again, in 1939, Lukumbuzya was a lad of nine years at the time of his election.

15. In addition to selecting the omukama, the Sita were specifically responsible for burial of the abakama, storing the omukama's official rainpot and rainstones, guarding the royal accoutrements of a ritual nature along with the head of the previous ruler in a special structure called *enzu ya menzi,* and guarding the abakama's burial ground. The Sita had divided themselves so that a particular elder was responsible for a particular task; the elder's son would then follow his father in the performance of a specific

duty. The elder Kaliga s/o Lwambali was a descendant of the keeper of the omukama's rainpot.

16. A markedly different situation existed in Buganda where the absence of a royal clan accounted for the variation; see A.I. Richards, "The Ganda," *East African Chiefs,* ed., A.I. Richards (London, 1960), 47.

17. A strand, or several strands, of hair from an elephant's or giraffe's tail was looped about the neck and tightened periodically until decomposition permitted the mechanism to sever the partially decomposed flesh. During the process, performed by members of the Gabe clan, the body was treated with "perfuming" agents.

18. This is Bahitwa's version; he also maintained that the lake level increased significantly and numerous islands came into being at this time, including Bukerebe itself and Kome, off the Buzinza coast.

19. Buyanza, Bahitwa, Magoma, and Kaliga.

20. Buyanza and Bahitwa

21. Palapala s/o Kazwegulu, Buyanza, and Bahitwa.

22. See, for example, Stanley, *Through the Dark Continent,* I, 194.

23. Buyanza, Palapala, and Bahitwa.

24. Simeo Rubuzi, Buyanza, Bahitwa, and Aniceti Kitereza.

25. Bahitwa, himself a Kula, did not portray a significantly different image than Silanga elders, such as Buyanza, Magoma, and Aniceti Kitereza.

26. Speke, *What Led to the Discovery of the Source of the Nile,* 317.

27. *Ibid.,* 308-18; Burton, *The Lake Regions of Central Africa,* 412, 415-16.

28. Speke, 317.

29. *Ibid.,* 325. Burton omitted any reference to a Kula ruler; *The Lake Regions,* 416.

30. Burton, 412.

31. Speke, 312-13.

32. Bahitwa, Buyanza, and Magoma.

33. Hurel, "Religion et vie domestique des Bakerewe," 62.

34. See note 7 above; also Hans H.J. Meyer, ed., "Ostafrika und Kamerun," *Das deutsche Kolonialreich* (Leipzig, 1909), I, 285.

35. Vicariats de Mwanza et de Maswa, "Table d'enquêtes sur les moeurs et coûtumes indigènes—Tribu des Basukuma," n.d., Archives of the White Fathers, Rome.

36. This implication comes from Bahitwa, Buyanza, Kaliga, and Makene.

37. "Historia ya Ukerewe," Teacher Training College, Murutunguru, Ukerewe. This is a sixteen-page cyclostyled manuscript that was prepared for the use of primary school teachers by the staff of the Teacher Training College. It is based upon Aniceti Kitereza's unpublished account of Kerebe history.

38. Data concerning Machunda was provided by Buyanza, Kaliga, and Bahitwa.

39. Buyanza.

40. Burton, *The Lake Regions,* 415-16.

41. Buyanza, Simeo Rubuzi, Bahitwa, and Kammando Mzinza.

42. Ralph A. Austen, "Ntemiship, Trade, and State-Building: Political Development among the Western Bantu of Tanzania," *Eastern African History,* eds., Daniel F. McCall, N.R. Bennett, and Jeffrey Butler, Boston University Papers on Africa, III (New York, 1969), 142-43; Ralph A. Austen, *Northwest Tanzania under German and British Rule* (New Haven, 1968), 16; Andrew Roberts, *Tanzania before 1900,* xv-xvii; Aylward Shorter, *Chiefship in Western Tanzania,* 387-92.

43. Kimambo, *A Political History of the Pare,* 127-28, 158, 164-65. Also see Cohen, *The Historical Tradition of Busoga,* 13-14.

44. Roberts, "Political Change in the Nineteenth Century," 83. While Donald Denoon and Adam Kuper are justified in requesting more specific evidence from Roberts to support his thesis, the Kerebe evidence certainly supports Roberts' hypothesis; see Denoon and Kuper, "Nationalist Historians in Search of a Nation," *African Affairs,* 69 (October 1970), 340-42.

45. Neither Bahitwa nor Buyanza seemed to have specific information on this although Kaliga of Chehaga's clan forthrightly declared that Chehaga wanted to become omukama.

46. Cohen, *The Historical Tradition of Busoga,* 12-13; Roberts, *Tanzania Before 1900,* xv; Roberts, "Political Change in the Nineteenth Century," 83.

47. Information on this subject is based on information from Buyanza, Bahitwa, Alipyo Mnyaga, Kaliga, and Aniceti Kitereza.

48. LaFontaine and Richards, "The Haya," 176.

49. Hartwig and Hartwig, "Aniceti Kitereza: A Kerebe Novelist," 167-68.

50. Buyanza, Bahitwa, Kaliga, and Kazimili s/o Mazige.

51. Buyanza and Bahitwa.

52. Bahitwa, Simeo Rubuzi, Kaliga, Magoma, Palapala, Alipyo Mnyaga, and Buyanza.

5 Social Consequences of Trade

The significant economic, political, and social changes that have been discussed in the preceding chapters could not have occurred without affecting basic religious conceptions of the Kerebe. The failure of the omukama's ritual power to control something as fundamental as death, particularly from new diseases, illustrates the nature of the problem confronting the Kerebe during the nineteenth century. Another manifestation of altering religious concepts is found in the social phenomenon of sorcery.[1] On the one hand it reflected the increased tensions following in the wake of internal responses to alien external stimuli. On the other hand it reflected the ontological means for comprehending an increased mortality from disease. Thus both social and religious consequences of change are manifested in sorcery. This chapter examines the evidence revealing the evolution of sorcery as a significant historical phenomenon. The consequences of forces unleashed during the early 1800s are readily apparent when the roles of the enfura and the *abafumu* (medicine men/diviners) are examined. The enfura's role exemplified erosive forces that modified former social relationships, while the abafuma's role illustrated the growing authority of nonascriptive specialists at the expense of royal and ascriptive authority.

Understanding the evolution of sorcery is extremely important in understanding the Kerebe. Briefly, it gave the Kerebe a means for comprehending death and personal misfortune. Comprehension of death among the Kerebe is similar to that described by John Mbiti. Although Africans have "accepted death as part of the natural rhythm of life," according to Mbiti, they paradoxically assume that "every human death . . . [has] external causes, making it both natural and unnatural. People must find and give immediate causes of death."[2] Mbiti identifies the most prevalent "cause" of death as magic, sorcery, and witchcraft. Other causes he mentions are the curse of a living person, activities of ancestors (living-dead) and spirits, and God. The latter rather nebulous category accounts for natural phenomena such as lightning or the "natural" death of a very old person, as well as the contravention of an important custom or prohibition (taboo). It is normally assumed, therefore, that death "is unnatural and preventable on the personal level because it is always caused by another agent."[3]

Sorcery among the Kerebe

The Kerebe use the term *obulogi* to describe the state or condition of sorcery. I use the word "sorcery" in preference to "witchcraft" because the Kerebe invariably associate obulogi with a person who willfully and secretly seeks to harm someone or someone's possessions, whether by purely magical means or by concrete actions involving medicines or poison.[4] The person who practices obulogi is called an *omulogi; abalogi* is the plural form. As described by Kerebe elders, sorcery frequently involved the use of poisons put into someone's food or drink, thus emphasizing in conception, though not necessarily in fact, that death was the net result of sorcery.[5] Not surprisingly, the omulogi—the sorcerer—is regarded as a person who used antisocial means for personal ends. As such he is a threat to the community and feared by it. Mbiti puts it this way:

> For African peoples sorcery stands for antisocial
> employment of mystical power, and sorcerers are
> the most feared and hated members of their com-
> munities. It is feared that they employ all sorts of
> ways to harm other people ... they send
> flies. . . . or other animals to attack their enemies
> or carry disease to them. . . . They feel and
> believe that all the various ills, misfortunes,
> sickness, accidents . . . which they encounter or
> experience, are caused by the use of this mystical
> power in the hands of a sorcerer, witch or
> wizard.[6]

Yet associating death with sorcery has no special
relevance in this study unless it can be demonstrated that
the significance of sorcery changed at some point in time.
Sorcery is too common a phenomenon, as Mbiti's general
comments illustrate. My own recognition of sorcery's
variable nature came about in a circuitous fashion.

The knowledgeable Buyanza made a chance, explanatory
remark during an early interview that alerted me to this
situation. At the time we were discussing various abakama
and he mentioned in passing that "before Ibanda became
omukama [ca. 1830] the Kerebe died natural deaths; during
and after Ibanda's time people died because someone killed
them"—because of obulogi. I did not question this unusual
assertion at the time since the interview was concentrating
on more mundane political affairs, nor did I regard it as
particularly significant. Only some weeks later did I become
concerned about Buyanza's statement, primarily because it
conflicted with my preconceived notion that sor-
cery/witchcraft was a static, integral feature of Kerebe life. I
was prematurely convinced that "it had always been this
way," to use a statement frequently heard from informants
who had no idea when or how a particular custom may have
started.

Buyanza later elaborated on his claim concerning the
"beginning" of obulogi. He associated two series of events
from Ibanda's reign with its introduction. One incident in-

volved a crocodile seizing and killing a man from the ritually powerful Sita clan while the victim was bathing in the lake. A dispute arose within the clan. One faction accused a member of another faction of "sending" the crocodile to kill the victim. The case eventually appeared before Ibanda, who for an unexplained reason refused to resolve it himself and instead requested the assistance of a Zinza omufumu (medicine man). The specialist came and by reading the intestines of a chicken identified the guilty party for Ibanda.

The second incident related by Buyanza involved a husband and wife. The wife feared that she was losing her husband's affections. To rectify this she approached a Jita woman who provided her with a special medicine that was to be mixed into food and consumed by her husband: It was intended to reawaken his affections for his wife. The prescription was administered as directed, but unfortunately the man died. Buyanza claims that the Kerebe learned the use of internal poison from this incident. The importance of these two events in relation to sorcery, as Buyanza related it, is that in one case poison taken internally with food or drink caused death—this is in contrast to poisons used on arrows and introduced directly into the blood stream, a Kerebe practice of long standing—and that in the other case an omufumu was called in to determine the guilty party.

Only two other informants, the historian Bahitwa and Kaliga s/o Lwambali, possessed oral data about the "commencement" of sorcery. Bahitwa's understanding of sorcery's introduction differs markedly from that of Buyanza. He claimed that it commenced during the reign of Katobaha III (early 1820s) when three clans immigrated into the chiefdom from Buzinza. Each of these families contained numerous abalogi (sorcerers) and during the remainder of the century they used their knowledge to kill and destroy the property of others. During the latter part of the 1800s the omukama attempted to eradicate sorcery by systematically killing members of these three clans. When I asked Bahitwa if this action succeeded, he readily acknowledged that it had failed but only because some women of the clans escaped, those who had married and were resident among other clans. Sorcery was perpetuated through them and their descendants. Bahitwa therefore associated the introduction and dissemination of sorcery with particular clans and their individual members, a common means of understanding the transmission of sorcery from one generation to another.[7] In contrast, Buyanza associated particular characteristics of sorcery—poison and medicine men—with specific events to arrive at a similar conclusion.

An interpretation of these diverse oral accounts cannot be based on the specifics of either informant's data, since there was insufficient corroborative evidence from other elders. But the common elements of both accounts are significant: Sorcery "began" at a specific time, that is, between the reigns of Mihigo II and Machunda, an estimated period of fifteen years. These commonalities indicated that social changes of an undetermined magnitude occurred during this period to account for these oral accounts, particularly for the contention that "natural deaths" were expected at one time but then "unnatural death" became prevalent. Natural death in this instance should be interpreted to mean normal or expected, which could be as a result of ancestral spirits, other spiritual forces or the breaking of a taboo. Spiritually caused deaths are distinguished from man-caused deaths. The central issue revolves around the assumption that death and misfortune were suddenly more common. The Kerebe apparently use the concept of obulogi to account for this development. Is there related evidence to support their contention?

Disease

European observers of the nineteenth century certainly noted the terrible devastation of diseases such as smallpox and cholera.[8] James Christie makes reference to an Arab-led caravan that transmitted cholera throughout the interior of East Africa. It visited Bukerebe in 1869 and may have been responsible, through the disease it carried, for the death of

Machunda about this time.[9] During the last quarter of the century, missionaries and travelers continued to mention the widespread mortality from smallpox. According to C. T. Wilson, for example, smallpox was "one of the most fatal diseases to which the Baganda [were] subject, coming at intervals in epidemics, and carrying off thousands of victims; few attacked ever [recovered]."[10]

The suggestion of these European sources is that people in eastern Africa did not possess an immunity, even a partial immunity, to some currently prevalent diseases. Hence the observations of Philip Curtin concerning the importance of the epidemiology—the disease environment—for a given area is especially relevant. Curtin reiterates the known fact, already mentioned in Chapter 2, that virulent new diseases cause extremely high death rates among a population with no biological immunity to them.[11] European sources of the 1800s indicate a general and tragic East African vulnerability to specific diseases. This was particularly true for the interior. Long-distance trade of course served to exacerbate the problem by insuring the diffusion of disease throughout the trading networks, a matter of increased communication.

Dr. E. J. Southon's comments on longevity in 1880 are valuable, even though he specifically refers to the Nyamwezi, who had participated in long-distance commercial ventures for about a century and thus should have developed some immunity to various diseases. He noted that "the average life of males in Unyamwezi does not exceed twenty to twenty-five years. Many men are every year killed in battle, and great numbers fall victim to epidemics and famines."[12]

Kerebe oral data concerning disease are imprecise, but sufficiently plentiful to warrant careful consideration.[13] Mihigo II's "introduction" of disease has been cited in Chapter 2. But it is also noteworthy that informants are reluctant to claim that those diseases associated with the east initially appeared during Mihigo's reign. In fact, they suspect an earlier arrival. Mihigo's manipulation of disease, however, is accepted. That it served to "kill his enemies" is also assumed. Even his "creation" of Butamile, the man/beast who terrorized the chiefdom, is widely assumed. Especially significant are numerous references to disease in unpublished but written local histories that emanate from the 1930s.[14] These unsolicited accounts mention the turmoil created as a consequence of disease and illness, with a concentration on the first half of the nineteenth century. Bahitwa's rendition of this unrest is decidedly exaggerated, but it illustrates his perception of what happened to Kerebe society following the death of Mihigo II. The following account is taken from a manuscript written for Bahitwa by a literate individual; Bahitwa had intended to have it published for use as a textbook in the local primary schools.

> After some time entire clans went away; they disappeared from this country. People started moving away when Katobaha mbaliro [Katobaha III] was ruling and no one was around when Golita started ruling. Gabriel Ruhumbika [1907-1938] started to rule the country properly again.[15]

It should be noted that Bahitwa attributes enlightened rule to Ruhumbika, whose appointment of the historian Bahitwa as a village headman may have had something to do with the attribution of ruling wisely.

The implication persists that depopulation occurred during the early 1800s. This development is definitely related to the specific rulers of the period and their control or lack of control over their environment. Regardless of Mihigo's alleged activities, whether participating in long-distance trade or bringing in deadly diseases, he is assigned the ultimate responsibility in oral sources.[16] It is because of his omnipotent authority that sorcery is not attributed to his reign. Concomitantly, Mihigo is not remembered as having denied responsibility for the misfortunes of his reign. He "acknowledged" his responsibility, hence the Kerebe by necessity did not have to seek a cause for disease, illness or Butamile. The cause was apparent and comprehended within the social context. Conversely, none of Mihigo's successors are attributed with an equal authority. And it is with this break in the perception of royal power that sorcery emerges.

Still, is it conceivable that the phenomenon of sorcery, so well entrenched in Kerebe society in the twentieth century, could have been absent before 1820 when Mihigo II died? The Kerebe generally acknowledged that some sorcerers, the abalogi, had the power to manipulate spiritual forces for antisocial purposes. Was this therefore an abuse of power that suddenly appeared during a period of political instability and adverse climatic conditions?

Differing Categories of Abalogi (Sorcerers)

The ability to manipulate spiritual forces for socially approved purposes is a "constant" within Kerebe oral accounts. Rainmakers, diviners, and above all, the abakama possessed this type of power and they composed the upper echelons of society, respected as well as feared. Before Mihigo's reign, for example, oral data refers to men from nonroyal clans who caused violent storms, prevented locusts from destroying crops, or served the community in some manner that required spiritual power. But there are no examples of socially harmful deeds that were not committed or sanctioned by an omukama. The absence of evidence one way or the other on this particular issue is, however, of little assistance in answering the question.

Fortunately there is valuable internal evidence which sheds considerable light on the role of the omulogi among the Kerebe. This evidence gradually took coherent form after intensive discussions with elders.[17] When discussing the harm an omulogi could cause, the elders' tendency was to describe the alleged consequence of sorcery, that is the death of someone, the loss of livestock, or the burning of a hut. The mental image of a scheming murderer or destroyer of property naturally took shape in my mind. Yet when requested to describe the physical and spiritual attributes these same elders portrayed the virtual replica of a European witch. Thus the omulogi had the power to make him/herself invisible and was frequently associated with animal or bird familiars—particularly hyenas and owls, both night creatures. In addition he/she would meet with other abalogi at night, at which time they would dance—always in the nude. The Kerebe abalogi also had a particular affinity for riding cattle during their nocturnal ventures.

This portrait of an omulogi possessed one inconsistency after another when compared with the former image of a murderer. One particular omulogi was much more a social nuisance rather than an indiscriminate destroyer. The anthropological literature on sorcery and witchcraft verifies this apparent dichotomy. Isaac Schapera noted this same distinction in Tswana society. He translated the Tswana designations as "night witches" and "day sorcerers" reporting virtually the same function for the divergent types as Kerebe informants.[18] Similar distinctions may have been present among the Amba, Kaguru, and Nyoro in eastern Africa.[19]

The role of the *omuhike* eventually emerged from arduous discussions as the key to resolving questions about sorcery. Discussions originally focused on the abalogi and those who possessed the ritual means to discern them, the abafumu or medicine men. But this merely clouded the past since the abafumu are important now and certainly have been for a century and a half. The abahike, on the other hand, are seldom mentioned. They are defined as persons with power superior to that of the abalogi so that they could literally "see" an omulogi even though he/she made him/herself invisible. With the identification of the omuhike and his supposed powers, it became evident that two distinct categories of abalogi existed. It was also clear that the omuhike's powers were no longer highly esteemed. His was virtually an historical role; he was important in the past but not today.[20]

An omuhike was invariably described as a man with political authority. The omukama was naturally the most powerful; therefore, he was an omuhike. In addition the headmen, the members of the council of elders and even some enfura had the power "to see" the invisible omulogi.

Yet when I discussed with informants the omulogi who killed, the specialist mentioned to determine the guilty party identified by them was not the omuhike. Rather it was the medicine man, the omufumu, who was not necessarily of the political elite. Once it became evident that two categories of abalogi existed, the two sets of specialists required to deal with the troublesome abalogi could be used to differentiate the conflicting data. From the wide geographical distribution of the root -logi or -loki in the vocabulary of people in the interlacustrine area, and further south, it is apparent that the Kerebe omulogi is a character of considerable antiquity whose attributes are widely shared.[21] There is no doubt that he was present among the Kerebe before the time of Mihigo II, as were the omufumu and omuhike.

Evolution of Sorcery

What altered between 1750 and 1850 was the conception of power attached to each role and the accompanying functions. This alteration occurred over time as the epidemiology of the region radically changed and as the community experienced political instability, a consequence of the abakama's failure to control the physical and spiritual environment. Before 1800, the society kept the abalogi in check through the power of the abahike. Sorcery as it was known in the nineteenth century probably did not exist; "witchcraft" may well be the preferable word to express the earlier situation. After the death of Mihigo II, with depopulation an ultimate concern and seemingly ineffectual abakama in power, sorcery arose as a means to explain the increasing deaths. These suspected man-caused deaths were not the responsibility of the invisible omulogi, but of an individual who relentlessly and secretly sought to cause irreparable harm to someone. For an unexplained reason the omuhike could not identify or "see" these particular abalogi. The former ascriptive leaders thus lost yet another attributed power.

Social anthropologists have recognized the altering

nature of sorcery and witchcraft within African societies during the twentieth century, although they have not as yet devoted their attention to analyzing this process of institutional or structural change.[22] The following statement by Aidan Southall illustrates the historical change which social scientists assume has transpired in the character of sorcery and witchcraft.

> Frequently and importantly, spirit possession and mediumship are associated with the new cults of Jok which seem to have appeared increasingly among the Alur since pressure of outside influence became intensified about eight years ago. . . . Formerly [the precolonial era] the regular, communal worship of chiefs, elders and people was sufficient to maintain harmony between spirit, man and nature. . . . Now they are upset in their feeling that witches are seriously on the increase and that nothing effective is done to control them, now that the powers of the chief are curtailed and former ordeals and punishment banned.[23]

Basil Davidson summarizes the presumed cause for the suspected increase in sorcery and witchcraft when he states that the "reason appears to lie in the disintegration of traditional structures and systems since the 1880s: in the passing of Africa's age of faith, and consequently in a growth of personal anxiety and alienation."[24] The assumption is implicit in Southall's statement and explicit in Davidson's that the advent of the colonial era introduced factors responsible for changes in the function of sorcery and witchcraft.

Yet it is apparent that earlier forces likewise operated to influence relationships and institutions. Referring specifically to Tanzania, Terence Ranger characterizes the entire nineteenth century as "a period in which insecurity and fear produced a widespread increase of witchcraft belief. . . ."[25] Edward Alpers has also inferred increasing accusations of witchcraft during the 1800s but he—misleadingly—associates the increase only with the demands of the slave trade.[26] A. J. H. Latham has recently described how economic developments and subsequent social tension gave rise to accusations of witchcraft in Old Calabar long before the colonial era.[27] Thus sorcery and/or witchcraft is now recognized by historians as a vital and elementary factor that requires analysis. Limits posed by available sources are a formidable barrier, but they can be partially overcome for the nineteenth century.[28]

A valuable historical study of sorcery or witchcraft, entitled *Witchcraft in Tudor and Stuart England,* was recently published by Alan Macfarlane. Unlike most of his contemporaries who are concerned with sorcery/witchcraft in Africa, Macfarlane concentrated solely on Essex, England, with its wealth of written records emanating from the sixteenth and seventeenth centuries. His is a detailed, microcosmic study. An interesting feature of his study is his use of hypotheses evolved by social anthropologists working in Africa. For this reason his interpretation of witchcraft's role in Essex has relevance for historians of Africa.

Macfarlane asserts that one vital function of witchcraft beliefs was "to explain events for which religious and medical knowledge were unable to provide a satisfactory answer." A second factor was sociological in nature. It was related to the conflict between social expectations and actual interpersonal relationships, "between an ideal of neighbourliness and the practical necessities enforced by economic and social change."[29] The growth of witchcraft during Tudor times in contrast to an earlier period is attributed by Macfarlane to changing social and economic conditions. The majority in the community adjusted satisfactorily. Persons accused of witchcraft appear in the records as social misfits, those who harassed their neighbors, if only by their seemingly threatening presence. Characteristically, a quarrel between the accused and accuser usually preceded the misfortune that triggered the accusation. Suspicion already existed. Macfarlane sees the "victims" of witchcraft accusations as persons who expected to be provided for within the comunity because their counterparts in pre-Tudor times had apparently received satisfactory consideration. But new conditions prompted the majority to embrace new values which did not adequately provide for the expectations of the minority. In one sense the values of those accused of witchcraft lagged behind the majority. They grumbled about their unfortunate lot. The majority in turn seized this expression of discontent to explain misfortune. They, the accusers, acted in self-defense while the accused acted on the premise that they were being ill-treated. According to earlier expectations this was true, but not according to the new values embraced by their contemporaries.

Religious beliefs, together with social attitudes and expectations, comprise the milieu in which the Kerebe, just as the Tudor English in Essex, had to adjust to the realities of the early nineteenth century. Economic opportunities as well as the presence of fatal diseases, both related to long-distance trade, set the changes in motion for the Kerebe. Social roles and relationships altered at a vastly accelerated rate. Nor was this an even transition. Some segments of the community lagged behind others, creating potentially antagonistic situations. With values in a state of flux there was heightened social tension, manifested in accusations of sorcery.

Factors Promoting Social Unrest

These accusations against sorcerers or witches can be understood within a context that is permeated with social tension. Max Marwick has formulated the following hypothesis that encompasses the general development in Bukerebe: "We may say that competition and tension arise more frequently where statuses are *achieved* than where they are *ascribed* [assigned by birth]." Marwick also contends that tensions emanating from an achievement-oriented environment "tend to be projected into witch

beliefs and subsequent conflict if there are no other adequate institutionalized outlets for it."[30]

Kerebe society was most assuredly shifting away from an
ascribed to an achieved social and political situation,
although the transition was definitely not as advanced
among the Kerebe as, for example, among the Ganda. But
the tensions associated with changing roles and expectations were clearly present. The aspiring enfura most
clearly illustrated the process. These men from nonroyal
clans were active in local trading activities. They were
achievers of the first order among the Kerebe. As indicated
in the preceding two chapters, the enfura sought material
gain only insofar as it enhanced their social and political
relationship with the omukama. They were not simply
seeking to increase agricultural production and to appropriate a servile labor force so that they could live a life of
ease and luxury. That they did modify agricultural production or change the role and function of the servile aberu and
abazana or become achievers is indirectly related to their essential goal of acquiring security a goal inextricably tied to
status.

The process of becoming an enfura encouraged com-
petitiveness and tension. It implied that these individuals
sought to elevate themselves to a position similar to the
ascribed position of elders and advisers. While this was a
challenge to men with ascriptive status, it was even more
disruptive to kin relationships. The entire lineage was not
involved in this achievement process. It was an individual
and his immediate nuclear family who participated, not all
kinsmen. Communal ties were sorely strained by this situation; within these familiar relationships accusations of
sorcery were most likely to occur. Sorcerers (or witches)
characteristically attacked their kinsmen or close neighbors,
not strangers.[31] The process of acquiring material
possessions to take to the omukama and to raise one's social
status aroused expectations within the lineage. According to
the communal ethic there was no reason to accumulate
wealth except insofar as it benefited the entire lineage. This
wealth was then the responsibility of the lineage's elders

who held it in trust for the extended family. An enfura represented only segments of a lineage and his acquired wealth was not necessarily shared to the degree expected by other segments of the lineage.

Thus an enfura simultaneously exacerbated one set of social relationships in his effort to seek another form of security from a new relationship with the omukama. The effort seems to have been counterproductive. In fact, it was no doubt worth the potential antagonism from some members of the lineage because the omukama could partially protect the enfura from hostile kinsmen, particularly if it came to accusations of sorcery. The essential concern, it must be emphasized, was to achieve security and protection from death. And the office of the omukama represented the best available shield, albeit a tarnished one. The procedure for discerning abalogi favored persons of high rank, including enfura; the enfura could certainly be accused of practicing obulogi but they had the means and status enabling them to appeal accusations. The process of appealing cases literally ate up possessions, thus favoring those with expendable wealth at their disposal. Persons without means to defend themselves who were accused of sorcery frequently found it expedient to seek refuge in other districts. That they were welcomed elsewhere does not necessarily testify to their innocence or to the spurious nature of sorcery and witchcraft accusations. Their reception was based upon the assumption that even if guilty they would not necessarily injure others; abalogi did not attack strangers. Concomitantly the desire by rulers to maintain or augment the numbers of their own subjects, in light of mortality rates and emigration related to sorcery/witchcraft accusations, lent itself to a policy of welcoming newcomers, whatever their background.

The development of the enfura as an achievement-oriented nucleus of society demonstrates the complex social repercussions stemming from a changing disease environment and the opportunities related to expanding commercial activities. The former value system and institutional structure had to adapt to these new forces. The expanding role of the medicine men—the abafuma—reveals another dimension of the change under way. Their increasing importance parallels that of the enfura.

Attenuation of the Omukama's Authority

The abafumu assumed the responsibility for determining the murderous abalogi within Kerebe society, a dramatically new development. Previously the abahike, the ascriptive political elite, had possessed the necessary power "to see" the abalogi and thereby control them. The acceptance of the abafumu by the rulers as essential to the process of controlling the dreaded sorcerers of the nineteenth century reinforces the fact that the office of omukama was becoming less effective in the spiritual and ritual sphere.

An examination of the legal system sheds light on the increasingly awkward position of the omukama. Normally, major legal problems had been handled by the omukama in his capacity as judge. Arbitration in these cases was possible because the litigants were known and their problems articulated. Disputes of this nature could be treated on their own merits. Sorcery stands in stark contrast to this situation. The alleged wrongdoer had carried out his nefarious activity secretly. There could be no arbitration. It became an extralegal matter by definition. Evidence was not available; only the misfortune, the end product, was readily discernible. Hence sorcery could not be systematically treated as a routine legal case. The guilty party had to be determined by ritual means.

Abafumu is a generic term used by the Kerebe to refer to specialists using a wide variety of ritual and mechanical devices to treat illnesses, to provide medicines for various purposes—some harmful—and to detect abalogi. They are generally regarded as an invaluable asset to the society, particularly in treating illnesses. The omufumu learned his skills from others, a particularly important characteristic. While he/she possessed ritual powers, they were of an acquired nature. No office as such existed. A novel problem usually required a novel solution; to seek this solution from someone else was a matter of course. It did not imply incompetence or inadequate power. The abafumu were practical individuals in this respect.

For them to have acquired the knowledge and means to identify abalogi was not a difficult matter. The basic question was whether or not the omukama would look to them for this function. It would be most interesting to know more about the apparent attenuated power of the omuhike. Why specifically did the abakama delegate responsibility for discerning sorcerers to the abafumu? Theoretically, the office of omukama retained superior power in comparison to any of his subjects, including abafumu. Yet there is an element of abdication of authority when the abafumu became essential in discovering abalogi. This has all the appearance of a royal admission that the ruler and his headmen and advisers could not "see" the disruptive abalogi. The facade of royal omnipotence was again marred.

Spiritual Ramifications

Other spiritual conceptions adjusted to the new realities of the 1800s. For example, a normal recourse in misfortune, particularly illness, was to appeal to ancestral spirits for assistance. Developments in the early 1800s complicated this process even though they did not displace it. When misfortune occurred, the dilemma confronting the victim or the victim's family was to determine what had caused the calamity. To know which spirits were involved, which taboo had been broken, and whether an omulogi was concerned was necessary before anything else could be accomplished. Increasingly, the omufumu was required to provide the answer. In this capacity he assumed priestlike powers in Bukerebe by 1900.[32] If an omulogi was indicated as responsible, then it became a matter of discovering who the omulogi was, again the function of an omufumu. On the other hand, if the misfortune was spiritually caused or related to a broken taboo, the clan elders possessed the necessary knowledge to restore harmonious relations.

Formerly the omufumu had not been an important intermediary for the elders. They had relied on their own means to resolve internal difficulties, only as a last resort appealing to the omukama. With dominant intrusive forces present, however, the elders sought aid outside the royal court. And it was the abafumu who responded and performed an invaluable service as social tensions mounted and as man-caused misfortunes seemingly increased. In this fashion the Kerebe adjusted and thereby retained a semblance of social order in spite of the ill-defined, intangible forces confronting every unit within the community.

What, then, is the historical significance of sorcery/witchcraft? The phenomenon itself is a particularly sensitive indicator of social tension. If it can be demonstrated to have evolved, or even significantly fluctuated in its intensity, at a particular time, it reveals to us that the society was experiencing acute stress. Whether or not victims of sorcery/witchcraft accusations were actually guilty of wrongdoing or were merely undesirables the society wanted to rid itself of cannot be actually determined in an historical context with inadequate data.

As an illustration, let us examine the assertion that chiefs frequently abused their power by accusing subjects of sorcery/witchcraft in order to exploit the accused and rob them of their positions.[33] This type of crass exploitation may, in fact, have occurred. But it should also be recognized that the widespread existence of sorcery/witchcraft was also a manifestation of a serious social malaise. It was an extralegal means of maintaining social control, as well as ontological framework for comprehending misfortune. Under normal circumstances initiative for an accusation did not come from the ruler himself but rather from within a village context. If the village legal structure could not resolve the situation it was then directed to higher authorities. It is unrealistic to allocate the primary responsibility for all sorcery accusations to the chiefs. A ruler could despoil a subject without resorting to extralegal means. They of course possessed the authority to enforce the decision of the diviners who determined the guilty parties. The manifested

desire in the 1800s to accumulate possessions naturally contributed to avarice among men in authority. Yet the ruler
was undoubtedly more interested in eradicating the causes
of sorcery and witchcraft than he was in increasing his
wealth by settling case after case. The position of the chief
did not assure immunity from the harmful practices of
sorcerers. The continual search by men of this rank for
magical powers to enhance their positions reflects their insecurity. Chiefs were in no position to remain aloof from the
affairs of the community. In fact, they were as deeply concerned about unsettling conditions over which they had little control as other members of their society. To regard
sorcery and witchcraft simply as a means of social control
and the chiefs as unscrupulous men taking advantage of
their subjects is to misconstrue the nature of sorcery and
witchcraft as well as to deny the anarchical nature of it. No
one was fully protected from sorcery or, in other terms,
from the diseases whose mortality rates encouraged the
search for a human agent on whom blame could be placed.
Why chiefs seemingly "exploited" sorcerers/witches is far
too complex an issue to blame on a single social echelon of
society. All were involved, along with their total value structure.

Rather than accusing some persons in the past of abusing
their power, a more productive enterprise is to examine
those factors responsible for the tension manifested by the
presence of sorcery/witchcraft. This enables us to view at
least partially the existing tangled web of relationships.
They reveal the ascending and descending mobility of some
social elements and the concomitant rigidity of others.
These fluctuating social relationships are themselves contingent upon factors which in turn require identification
and analysis. Given this perspective of sorcery, its evolution
among the Kerebe illustrates the magnitude of adjustment
required in a community that was being "opened up," that
was becoming a participant within the extended international community.

It is inadequate simply to discern the changing roles of
the omukama, the enfura, the abalogi, or the abafumu. It is

essential to determine why the alteration of roles occurred and how this was perceived by the society. Otherwise the omnipotence attributed to Mihigo II makes little sense when contrasted to his ritually less well-endowed successors. The access to ritual or spiritual power by an omukama or an omufumu also has little meaning unless explained in a religious or ontological framework. Because an analysis of sorcery requires consideration of intangible beliefs, it explicitly emphasizes the fundamental nature of change in progress during the nineteenth century and serves to clarify the extent that the old order had changed before the twentieth century.

Notes

1. This subject was initially analyzed and published in a paper entitled "Long-Distance Trade and the Evolution of Sorcery Among the Kerebe," *African Historical Studies*, IV, 3 (1971), 505-24.

2. Mbiti, *African Religions and Philosophy*, 155.

3. *Ibid.*, 156.

4. See E. E. Evans-Pritchard, *Witchcraft, Oracles and Magic among the Azande* (Oxford, 1937), 387.

5. In addition to Buyanza, Bahitwa, Kaliga, and Simeo Rubuzi provided valuable information on sorcery.

6. Mbiti, *African Religions and Philosophy*, 200.

7. See Beidelman, "Witchcraft in Ukaguru," 67-68; Gray, "Structural Aspects of Mbugwe Witchcraft," 168-70; LeVine, "Witchcraft and Sorcery in a Gusii Community," 228-29.

8. Burton, *The Lake Regions of Central Africa*, II, 318-21.

9. Christie, *Cholera Epidemics in East Africa*, xi-xii.

10. Wilson and Felkin, *Uganda and the Egyptian Soudan*, I, 183; also *ibid.*, II, 48.

11. Curtin, "Epidemiology and the Slave Trade," 195.

12. Southon, "History, Country, and People of the Unyamwezi District."

13. Alipyo Mnyaga, Bahitwa, and Buyanza.

14. See Zimon, "Geschichte des Herrscher-Klans Abasiranga," 366, 368.

15. Bahitwa s/o Lugambage, "Kerebe Manuscripts from Nansio, Ukerewe," Book A2, 18-19 (microfilm, University of Dar es Salaam Library, Tanzania).

16. Buyanza, Bahitwa, Magoma, Makene, and Kaliga.

17. Buyanza, Simeo Rubuzi, Bahitwa, and Kaliga.

18. Isaac Schapera, "Sorcery and Witchcraft in Bechuanaland," *Witchcraft and Sorcery*, ed., Max Marwick (Baltimore, 1970), 110-12. Michael Gelfand reports a similar division among the Shona in *The African Witch* (Edinburgh, 1967), 23-46.

19. E.H. Winter, "The Enemy Within: Amba Witchcraft," *Witchcraft and Sorcery in East Africa*, eds., John Middleton and E.H. Winter (London, 1963), 279-281, 291-293; John Beattie, "Sorcery in Bunyoro," *Witchcraft and Sorcery in East Africa*, eds., John Middleton and E.H. Winter (London, 1963), 29-30; Beidelman, "Witchcraft in Ukaguru," 61-63.

20. Neither Buyanza nor Bahitwa mentioned the omuhike. The term eventually emerged in an interview with Simeo Rubuzi whose information was subsequently verified by Buyanza and Bahitwa.

21. See Wyatt MacGaffey, "Comparative Analysis of Central African Religions," *Africa*, XLII, 1 (1972), 23-24.

22. A notable and valuable exception is the analysis by Monica Wilson of "Changes in Social Structure in Southern Africa: The Relevance of Kinship Studies to the Historian"; another example is provided by Martin Southwold in "The History of a History: Royal Succession in Buganda," *History and Social Anthropology*, ed., I. M. Lewis (London, 1968), 136-37. Thomas O. Beidelman in "Myth, Legend and Oral History: A Kaguru Traditional Text,"

Anthropos, 65, 1/2 (1970), 74-77, criticizes historians working with oral sources, particularly their misuse of anthropological evidence.

23. Aidan Southall, "Spirit Possession and Mediumship Among the Alur," *Spirit Mediumship and Society in Africa,* eds., John Beattie and John Middleton (London, 1969), 258-59. Similar comments are found in the following: Elizabeth Colson, "Spirit Possession Among the Tonga of Zambia," *Spirit Mediumship and Society in Africa,* eds., John Beattie and John Middleton (London, 1969), 94; S. G. Lee, "Spirit Possession among the Zulu," *Spirit Mediumship and Society in Africa,* eds., John Beattie and John Middleton (London, 1969), 130; John Beattie, "Spirit Mediumship in Bunyoro," *Spirit Mediumship and Society in Africa,* eds., John Beattie and John Middleton (London, 1969), 161; Godfrey Lienhardt, *Divinity and Experience* (Oxford, 1961), 259-61; E. E. Evans-Pritchard, *Nuer Religion* (London, 1956), 308-09; Bronislaw Stefaniszyn, *Social and Ritual Life of the Ambo of Northern Rhodesia* (London, 1964), 157; M. G. Marwick, "The Sociology of Sorcery in a Central African Tribe," *African Studies,* 22, 1 (1963), 10; J.H.M. Beattie, "Initiation into the Cwezi Spirit Possession Cult in Bunyoro," *African Studies,* 16, 3 (1957), 150-51; John Middleton, "Witchcraft and Sorcery in Lugbara," *Witchcraft and Sorcery in East Africa,* eds., John Middleton and E. H. Winter (London, 1963), 271; John Beattie, "Sorcery in Bunyoro," 40; Audrey I. Richards, "A Modern Movement of Witch-Finders," *Africa,* VIII, 4 (1935), 457-59.

24. Basil Davidson, *The African Genius* (Boston, 1969), 125.

25. Ranger, "The Movement of Ideas," 169.

26. Alpers, "The East African Slave Trade," 19.

27. Latham, "Witchcraft Accusations and Economic Tension in Pre-Colonial Old Calabar," 249, 259-60.

28. See T. O. Ranger and Isaria Kimambo, eds., *The Historical Study of African Religion* (Berkeley, 1972).

29. Alan Macfarlane, "Witchcraft in Tudor and Stuart Essex," *Witchcraft Confessions and Accusations,* ed., Mary Douglas

(London, 1970), 82; also Alan Macfarlane, *Witchcraft in Tudor and Stuart England* (New York, 1970), 249-52.

30. Max Marwick, "The Social Context of Cewa Witch Beliefs," *Africa,* 22, 2 (1952), 129-30.

31. See M. G. Marwick, *Sorcery in Its Social Setting* (Manchester, England, 1965), 3.

32. Hurel, "Religion et vie domestique des Bakerewe," 83-87; also see Mbiti, *African Religions and Philosophy,* 169.

33. Alpers, "The East African Slave Trade," 19.

6 The Kerebe Experience within East African Historiography

I have attempted here to utilize social and ontological factors as well as political and economic developments to make Kerebe oral data comprehensible and meaningful. This means of interpreting oral data adds a dimension to Kerebe history that conceivably could embrace all aspects of the society's development in the nineteenth century, although this monograph does not pretend to be so comprehensive. This approach does enable one to examine the entire society, however, thereby avoiding the emphasis inherently suggested by much of the data, whether oral or archival: concentration on the ruling class, a mere "chronicle of the aristocracy."[1] The available published monographs on East African societies are clearly difficult to appreciate if they concentrate solely on internal political and economic affairs. The reader too frequently infers from them that the characteristics of specific East African societies are parochial rather than general phenomena, even though this may well be a misleading impression. Analysis of social and ontological factors fleshes out political and economic data, making more easily discernible those historical trends that transcend a specific society and are potentially relevant to the general region.

What happened to an East African society that participated in long-distance trade? This basic question provided the rationale for my organization, analysis, and interpretation of Kerebe oral evidence which make it apparent that the plethora of Kerebe responses emanated from two prevailing external stimuli: new economic opportunities and alien diseases. The latter factor has all too often been overlooked, although to East Africans during the era of long-distance trade it was as significant as new trading opportunities, if not more so.[2]

In view of the two fundamental external stimuli, it is essential to again raise the questions posed in the Introduction. They incorporate the advantages and disadvantages to a community for participating in long-distance trade:

> What economic changes occurred as a consequence of long-distance trade? How did participation in trade, regional and long-distance, affect relationships between social groups, between neighboring political entities?

> How did these presumably altered relationships affect the authority of ascriptive leaders, i.e., those whose role was basically defined by birth? How did these leaders respond? If these leaders were displaced, by whom?

> How did commoners respond to the fluctuating economic, social, and political conditions?

> Did the role of the servile population alter?

> Did increased mortality characterize participation in long-distance trade through disease and/or violence? Was there depopulation? Did new food crops offset depopulation forces?

> Did individual and lineage insecurity increase? How was this manifested?

Were religious or ontological beliefs altered or in
any way adjusted during this era?

Answers to these questions are found in the preceding
four chapters. The manifold dimension of each question
precludes a succinct response. This can be demonstrated
with the first question dealing with economic changes.

Kerebe participation in long-distance trade encouraged
an array of economic responses, some in the sphere of the
omukama who monopolized the export-import commodities contingent upon long-distance trade, and some in
the sphere of commoners who substantially increased
regional trading ventures. It is in the latter realm that the
Kerebe offer substantially new data, although their activities cannot be characterized as representative.
Geographic factors—climate much more favorable than
that of immediate neighbors, a peripheral position in relation to long-distance trade routes and a reasonable distance
from militaristic neighbors, particularly the Ganda—to a
great degree defined the unique economic sphere of the
Kerebe. Even within Kerebe society itself not all nuclear
family units exhibited similar responses to economic forces,
and any generalization must take this into consideration.

As fruitful and revealing as an economic analysis of
Kerebe evidence may be, however, it leaves many questions
unanswered. This may be partially a consequence of the
nature of the Kerebe economy. That it remained essentially
subsistence-oriented throughout the 1800s is clear, but that
the system was significantly different in 1800 than in 1900
is also evident. Why did economic changes occur? An
answer couched exclusively in economic terms falls short of
a satisfactory explanation. The Kerebe data make sense only
when placed within an ontological and social context.

The overriding concern of the Kerebe during the
nineteenth century was not economic gain or social status
but survival. Of course survival was inextricably linked to
long-distance trade; thus it is misleading to separate trade
from survival, to separate economic affairs from physical

and related ontological affairs. Precisely how these components meshed is impossible to determine. They appeared
simultaneously and intangibly behind the facade of beads,
cloth, wire, and elephant tusks. But the evidence makes it
sufficiently clear that the Kerebe were more concerned
about the increasing mortality rate during the nineteenth
century than about improving their social status. When this
assumption is accepted, the oral data, including the
economic factors, can be organized and interpreted
meaningfully.

Illness and death, particularly from smallpox and cholera,
loom as the dominant concern of the Kerebe. The inability
of the abakama and other ascriptive leaders to control illness and death required the people to adjust their views concerning ritual and spiritual authority. This may be described
as a loss of ritual authority or as a failure of that authority to
meet the challenge of new conditions. In either case, the ultimate consequence was that the power of the abakama was
perceived as inadequate to control the physical environment of Bukerebe. The leadership responded to its dilemma
by consciously resorting to tangible means of supplement-
ing its increasingly ineffectual ritual power. Although
ritual means were not forsaken during the nineteenth century, as demonstrated by the abakama's continual search for
effective "medicine," the creation of a strong military force
or the availability of one that could be used—e.g., the
Ganda—appeared more effective than rituals in resolving
some issues. A desire to influence one's life by active
processes became more prevalent than the passive method
of utilizing ritual means.

Altering social roles reflect the forces of change within
the community. The abakama remained the single most
powerful constituent even though they functioned with increasingly ineffectual ritual power. They depended more
upon the achievement-oriented enfura than upon the
ascriptive leaders for political support. The enfura
themselves were representatives par excellence of the
minority of Kerebe who took advantage of economic opportunities to gain material possessions. These possessions

enhanced their social status while simultaneously enabling them to gain access to the abakama. In return for their support of the abakama, the enfura acquired a measure of security through access to the abakama's ritual authority and his sympathetic hearing of legal or extralegal disputes. An examination of the abafumu's (medicine men) role reveals an increasing reliance upon their acquired mechanical and ritual procedures for resolving extralegal disputes, i.e., sorcery. Their changing role again illustrates the need for new means to counteract novel conditions, in the face of which former methods were ineffectual. Finally, the lowly aberu and abazana reveal how an institution formerly associated with punishment and welfare was transformed into an institution designed to provide labor as well as to augment a clan's numbers. These are examples of the complex social responses to circumstance attending long-distance trade.

Even the increase in Kerebe agricultural productivity was a response to specific needs. In this sphere the society displayed an aggressive, productive attempt to overcome its basic insecurity. Surplus grain was produced and then exchanged with neighboring communities that had an urgent need for this commodity, a need usually associated with drought and subsequent famine. The acquired product, whether cattle, goats, aberu/abazana, hoes, hides, or tobacco, was then used to enhance or to fortify one's position. Those who aspired to become enfura—achievers—sought greater security within a troubled environment.

The intertwined relationship of medical, economic, social, and political developments militates against a compartmentalized and isolated analysis of any single component. For example, it has been stated that the introduction of new crops to Tanzania offset effects of warfare, slave trading, and famine to the degree "that the country's total population grew significantly in the nineteenth century. . . ."[3] New crops such as rice, maize, and cassava certainly had an impact upon those people who adopted them, but to give them credit for significantly increasing the country's population does not take into adequate consideration concomitant developments in other spheres, particularly the medical. "Some evidence" cited for population increase includes the "growing fragmentation of clan land and an increasing number of inter-clan disputes," the "spread of settlement up and down the slopes of Kilimanjaro and Meru and . . . the colonization of new land in Unyanyembe and Usukuma."[4] In all cited cases the apparent population increase is more likely to have been a product of commercial opportunities and intraclan as well as interclan sorcery/witchcraft problems, that is, the movement of people as a result of tensions stemming from sickness, death and strained clan relations. The signs of assumed population increase actually may have been signs of population decline.

There is every reason to assume that the era of long-distance trade was characterized by a remarkable increase in the extent of violence and civil strife in East Africa. What Kiwanuka has observed among the Ganda certainly holds true for the Kerebe: "For all people, particularly those in politics, Kiganda society concealed a life of fear and anxiety. . . ."[5] Indicators of tension such as internal political strife and sorcery accusations, just as much as the importation of serviles into a community, reveal an abnormal social situation, an aberration of an earlier condition. They are manifestations of an unhealthy society, that at the same time demonstrate the desire to overcome disruptive influences.

The perspective offered by the Kerebe is in some ways unusual. They represent a small but enterprising trading population that apprehensively and opportunistically viewed the activities of aliens and stronger neighbors, a society that advanced its own welfare when the opportunity arose. With other societies in eastern Africa, they also experienced the external stimuli symbolized by the presence of Swahili and Arab traders—trading opportunities and disease. In this respect their historical experience does not contrast significantly with those of other societies. This shared experience was the bond of commonality among East

African peoples of the nineteenth century. During this eventful period these peoples manifested a strong, forthright determination to take advantage of opportunities and to overcome enormous, novel obstacles. The resultant social tensions emanating from radically altered social roles is not difficult to understand. It was the price required in developing the art of survival.

Notes

1. Terence Ranger, "Introduction," *Emerging Themes of African History,* ed., T.O. Ranger (Nairobi, 1968), xiii.

2. Kiwanuka also notes the substantial impact diseases made upon the Ganda in the late nineteenth century; see *A History of Buganda,* 151.

3. John Iliffe, "Agricultural Change in Modern Tanganyika," Historical Association of Tanzania Paper No. 10 (Nairobi, 1971), 9.

4. *Ibid.*

5. Kiwanuka, *A History of Buganda,* 154.

Sources

Oral Sources

Oral information provides the bulk of the evidence used in reconstructing Kerebe history. Each informant is identified by name, clan (when Jita or Kara appear in parenthesis it refers to an ethnic group rather than a clan), village and approximate age in 1968. The letters s/o mean "son of." An asterisk indicates that the individual was literate.

Adolf Malimu s/o Kalimanzila (Jita), Namagamba, 60s. Malimu provided information about his father's journeys as an envoy for Omukama Rukonge. Interviewed on January 24, 1969.

Alipyo Mnyaga, * Miro, Bukonyo, 60s. As a former secretary of Omukama Ruhumbika, and as a district court magistrate in 1968, Mr. Mnyaga was in a position to learn significant information about the royal clan and has made an effort to remember it. Interviewed on September 7, 1968.

Alphonce Golita Mukamabili s/o Mukaka, * Silanga, Lugongo, 70s. During the regency of Omukama Lukumbuzya, this man, a son of Omukama Mukaka, acted as regent for over a decade. His knowledge of the precolonial period was meager, in contrast to the information he possessed on political activities since the 1930s. Interviewed on November 7, 1968.

Aniceti Kitereza, * Silanga, Nakisilila, 73. Mr. Kitereza has produced a number of lengthy accounts of Kerebe customs. His recorded version of the royal clan's history provides the basis for a history used within the primary schools of the community. He is not regarded as an historian nor is his collected historical information outstanding, but within the ethnographic sphere he is one of the most sensitive and lucid informants. Periodic interviews between July 15, 1968, and March 15, 1969.

Bahitwa s/o Lugambage, Kula, Harwego, 82. Bahitwa is the remaining official Kerebe historian of the old order. His information has significant potential for assisting in shedding light on the pre-1700 era. He is not renowned for his accuracy on specific details, but his breadth of history permits a cautious interpretation of the major trends. Periodic interviews between July 15, 1968, and March 15, 1969, with increasing frequency after January, 1969.

Bundala Kakenki, Kula, —, 60s. He provided information concerning his clan. Interviewed September 13, 1968.

Buyanza Bernardino "Musa" s/o Nansagate, * Silanga, Kiyozu, 86. His information on nineteenth century political, social, and economic developments provides the basis for much of the material of that century discussed above. He was an extremely valuable informant for all subjects that fell within his period of expertise. His service within the German military forces from 1904 to 1918 exposed him to cosmopolitan perspectives denied to men of more insular experiences. Frequent interviews between September 1, 1968, and March 15, 1969.

Celestine Mahoro, Miro, Musozi, 90s. He provided limited information on life at the end of the 1800s. Interviewed July 25, 1968.

Chavery Wanzura s/o Magoyelo (Kara), Bulamba, 70s. Information about his father's two journeys to Takama during the reign of Machunda was extremely valuable in reconstructing the early contacts between the Kerebe and Ganda. Interviewed November 7, 1968.

Darmas Biseko, Lanzi, Nakabungo, 30s. He provided information concerning his father, who was reported to be one of the first Kerebe to speak Swahili and consequently was one of the first non-Silanga appointed to the position of headman during the reign of Rukonge. Interviewed August 8, 1968.

Daudi Musombwa, * Gembe, Kibara, 70s. He related numerous traditions and was able to portray a view of the nineteenth century that was in essential agreement with Buyanza's traditions. Interviewed August 9, 1968.

Donald Mganga s/o Rulago, Nampanga, Bwiro, 40s. He had uncovered a number of metal implements, including two hoes, in his field. The hoes were not of the Zinza shape and he consequently inquired about their origin. I visited him, acquired one of the hoes, and proceeded to determine its possible origin. One of the old smiths on the island identified the hoe as a product of Ngurimi. The hoe was subsequently placed in the National Museum in Dar es Salaam. Interviewed September 13, 1968.

Gregory Nkomangi s/o Babili (Ruri), Musozi, 40s. He provided excellent information on musicians and musical games in the present century. Interviewed December 16, 1968.

Jeremi Mukama Baruza, * Singo (Jita), Bulamba, 70s. He gave information about his father's migration to Bukerebe from Majita. Interviewed September 12, 1968.

Johanna Constantine, Zubwa –, 60s. He provided information concerning his clan. Interviewed September 7, 1968.

Josephat Mdono s/o Katundali, * Hira, Musozi, 30s. He acted as my research assistant for three months and was instrumental in introducing me to the Kerebe and their way of life from July 10, 1968, through October, 1968.

Joseph Samula, * Gembe, Hamkoko, 70s. He contributed information on his clan and his own educational experience. Interviewed July 26, 1968.

Kabunazya, Tundu, –, 60s. He provided information on his clan's history. Interviewed August 23, 1968.

Kaliga s/o Lwambali, Sita, Kitale, 70s. Obtaining information from men residing around the residence of the former omukama proved to be difficult; uncooperativeness and suspicion were common traits of potentially valuable informants. Kaliga was one of the few men representing the former power structure who readily provided information about his clan and their relation to the royal clan. His father had been guardian of the omukama's rainpot. Interviewed August 30 and December 17 and 19, 1968.

Kammando Mzinza, * Kula, Buye, 60s. His information on the Kula clan was incomplete, but did corroborate Bahitwa's account to a degree. Interviewed September 17, 1968.

Kazimili s/o Mazige, Zubwa, Hekerege, 60s. An accomplished *enanga* player, he gave valuable information on the role of this instrument in Kerebe society as well as providing a number of song texts from the 1800s. Interviewed November 4, 1968.

Kilemezi, Mwizarubi (Jita), Bukonyo, 70s. An accomplished musician from the pre-1940 era, he gave an account of musical developments in the present century. Interviewed December 13, 1968.

Lazali Katundali, Hira, Musozi, 50s. He provided information on his clan's history. Interviewed July 25, 1968.

Lazaro s/o Machunda, Silanga, Dar es Salaam, 110. The sole surviving son of Omukama Machunda (died ca. 1869) he went into exile during Rukonge's reign and eventually became a part of an Arab caravan to the coast, where he remained. He unfortunately could recall few events from the 1800s, with the interesting exception of a few key lines from songs he had sung over seventy-five years ago. Interviewed July 10, 1968.

Luguga s/o Tuuna, Songe, Buzunze, 70s. He provided information on his clan's history. Interviewed August 23, 2968.

Lwakanyaga, Songe, Nakatunguru, 70s. He provided information on his clan's role during the 1800s. The Songe clan made wooden utensils for the omukama, and it was therefore assumed that they were responsible for producing the piece of wooden sculpture which the Germans took from Rukonge in 1895. In fact a Nyamwezi had produced the figure. Interviewed August 23, 1968.

Magoma s/o Kitina, Silanga, Nebuye, 60s. Magoma prided

himself on being knowledgeable about his clan's traditions, and in fact he gave an extensive narrative of the royal clan's trek from Isene to Ihangiro to Bukerebe. He was not as knowledgeable about other topics. Interviewed January 22, 1969.

Makene s/o Ikongolero, Hira, Kihungula, 70s. Makene was the most knowledgeable member of the Hira clan on its history especially for the pre-Silanga era. His information paled along-side that of Bahitwa, but it provided a valuable corroboration of Bahitwa's information. This was particularly important for obtaining evidence concerning blacksmithing before 1700. Makene confirmed that his clan had at one time "beat" iron, an admission that gave credence to Bahitwa's traditions on this sensitive topic. Interviewed occasionally between July 20, 1968, and March 1, 1969.

Makeremu s/o Manyanga, Hesera, Harwego, 30s. All senior members of this clan are deceased, but Makeremu shed light on his ancestors' introduction of the elephant-hunting association into Bukerebe from Usukuma. Interviewed January 16, 1969.

Makomba, Kula, Nakatunguru, 50s. A musician and craftsman, Makomba shed considerable light upon the Kerebe musical games of the present century. Some of his pieces of sculpture were used as *amaleba* in games; one piece is now within the Fine Arts Museum, Indiana University. Interviewed occasionally between September, 1968, and February, 1969.

Malobo Bangala s/o Makene, Hira, Kihungula, 40s. He provided information on musical games of the present century. Interviewed October 3, 1968.

Manumbi, Zandwa (Jita), Kilimabuye, 60s. He provided information about his father's migration to Bukerebe. Interviewed September 6, 1968.

Manyanya s/o Nyawawa, Lega, Butimba, 90s. Manyanya is not a Kerebe, but he was questioned about sculpturing in Butimba in the late nineteenth century. His information was useful in revealing the nature of trading activities in the region before 1900. Interviewed September 27, 1968.

Masalu Kapongo, royal clan, Chumve, Nassa chiefdom, Usukuma, 90s. His information was helpful in disclosing the relationship between the related royal clans of Bukerebe and Nassa. Interviewed September 21, 1968.

Matabi s/o Kumaya, Songe, Musozi, 90s. Matabi related information about his clan and musical practices at the turn of the present century. Interviewed August 22, and September 10, 1968.

Matuli, Yango, Nakatunguru, 60s. He provided information concerning his clan's history and considerable information on musical games in the present century. His personal experiences revealed a great deal about Kerebe attitudes during the time of my stay on the island. Interviewed occasionally between August, 1968, and January, 1969.

Mbaruku Nyamlazi, Kana, —, 70s. His ancestors came to Bukerebe from Irugwa, an island that came under Silanga control in the 1600s. Interviewed September 17, 1968.

Mfaume s/o Gatalya, * Silanga, Nampanga, 60s. Mfaume had been an interpreter for the British colonial government and had remained away from Bukerebe for a number of years before retiring on the island. While he did not possess much information, he was extremely helpful in explaining the purpose of my activities to Buyanza, who was initially skeptical of my intentions. Consequently, Mfaume's intervention on my behalf persuaded the man who eventually contributed most to my collection of oral data to cooperate with me. Occasional meetings between September, 1968, through March, 1969.

Mpehi s/o Magesa, Himba, Musozi, 70s. Mpehi contributed substantially to my understanding of the role played by hippo hunters in Kerebe life. Interviewed August 8, 22, and November 6, 1968, and January 30, 1969.

Mongelele Bulolima s/o Manoko, Gamba (Jita), Kilimabuye, 50s. He is an outstanding musician on the island. He contributed information about the introduction and role of the *endongo,* a single-stringed bowed instrument. A number of his songs were recorded and are on tapes preserved by the Archives of Traditional Music, Indiana University and the Music Conservatoire of Tanzania situated in Dar es Salaam. Interviewed occasionally between August, 1968, and February, 1969.

Muganga Golita, Silanga, Mahande, 60s. A renowned musician, he gave historical information on the development of Kerebe musical traditions during the past century. Interviewed December 12, 1968.

Muganzansoni, Yango, Kagunguli, 60s. Provided information on the history of his clan. Interviewed September 10, 1968.

Musumali, Gamba (Jita), Kilimabuye, 70s. He provided information about the migration of his father to Bukerebe. Interviewed September 6, 1968.

Mzugulu Ndozero, Bwarumi, Lutali, 80s. Mzugulu provided information about his clan and about the relationship of the people on Irugwa Island to Bukerebe. Interviewed September 17, 1968.

Namtamwa, * Songe, Gallu settlement scheme, 60s. He gave information concerning his educational experience. Although he knew limited amounts of history about his clan, he was most knowledgeable about administrative structure and developments since the 1930s. Interviewed August 26, 1968.

Neki Kageri, Bwarumi, —, 60s. He provided information about his clan. Interviewed August 23, 1968.

Ngilimba, Songe, Buzunze, 60s. He provided information about his clan. Interviewed August 31, 1968.

Ngoloma s/o Lamusyeta, Sindi, Musozi, 50s. He gave information concerning his clan's origins. Interviewed January 7, 1969.

Nfuma, Miro, Bukindo, 70s. He provided information about his clan. Interviewed August 31, 1968.

Ntobesya Halanga, Hindi, Nakabungo, 70s. He provided information about his clan. Interviewed August 8, 1968.

Palapala s/o Kazwegulu, Silanga, Kitale, 60s. His father was a former Siba. His information about the royal clan was reasonably broad and his information shed light on the administrative role of the Siba within the Silanga administrative hierarchy. Interviewed September 30, 1968.

Padre Petro s/o Chavery, * (Kara), Itira Parish, 50s. Padre Petro informed me about his grandfather's exploits under Machunda and directed me to his father. He shared and discussed ideas concerning Kerebe history. Interviewed August 26, 1968.

Petro Mahugo, Chuma, — 60s. He provided information about his clan. Interviewed September 12, 1968.

Rukonge Biseko, Kula, Butiriti, 60s. He provided information about his clan. Interviewed July 26, 1968.

Simeo Rubuzi, * Siba (Kara), Murutunguru, 60s. He is an aspiring historian, emulating both Aniceti Kitereza and Bahitwa. Since he is of Kara origin, his view of Kerebe history is valuable. He has attempted to write history, and lives for the day when he can get his material published. I was unable to use much of his information because it had been greatly influenced by Kitereza and Bahitwa and he had extracted portions from the material used by primary school teachers. He was not in the tradition of a Kerebe historian, nor were his ancestors important within the chiefdom. His information was collected for a utilitarian purpose, to publish a history book that would be used by the local schools and provide an income for himself. Interviewed occasionally between August, 1968, and February, 1969.

Walji Rahani, —, Nansio, 80s. As one of the first Asian shopkeepers to establish a *duka* (shop) on the island, Walji provided valuable comments concerning his half-century as an alien businessman on the island. Interviewed January 29, 1969.

Wanzala s/o Buzuzya, Miro, Rubya, 50s. He provided information about his father's exploits as a sculptor in the twentieth century and thereby helped to resolve a vexing problem focusing on the sculpturing tradition of the Kerebe. Interviewed September 30, 1968.

Zumbula s/o Gilolo, Yango (Jita), Guguyu, 80s. A retired blacksmith, Zumbula provided significant information about his own family, who immigrated into Bukerebe during Machunda's reign and who continue as blacksmiths on the island. Although referred to as Jita, the clan's origins go back to Buha and Bunyoro. Zumbula was able to identify two non-Zinza hoes that were found on the island. Interviewed occasionally between October, 1968, and February, 1969.

Documentary Sources

Tanzania: Tanzania National Archives, Dar es Salaam

The National Archives contains copies of correspondence from members of the German Antislavery Society to the parent organization in Coblenz, in addition to German colonial officials' correspondence pertaining to the Society (G. 1/30).

The Mwanza District (Province) Book in the Archives also contains valuable historical notes on the Kerebe and neighboring societies.

Anon. "The Ukerewe Tradition (concerning the foundation of Ruhinda's kingdom)." Enclosed in A. M. D. Turnbull. "Notes on the History of Uzinza."

Turnbull, A. M. D. "Tribal History and Legends on Ukerewe Chiefdom."

————. "Notes on the History of Uzinza, Its Rulers and People." Williams, O. Guise. "Tribal History and Legends—Sukuma."

Tanzania: University of Dar es Salaam, Library

Relevant papers within the Hans Cory collection include the following:

Anon. "History of Ukerewe Chiefdom." No. 290.

Baker, E. C. "Report on Administrative and Social Conditions in the Ukerewe Chiefdom." No. 9.

Cory, Hans. "The Bahinda in Bumbwiga (a Bukoba Chiefdom)." No. 40.

―――――― . "(Banyamwezi) The Country and Its Inhabitants." No. 43.

―――――― . "The Coming of the Wasilanga Chiefs." No. 30.

―――――― . "The Earliest History of Bukoba." No. 41.

―――――― . "Report on the Pre-European Tribal Organizations in Musoma District." No. 173.

―――――― . "Ukerewe Local Government and Land Tenure." No. 420.

Turnbull, A. M. D. "Usambiro Sultanate, . . . ; History of the Bahinda Rule in Uzinza." No. 416.

―――――― . "Wahima." No. 231.

"Kerebe manuscripts from Nansio, Ukerewe." Microfilm. These recorded historical traditions of Bahitwa s/o Lugambage and Simeo Rubuzi are available in English translation for examination in the University of Dar es Salaam Library.

Tanzania: Ukerewe (Bukerebe)

Valuable written but unpublished sources of information in French and Kikerebe are available in the Roman Catholic parishes at Kagunguli and Murutunguru:

Anon. "Historia ya Ukerewe." Mimeographed manuscript, Teacher Training College, Murutunguru.

Kitereza, Aniceti. "Omwanzuro gw' Abakama ba Bukerebe." Typed Kikerebe manuscript.

Simard, J.A. "Religion d'Ukerewe ou résumé des connaissances religieuses des Bakerewe." Typed manuscript.

_____. "Vocabulaire Français-Kikerewe." Typed manuscript.

_____. "Vocabulaire Kikerewe-Français." Typed manuscript.

**Tanzania: Nyegezi (near Mwanza),
Regional House, White Fathers**

Extant diaries of the Roman Catholic White Fathers are available from numerous missions in the district for perusal. Those consulted included the following:

Diary: Notre Dame de Kamoga (Bukumbi), 1883-1888, 1893-1899.

Rome: Mother House of the White Fathers (Padri Bianchi)

Much of the information extracted from diaries that was sent by missionaries to the Mother House and subsequently published in the order's periodical, the Chronique de la Société des Missionnaires d'Afrique, *is preserved in Rome. The complete diaries themselves, however, remain at Nyegezi in Tanzania if extant. Reports and survey information is also available for perusal in Rome. The consulted diaries and reports of the White Fathers, written in French, include the following:*

Diary: La Mission du Bukumbi (alias Kamoga), 1889-1893.

Diary: Ukerewe, 1897-1904.

Correspondence from Ukerewe, 1896-1922.

R. P. Bourget. "Notes sur les Bagwe."

R. P. Joseph Gass. "Les Bagwe: Croyances, Superstitions, Sorcelleries," 1927.

Vicariats de Mwanza et de Maswa. "Table d'enquetes sur les moeurs et coutumes indigènes—Tribu des Basukuma."

Chronique de la Société des Missionnaires d'Afrique, 1878-1898.

London: Church Missionary Society

Correspondence to and from missionaries in eastern Africa is available for research. The earliest letters from any given area frequently contain valuable information on the community in which the missionary was residing at the time. The consulted information included the following:

The Nyanza Mission, 1876-1898.

Walker Papers, the personal correspondence of R.H. Walker to members of his family and friends—a keen observer.

London: London Missionary Society

The Observations recorded by Dr. E. J. Southon are particularly valuable in assessing the effects of long-distance trade upon some of the Nyamwezi.

Central Africa, 1876-1885.

Relevant Published Primary and Secondary Works

Alpers, Edward A. "The Coast and the Development of the Caravan Trade." *A History of Tanzania,* ed. I. N. Kimambo and A. J. Temu. Nairobi: East African Publishing House, 1969.

_____ . "The East African Slave Trade." Historical Association of Tanzania, Paper No. 3. Nairobi: East African Publishing House, 1967.

_____ . "The Nineteenth Century: Prelude to Colonialism." *Zamani; A Survey of East African History,* ed. B. A. Ogot and J. A. Kieran. Nairobi: East African Publishing House, 1968.

————. "Re-thinking African Economic History: A Contribution to the Discussion of the Roots of Under-Development." *Ufahamu,* 3, 3 (1973), 97-129.

Anon. "Excerpt from Proceedings of the Royal Geographical Society Concerning Erhardt's Map." *Church Missionary Intelligencer,* VII (1856), 190-92.

Anon. *Près des Grand Lacs, par les missionnaires de S. Em. le Cardinal Lavigerie.* Paris, 1885.

Austen, Ralph A. *Northwest Tanzania under German and British Rule.* New Haven: Yale University Press, 1968.

————. "Ntemiship, Trade, and State-Building: Political Development among the Western Bantu of Tanzania." *Eastern African History,* ed. Daniel F. McCall, N.R. Bennett, and Jeffrey Butler. Boston University Papers on Africa, III. New York: Praeger, 1969.

————. "Patterns of Development in Nineteenth-Century East Africa." *African Historical Studies,* IV, 3 (1971), 645-57.

Beachey, R. W. "The Arms Trade in East Africa in the Late Nineteenth Century." *Journal of African History,* III, 3 (1962), 451-67.

Beattie, J. H. M. "Initiation into the Cwezi Spirit Possession Cult in Bunyoro." *African Studies,* 16, 3 (1957), 150-61.

————. "Sorcery in Bunyoro." *Witchcraft and Sorcery in East Africa,* ed. John Middleton and E. H. Winter. London: Routledge and Kegan Paul, 1963.

————. "Spirit Mediumship in Bunyoro." *Spirit Mediumship and Society in Africa,* ed. John Beattie and John Middleton. London: Routledge and Kegan Paul, 1969.

Becker, Jérôme. *La Vie en Afrique; ou, Trois ans dans l'Afrique centrale.* 2 vols. Paris: J. Lebègue, 1887.

Beidelman, Thomas O. "Myth, Legend and Oral History: A Kaguru Traditional Text." *Anthropos,* 65, 1/2 (1970), 74-97.

_____ . "Witchcraft in Ukaguru." *Witchcraft and Sorcery in East Africa,* ed. John Middleton and E. A. Winter. London: Routledge and Kegan Paul, 1963.

Bennett, Norman R. "The Arab Impact." *Zamani; A Survey of East African History,* ed. B. A. Ogot and J. A. Kieran. Nairobi: East African Publishing House, 1968.

_____ . *Mirambo of Tanzania, ca. 1840-1884.* New York: Oxford University Press, 1971.

_____ . ed. *Stanley's Despatches to the New York Herald, 1871-1872, 1874-1877.* Boston: Boston University Press, 1970.

Betbeder, Paul. "The Kingdom of Buzinza." *Journal of World History,* XIII, 4 (1971), 736-60.

Brard, Père. "Rapport du P. Brard sur les tribus insulaires du Nyanza Meridional." *Chronique trimestrielle de la Société des missionnaires d'Afrique,* 73 (1897), 152-57.

Bridges, R. C. "Introduction to the Second Edition." *Travels, Researches, and Missionary Labours.* J. Lewis Krapf. London: Frank Cass, 1968.

Burdo, Adolphe. *Les Belges dans l'Afrique Centrale.* Vol. I. *De Zanzibar du Lac Tanganika.* Bruxelles: P. Maes, 1886.

Burton, Richard F. *The Lake Regions of Central Africa.* 2 vols. London: Longman Green, 1860.

_____ . "The Lake Regions of Central Equatorial Africa." *Journal of the Royal Geographical Society,* XXIX (1859), 1-454.

Cameron, Verney L. *Across Africa.* New York: Harper Bros., 1877.

Chacker, Eunice A. "Early Arab and European Contacts with Ukerewe." *Tanzania Notes and Records,* 68 (1968), 75-86.

Christie, James. *Cholera Epidemics in East Africa.* London: Macmillan, 1876.

Cohen, David. "Agenda for African Economic History." *The Journal of Economic History,* XXXI, 1 (1971), 208-21.

_____ . *The Historical Tradition of Busoga: Mukama and Kintu.* Oxford: Clarendon Press, 1972.

_____ . "A Survey of Interlacustrine Chronology." *Journal of African History,* XI, 2 (1970), 177-202.

Colson, Elizabeth. "Spirit Possession among the Tonga of Zambia." *Spirit Mediumship and Society in Africa,* ed. John Beattie and John Middleton. London: Routledge and Kegan Paul, 1969.

Curtin, Philip D. "Epidemiology and the Slave Trade." *Political Science Quarterly,* LXXXIII, 2 (1968), 190-216.

_____ . "Field Techniques for Collecting and Processing Oral Data." *Journal of African History,* IX, 3 (1968), 367-85.

Davidson, Basil. *The African Genius; An Introduction to African Cultural and Social History.* Boston: Little, Brown, 1970.

Denoon, Donald and Adam Kuper. "Nationalist Historians in Search of a Nation." *African Affairs,* 69 (1970), 429-49.

De Rosemond, C. C. "Iron Smelting in the Kahama District." *Tanganyika Notes and Records,* 16 (1943), 79-84.

Dike, K. O. *Trade and Politics in the Niger Delta, 1830-1885.* Oxford: Clarendon Press, 1956.

Ehret, Christopher. "Cattle-Keeping and Milking in Eastern and Southern African History: The Linguistic Evidence." *Journal of African History,* VIII, 1 (1967), 1-17.

_____ . "Cushites and the Highland and Plains Nilotes." *Zamani; A Survey of East African History,* ed. B. A. Ogot and J. A. Kieran. Nairobi: East African Publishing House, 1968.

_____. *Southern Nilotic History.* Evanston: Northwestern University Press, 1971.

Emin Pasha in Central Africa; Being a Collection of His Letters and Journals. Ed. G. Schweinfurth et al.; tr. Mrs. R. W. Felkin. London: G. Philip, 1888.

Evans-Pritchard, E. E. *Nuer Religion.* Oxford: Clarendon Press, 1956.

———— . *Witchcraft, Oracles and Magic among the Azande.* Oxford: Clarendon Press, 1937.

Felkin, Robert W. "Notes on the Waganda Tribe of Central Africa." *Proceedings of the Royal Society of Edinburgh,* 13, (1886), 699-770.

———— . "Uganda." *The Scottish Geographical Magazine,* II (1886), 208-26.

Fosbrooke, H. A. "Some Aspects of the Kimwani Fishing Culture." *Journal of the Royal Anthropological Institute,* LXIV (1934), 1-22.

Gelfand, Michael. *The African Witch; With Particular Reference to Witchcraft Beliefs and Practice among the Shona of Rhodesia.* Edinburgh: E. and S. Livingstone, 1967.

Good, Charles M. *Rural Markets and Trade in East Africa.* The University of Chicago, Department of Geography, Research Paper No. 128. Chicago: University of Chicago, 1970.

Grant, J. A. "Summary of Observation on the Geography, Climate, and Natural History of the Lake Region of Equatorial Africa, Made by the Speke and Grant Expedition, 1860-1863." *Journal of the Royal Geographical Society,* XLII (1872), 243-342.

Gray, John M. "Arabs on Lake Victoria. Some Revisions." *Uganda Journal,* XXII (1958), 76-81.

Gray, Richard and David Birmingham, eds. *Pre-Colonial African Trade; Essays on Trade in Central and Eastern Africa before 1900.* New York: Oxford University Press, 1970.

Gray, Robert F. "Structural Aspects of Mbugwe Witchcraft." *Witchcraft and Sorcery in East Africa,* ed. John Middleton and E. H. Winter. London: Routledge and Kegan Paul, 1963.

Gulliver, P. H. "A Tribal Map of Tanganyika." *Tanganyika Notes and Records,* 52 (1959), 61-74.

Guthrie, Malcolm. *The Classification of the Bantu Language.* London: International African Institute, 1948.

————. *Comparative Bantu.* Vol III. Farnborough, England: Gregg International Publishers, 1970.

Hartwig, Charlotte M. "Music in Kerebe Culture." *Anthropos,* 67 (1972), 449-64.

Hartwig, Charlotte M. and Gerald W. "Aniceti Kitereza: A Kerebe Novelist." *Research in African Literatures,* III, 2 (1972), 162-70.

Hartwig, Gerald W. "The Bakerebe." *Journal of World History,* XIV, 2 (1972), 353-76.

————. "Bukerebe, the Church Missionary Society, and East African Politics, 1877-1878." *African Historical Studies,* I, 2 (1968), 211-32.

————. "A Historical Perspective of Kerebe Sculpturing-Tanzania." *Tribus,* 18 (1969), 85-102.

————. "The Historical and Social Role of Kerebe Music." *Tanzania Notes and Records,* 70 (1969), 41-56.

————. "Long-Distance Trade and the Evolution of Sorcery among the Kerebe." *African Historical Studies,* IV, 3 (1971), 505-24.

————. "Oral Data and Its Historical Function in East Africa." *The International Journal of African Historical Studies,* VII, 3 (1974).

————. "Oral Traditions Concerning the Early Iron Age in Northwestern Tanzania." *African Historical Studies,* IV, 1 (1971), 93-114.

————. "The Victoria Nyanza as a Trade Route in the Nineteenth Century." *Journal of African History,* XI, 4 (1970), 535-52.

Henige, David P. "Reflections on Early Interlacustrine Chronology: An Essay in Source Criticism." *Journal of African History,* XV, 1 (1974), 27-46.

Holmes, C. F. and R. A. Austen. "The Pre-Colonial Sukuma." *Journal of World History,* XIV, 2 (1972), 377-405.

Hopkins, A. G. *An Economic History of West Africa.* New York: Columbia University Press, 1973.

Hurel, Eugene. "Religion et vie domestique des Bakerewe." *Anthropos,* VI (1911), 62-94, 276-301.

Iliffe, John. "Agricultural Change in Modern Tanganyika." Historical Association of Tanzania, Paper No. 10. Nairobi: East African Publishing House, 1971.

Isaacman, Allen. "The Origin, Formation and Early History of the Chikunda of South Central Africa." *Journal of African History,* XIII, 3 (1972), 443-61.

Ishumi, Abel G. M. "The Kingdom of Kiziba." *Journal of World History,* XIII, 4 (1971), 714-35.

Jones, D. H. "Problems of African Chronology." *Journal of African History,* XI, 2 (1970), 161-76.

Jones, William O. *Manioc in Africa.* Stanford: Stanford University Press, 1959.

Kaijage, Frederick J. "Kyamutwara." *Journal of World History,* XIII, 3 (1971), 542-74.

Karugire, Samwiri Rubaraza. *A History of the Kingdom of Nkore in Western Uganda to 1896.* Oxford: Clarendon Press, 1971.

Katoke, I. K. "Karagwe: A Pre-Colonial State." *Journal of World History,* XIII, 3 (1971), 515-41.

————. "The Kingdom of Ihangiro." *Journal of World History,* XIII, 4 (1971), 700-14.

Kimambo, Isaria N. "The Economic History of the Kamba, 1850-1950." *Hadith,* 2 (1970), 79-103.

————. *A Political History of the Pare of Tanzania, c. 1500-1900.* Nairobi: East African Publishing House, 1969.

Kitereza, Aniceti. "How Men and Women Came to Live Together," ed. and intro. Charlotte and Gerald Hartwig. *Natural History,* LXXIX, 1 (1970), 9-20.

30 THE ART OF SURVIVAL

Kiwanuka, M. S. M. Semakula. *A History of Buganda; From the Foundation of the Kingdom to 1900.* New York: Africana Publishing Corporation, 1972.

LaFontaine, J. "The Zinza." *East African Chiefs,* ed. Audrey I. Richards. London: Faber and Faber, 1960.

LaFontaine, J. and A. I. Richards. "The Haya." *East African Chiefs,* ed. Audrey Richards. London: Faber and Faber, 1960.

Latham, A. J. H. "Witchcraft Accusations and Economic Tension in Pre-Colonial Old Calabar." *Journal of African History,* XIII, 2 (1972), 349-60.

Lee, S. G. "Spirit Possession among the Zulu." *Spirit Mediumship and Society in Africa,* ed. John Beattie and John Middleton. London: Routledge and Kegan Paul, 1969.

LeVine, Robert A. "Witchcraft and Sorcery in a Gusii Community." *Witchcraft and Sorcery in East Africa,* ed. John Middleton and E. H. Winter. London: Routledge and Kegan Paul, 1963.

Lienhardt, Godfrey. *Divinity and Experience; The Religion of the Dinka.* Oxford: Clarendon Press, 1961.

Ludwig, Heinz Dieter. *Ukara—Ein Sonderfall tropischer Bodennutzung im Raum des Victoria-Sees.* Ifo-Institute für Wirtschaftsforschung München, Afrika-Studien Nr. 22. München: Weltforum Verlag, 1967.

Macfarlane, Alan. *Witchcraft in Tudor and Stuart England.* New York: Harper and Row, 1970.

————. "Witchcraft in Tudor and Stuart Essex." *Witchcraft Confessions and Accusations,* ed. Mary Douglas. London: Tavistock, 1970.

MacGaffey, Wyatt. "Comparative Analysis of Central African Religions." *Africa,* XLII, 1 (1972), 21-31.

McMaster, David N. *A Subsistence Crop Geography of Uganda.* The World Land Use Survey, Occasional Papers No. 2. Ed. L. Dudley Stamp. Bude, England: Geographical Publications, 1962.

Marwick, Max. "The Social Context of Cewa Witch Beliefs." *Africa,* XXII, 2 (1952), 120-35.

———. "The Sociology of Sorcery in a Central African Tribe." *African Studies,* 22, 1 (1963), 1-21.

———. *Sorcery in Its Social Setting.* Manchester, England: Manchester University Press, 1965.

Mbiti, John S. *African Religions and Philosophy.* London: Heinemann Educational Books, 1969.

Meillassoux, Claude, ed. *The Development of Indigenous Trade and Markets in West Africa.* London: Oxford University Press, 1971.

Meyer, Hans Heinrich J., ed. "Ostafrika und Kamerun." *Das Deutsch Kolonialreich.* Bd. I. Leipzig: Verlag des Bibliographischen-instituts, 1909.

Middleton, John. "Witchcraft and Sorcery in Lugbara." *Witchcraft and Sorcery in East Africa,* ed. John Middleton and E. H. Winter. London: Routledge and Kegan Paul, 1963.

Nicholls, Christine S. *The Swahili Coast: Politics, Diplomacy and Trade on the East African Littoral, 1798-1856.* London: Allen and Unwin, 1971.

Ogot, B. A. *History of the Southern Luo; Migration and Settlement.* Nairobi: East African Publishing House, 1967.

Oliver, Roland. "Discernible Developments in the Interior, c. 1500-1840." *History of East Africa.* Vol. I. Ed. Roland Oliver and Gervase Mathew. Oxford: Clarendon Press, 1963.

Omer-Cooper, J. D. *The Zulu Aftermath.* London: Longmans, 1966.

Pender-Cudlip, Patrick. "Encyclopedic Informants and Early Interlacustrine History." *The International Journal of African Historical Studies,* VI, 2 (1973), 198-210.

———. "Oral Traditions and Anthropological Analysis: Some Contemporary Myths." *Azania,* VII (1972), 3-24.

Posnansky, Merrick. "The Excavation of an Ankole Capital Site at Bweyorere." *Uganda Journal*, XXXII, 2 (1968), 165-82.

Pruen, S. Tristram. *The Arab and the African*. London: Seeley and Co., 1891.

Ranger, Terence, ed. *Emerging Themes of African History*. Nairobi: East African Publishing House, 1968.

──── . "The Movement of Ideas, 1850-1939." *A History of Tanzania*, ed. I. N. Kimambo and A. J. Temu. Nairobi: East African Publishing House, 1969.

──── . "The 'New Historiography' in Dar es Salaam: An Answer." *African Affairs*, 70, 278 (1971), 50-61.

──── . "Recent Developments in the Study of African Religious and Cultural History and Their Relevance for the Historiography of the Diaspora." *Ufahamu*, IV, 2 (1973), 17-34.

Ranger, T. O. and I. N. Kimambo, eds. *The Historical Study of African Religion*. Berkeley and Los Angeles: University of California Press, 1972.

Redmayne, Alison. "The War Trumpets and Other Mistakes in the History of the Hehe." *Anthropos*, 65, 1/2 (1970), 98-109.

Richards, Audrey I. "The Ganda." *East African Chiefs*, ed. Audrey I. Richards. London: Faber and Faber, 1960.

──── . "A Modern Movement of Witch-Finders." *Africa*, VIII, 4 (1935), 448-61.

Roberts, Andrew D. *A History of the Bemba: Political Growth and Change in North-Eastern Zambia Before 1900*. London: Longman, 1973.

──── . "The Nineteenth Century in Zambia." *Aspects of Central African History*, ed. T. O. Ranger. London: Heinemann Educational Books, 1968.

──── . "The Nyamwezi." *Tanzania Before 1900*, ed. Andrew Roberts. Nairobi: East African Publishing House, 1968.

──── . "Nyamwezi Trade." *Pre-Colonial African Trade*, ed.

Richard Gray and David Birmingham. New York: Oxford University Press, 1970.

_____ . "Political Change in the Nineteenth Century." *A History of Tanzania,* ed. I. N. Kimambo and A. J. Temu. Nairobi: East African Publishing House, 1969.

_____ . *Recording East Africa's Past; A Brief Guide for the Amateur Historian.* Nairobi: East African Publishing House, 1968.

_____ . ed. *Tanzania Before 1900.* Nairobi: East African Publishing House, 1968.

Rodney, Walter. *How Europe Underdeveloped Africa.* London: Bogle-L'Ouverture Publication, 1972.

Roscoe, John. *The Baganda.* London: Macmillan, 1911.

Russell, E. W., ed. *The Natural Resources of East Africa.* Nairobi: East African Literature Bureau, 1962.

Schapera, Isaac. "Sorcery and Witchcraft in Bechuanaland." *Witchcraft and Sorcery,* ed. Max Marwick. Baltimore: Penguin, 1970.

Schynse, August. *A travers l'Afrique avec Stanley et Emin Pasha.* Paris: C. Hespers, 1890.

Senior, H. S. "Sukuma Salt Caravans to Lake Eyasi." *Tanganyika Notes and Records,* 6 (1938), 87-90.

Shorter, Aylward. *Chiefship in Western Tanzania; A Political History of the Kimbu.* Oxford: Clarendon Press, 1972.

_____ . "The Kimbu." *Tanzania Before 1900,* ed. Andrew Roberts. Nairobi: East African Publishing House, 1968.

Soper, R. C. "A General Review of the Early Iron Age of the Southern Half of Africa." *Azania,* VI (1971), 5-38.

_____ . "Iron Age Sites in Chobi Sector, Murchison Falls National Park, Uganda." *Azania,* VI (1971), 53-88.

Soper, R. C. and B. Golden. "An Archaeological Survey of Mwanza Region, Tanzania." *Azania,* IV (1969), 15-80.

Southall, Aidan. "Spirit Possession and Mediumship among the Alur." *Spirit Mediumship and Society in Africa,* ed. John Beattie and John Middleton. London: Routledge and Kegan Paul, 1969.

Southwold, Martin. "The History of a History: Royal Succession in Buganda." *History and Social Anthropology,* ed. I. M. Lewis. London: Tavistock, 1968.

Speke, John H. *Journal of the Discovery of the Source of the Nile.* Edinburgh: Blackwood, 1863.

———. *What Led to the Discovery of the Source of the Nile.* Edinburgh: Blackwood, 1864.

Stahl, Kathleen M. *History of the Chagga People of Kilimanjaro.* London: Mouton, 1964.

Stanley, Henry M. *Through the Dark Continent.* 2 vols. New York: Harper and Brothers, 1878.

Stefaniszyn, Bronislaw. *Social and Ritual Life of the Ambo of Northern Rhodesia.* London: Oxford University Press, 1964.

Stenning, D. J. "The Nyankole." *East African Chiefs,* ed. Audrey I. Richards. London: Faber and Faber, 1960.

Storms, Capitaine. "L'esclavage entre le Tanganika et la côte est." *Le Mouvement Antisclavagiste,* I (1888-89), 14-18.

Stuhlmann, Franz. *Mit Emin Pascha ins Herz von Afrika.* Berlin: D. Reimer, 1894.

Sutton, J. E. G. "The Interior of East Africa." *The African Iron Age,* ed. P. L. Shinnie. Oxford: Clarendon Press, 1971.

———. "The Settlement of East Africa." *Zamani; A Survey of East African History,* ed. B. A. Ogot and J. A. Kieran. Nairobi: East African Publishing House, 1968.

Sutton, J. E. G. and A. D. Roberts. "Uvinza and Its Salt Industry." *Azania,* III (1968), 45-86.

Tanner, R. E. S. "A Prehistoric Culture in Mwanza District, Tanganyika." *Tanganyika Notes and Records,* 47 (1957), 175-86.

_____. "A Series of Rock Paintings Near Mwanza." *Tanganyika Notes and Records,* 34 (1953), 62-7.

Taylor, Brian K. "The Western Lacustrine Bantu." *Ethnographic Survey of Africa; East Central Africa,* Part XIII, ed. Daryll Forde. London: International African Institute, 1962.

ten Raa, Eric. "Sandawe Prehistory and the Vernacular Tradition." *Azania,* IV (1969), 91-104.

Tuden, Arthur and Leonard Plotnicov, ed. *Social Stratification in Africa.* New York: The Free Press, 1970.

Vansina, Jan. "Once Upon a Time: Oral Traditions as History in Africa." *Daedalus,* 100, 2 (1971), 442-68.

Were, Gideon S. *A History of the Abaluyia of Western Kenya.* Nairobi: East African Publishing House, 1967.

Werther, C. Waldemar. *Zum Victoria Nyanza; Eine Antisklaverei-Expedition und Forschungsreise.* Berlin: H. Paetel, n.d. (1894).

Wilson, Charles T. and Robert W. Felkin. *Uganda and the Egyptian Soudan.* 2 vols. London: S. Low Marston, Searle and Rivington, 1882.

Wilson, Monica. "Changes in Social Structure in Southern Africa: The Relevance of Kinship Studies to the Historian." *African Societies in Southern Africa,* ed. Leonard Thompson. New York: Praeger, 1969.

Winter, E. H. "The Enemy Within: Amba Witchcraft." *Witchcraft and Sorcery in East Africa,* ed. John Middleton and E. H. Winter. London: Routledge and Kegan Paul, 1963.

Zimoń, Henryk. "Geschichte des Herrscher-Klans Abasiranga auf der Insel Bukerebe (Tanzania) bis 1895." *Anthropos,* 66, 3/4 (1971), 321-72; 66, 5/6 (1971), 719-52.

Unpublished Secondary Works

Buchanan, Carole A. "The Kitara Complex: The Historical

Tradition of Western Uganda to the 16th Century." Ph.D. dissertation, Indiana University, 1973.

Holmes, Charles F. "A History of the Bakwimba of Usukuma, Tanzania, from Earliest Times to 1945." Ph. D. dissertation, Boston University, 1969.

Jackson, Jr., Kennell A. "An Ethnohistorical Study of the Oral Traditions of the Akamba of Kenya." Ph.D. dissertation, University of California, Los Angeles, 1972.

Katoke, Israel K. "A History of Karagwe: Northwestern Tanzania, ca. 1400-1915." Ph. D. dissertation, Boston University, 1969.

Rowe, John A. "Revolution in Buganda, 1856-1900. Part One: The Reign of Kabaka Mukabya Mutesa, 1856-1884." Ph. D. dissertation, University of Wisconsin, 1966.

Appendixes

Appendix 1

The tentative clan information below is primarily the contribution of Bahitwa and represents clans who have lived at some time in the past in the district of Bukerebe. The approximate time a particular omukama ruled is provided in Appendix 2.

CLAN	TIME OF ARRIVAL	ROUTE TO BUKEREBE	TOTEM
Bago	Omukama Nago	A	bushbuck
Bilizi	pre-Silanga	A	?
Bo (Mbeba)	pre-Silanga	A	?
Bogo	pre-Silanga	A	bushbuck and tri-colored cow (a mottled animal with black, brown, and white coloration)
Bwarumi	pre-Silanga	A	mud fish
Bya	post-Silanga	C	?
Chamba (sub-clan of Timba)	post-Silanga	D	tri-colored cow and warthog

Chambi (sub-clan of Yango)	post-Silanga	D	tri-colored cow
Chuma	post-Silanga	D	hippopotamus
Chwela	pre-Silanga	E	?
Gabe	pre-Silanga	D	bushbuck
Gana (sub-clan of Gara)	pre-Silanga	D	tri-colored cow
Gabo (sub-clan of Gabe)	Omukama Mihigo I		tri-colored cow and wren-like bird
Ganga (sub-clan of Lanzi)	post-Silanga	D	hippopotamus
Ganza (sub-clan of Yanza on Bukara)	pre-Silanga	A	tri-colored cow
Gara	pre-Silanga	D	bushbuck
Gembe (sub-clan of Silanga)	with Silanga	E	wren-like bird and mud fish
Gere (Fwe'ngere)	pre-Silanga	A	?
Geru	pre-Silanga	A	?
Gobera	pre-Silanga	C	?
Goma (sub-clan of Zigaba)	pre-Silanga	A	bushbuck and a guinea fowl
Gulye	pre-Silanga	A	?
Guza (sub-clan of Gembe)	post-Silanga		wren-like bird and mud fish
Haza (sub-clan of Tundu)	with Silanga	F	?
Hembe	with Silanga	F	a type of grass
Hesere	Omukama Mihigo II	A	wren-like bird

Hima	pre-Silanga	A	?
Himba	Omukama Kaseza	?	buffalo
Hindi	Omukama Mihigo	A	mud fish
Hinga	pre-Silanga	A	hartebeest
Hira	pre-Silanga	A	wren-like bird and tri-colored cow
Horo (Horu)	pre-Silanga	A	?
Hunga	post-Silanga	A	bushbuck
Kamba	pre-Silanga	A	tri-colored cow
Kana (sub-clan of Miro)	?	D	tri-colored cow
Kanda	pre-Silanga	A	?
Kangara (Tatog)	pre-Silanga		
Kayebe	Omukama Katobaha	A	mixture of millet and sand ready for sowing
Kerekeke	pre-Silanga	A	monkey
Kokwa	pre-Silanga	C	?
Koni	pre-Silanga	A	?
Kula	pre-Silanga	A	tri-colored cow
Kulitira	pre-Silanga	A	wren-like bird and mud fish
Kumi (sub-clan of Kula)	?	A	tri-colored cow
Lanzi	pre-Silanga	A	hippopotamus
Lera (sub-clan of Kula)	Omukama Mihigo	A	tri-colored cow
Lima (sub-clan of Lanzi)	?	A	hippopotamus
Linda (sub-clan of Sekabwiname)	pre-Silanga	C	tri-colored cow
Liro	pre-Silanga	A	?
Lubizi	with Silanga	F	buffalo

Lwa	pre-Silanga	A	bushbuck and tri-colored cow
Mara	pre-Silanga	B	?
Manda	pre-Silanga	A	?
Maro	pre-Silanga	A	?
Milwa	pre-Silanga	B	?
Miro	Omukama Katobaha II	E	baboon and tri-colored cow
Mpeke	pre-Silanga	C	?
Nange	pre-Silanga	A	?
Ndu	pre-Silanga	E	?
Nene	pre-Silanga	E	?
Ngu	pre-Silanga	A	?
Nonza	pre-Silanga	A	?
Noro	pre-Silanga	E	?
Nuge	pre-Silanga	E	tri-colored cow
Nzozwa	pre-Silanga	A	tri-colored cow
Ombezi	pre-Silanga	A	?
Onzi	pre-Silanga	B	?
Ruhu (sub-clan of Hembe)	Omukama Kahana	A	a type of grass
Sa (Siba)	pre-Silanga	A	?
Sandasya (Sandawe)	pre-Silanga		
Segena	Omukama Katobaha II	E	wren-like bird and mud fish
Segi	Omukama Kahana	A	?
Segu (sub-clan of Miro)	Omukama Katobaha II	E	baboon and tri-colored cow
Sekabwiname	pre-Silanga	A	tri-colored cow
Senzi (sub-clan of Gara)	?	D	tri-colored cow and two types of brush not used for firewood
Shosho	pre-Silanga	A	monkey
Si	pre-Silanga	B	wren-like bird

Silanga (sub-clan of Segena)		E	wren-like bird and mud fish
Sindi	Omukama Kahana	A	tri-colored cow
Singo	with Silanga	F	bushbuck and tri-colored cow
Sita	with Silanga	E, F	hippopotamus
Sohera	pre-Silanga	D	?
Songe	post-Silanga	D	black-headed weaver
Sosi	pre-Silanga	D	tri-colored cow
Sumba (sub-clan of Gara)	?	D	tri-colored cow
Swiza	pre-Silanga	B	?
Syora (sub-clan of Bwarumi)	?	A	lungfish
Tamba	pre-Silanga	B	?
Tiama (sub-clan of Kamba)	?	A	crow ?
Timba	Omukama Katobaha II	B	bushbuck
Tongera	Omukama Kahana	D	tri-colored cow
Toto	?	?	helmet guinea fowl
Tundu	with Silanga	D, F	leopard
Twa	pre-Silanga	D	?
Twiga	pre-Silanga	D,E	?
Yambi (sub-clan of Silanga)	Omukama Mihigo	E	wren-like bird and mud fish
Yange	pre-Silanga	A	?
Yango	with Silanga	D, F	?
Yozu	pre-Silanga	D	?
Zaga	pre-Silanga	E	?
Zeru (sub-clan of Senzi)	?	D	bushbuck

Zigaba	Omukama Mihigo	D	tri-colored cow and intestines of any eatable animal
Zigu (sub-clan of Timba)	?	A	bushbuck
Zila	pre-Silanga	E	?
Zime	pre-Silanga	E	tri-colored cow
Zimuzimu (Nwi)	pre-Silanga	E	?
Zubwa	with Silanga	D, F	tri-colored cow and hartebeest
Zugumi (became part of Kula)	?	A	tri-colored cow
Zuke	pre-Silanga	B	tri-colored cow

1. *Legend to routes taken to Bukerebe:*
    A: *Buha to Buzinza to Usukuma to Bukerebe*
    B: *Buha to Buhaya to Buzinza to Usukuma to Bukerebe*
    C: *Buha to Buhaya to Buganda to east side of lake to Bukerebe*
    D: *Bunyoro to Buhaya to Buzinza (or Buha) to Usukuma to Bukerebe*
    E: *Bunyoro to east side of lake to Bukerebe*
    F: *Buhaya across the lake to Bukerebe*
2. *Kikerebe names for totems:*

Engabe: bushbuck   *Enemela: hartebeest*
Enkanga: helmet guinea fowl   *Enzubu: hippopotamus*
Enfunzi: wren-like bird   *Endara: leopard*
Enkobe: baboon   *Ensole: black-headed weaver*
Enkende: monkey   *Omusilionjo: mud fish*
Embogo: buffalo   *Namulimi: anteater*
Empunu: warthog   *Runa: tri-colored mottled*
Emamba: lungfish   *cow or bull: black,*
                                     white, brown

Appendix 2

The following list of Kerebe abakama is based upon the evidence of numerous informants. The only serious deviation from this list comes from Bahitwa who claims that Golita was the third and Ruhinda the fourth omukama in place of Katobaha II, giving his list a total of eighteen abakama. An asterisk before a name indicates that the ruler was deposed.

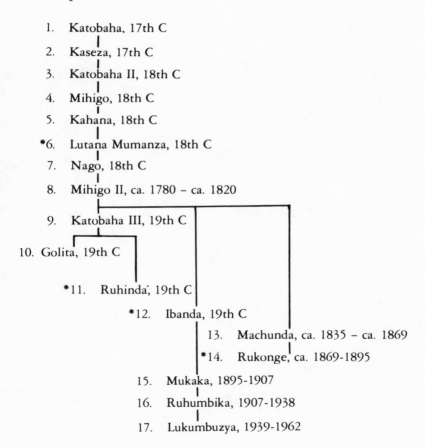

1. Katobaha, 17th C
2. Kaseza, 17th C
3. Katobaha II, 18th C
4. Mihigo, 18th C
5. Kahana, 18th C
*6. Lutana Mumanza, 18th C
7. Nago, 18th C
8. Mihigo II, ca. 1780 – ca. 1820
9. Katobaha III, 19th C
10. Golita, 19th C
*11. Ruhinda, 19th C
*12. Ibanda, 19th C
13. Machunda, ca. 1835 – ca. 1869
*14. Rukonge, ca. 1869-1895
15. Mukaka, 1895-1907
16. Ruhumbika, 1907-1938
17. Lukumbuzya, 1939-1962

INDEX